**M** acca's **A** ustralia

IAN  McNAMARA

# Macca's Australia

Australia All Over

ABC
BOOKS

# Acknowledgements

Compiling a book takes many skills, so thanks to all those who helped make it possible again: Andrew Rankin for the cover picture, Dawn Webb's transcription of interviews, Helen Semmler's design (for the third time), Helen Dash and Neil Conning for sub-editing and proof checking, and Lee's ability to answer many queries at the same time as producing the program.

Thanks to the following for sending in pictures used in the book: Alan Gibb, picture 5; Allan Habermann, 6; G. Player, 7; Betty Thatcher, 8; Sue, daughter of Dulcie Hall, 9; Lyn Burdon, 11; Chaplain Robert Morgan, 13; H. J. Wright, 14; Jenny O'Hallorn, 17; Rita Watson, 19; Joy Stott, 21; Katherine and family, 22; Nikki Lloyd and family, 23; K. Buckley, 25; Ronda Finnigan, 31 and 69; David Bearup, 34–38; Mary from Walla Walla, 45–47; Irene Witcher, 53; the Langmans, 55; Anne Simpson, 58; Georgie Frogley, 65; Philippa Merchant, 67; Bruce, son of Laurel Naylor, 68; Bradley Russell, 72; Glennis Crawford, 73–75; Andrew Rankin, 78 and cover. Apologies to anyone whose picture's been used without credit, but sometimes pictures are sent in without an owner's name.

• • • • • • • • • • • • • • • • • • • • • • • • • • • • • • • • • • • • • • • • • • • • • • • • • • • •

Published by ABC Books for the
AUSTRALIAN BROADCASTING CORPORATION
GPO Box 9994, Sydney, NSW 2001

Copyright © Currawong Music Pty Ltd, 1997
First published October 1997

National Library of Australia
Cataloguing-in-Publication entry
McNamara, Ian
  Macca's Australia
  ISBN 0 7333 0608 X
  1. Australia - Social conditions. 2. Australia - Social
  life and customs. I. Australian Broadcasting Corporation.
  II. Title. III: Australia All Over (Radio program).
  IV. Title: Macca's Australia
994

Publication co-ordinated by
RICHARD SMART PUBLISHING, SYDNEY

Illustrated and designed by Helen Semmler
Typset in 11/14 Garamond light
Colour separations by First Media, Adelaide
Printed in Australia by Sands Print Group, Perth

5 4 3 2 1

# *C ontents*

# **F**or the **P**eople

# *Introduction*

'There's a radio show that Australians all know about explorers and shearers and drovers.' So go the words of the poem written by Vince Clancy in 1986 that became the lyrics to the song 'Australia All Over'.

If you are a listener you'll know that only occasionally do we talk about explorers, shearers and drovers, and usually only when they ring up. We get modern-day explorers, I suppose—the bloke up in the Gulf Country recently who had found Burke and Wills' Camp Number 120 and was out there exploring.

All sorts of people ring: truckies carrying rolls of toilet paper or ballot boxes or ostriches or 'just general'; scientists at Maralinga; teachers; judges; youngsters. I call them 'enthusiasts'. You can hear it in their voices and I not only like what they say but how they say it.

I love the regulars like Gilbert, and Marion Leiba—the bombs and earthquakes (and landslides) lady. When I say 'regulars', they might ring once every six months, but they've got something to say, something to give.

Recently a listener brought to my attention an article by an academic who, I think, claims that my program is about nostalgia. It's a common tool of those who seek to criticise, to invoke the nostalgia critique. Someone told me a former Liberal politician apparently said the same thing. They obviously don't listen to the program. Unlike the rest of the media, I never hesitate to recall the wonderful events of our past, but the program is about now. That's why phone calls from Australians talking about what they are doing and thinking *now* receive such prominence, although we sometimes blend the past and the present, like with Keith Oliver who walked Australia from north to south following in the steps of Morrison of Peking. Over a series of months, those phone calls became a delightful blend of the history of George Morrison; a geography lesson during Keith's stays at places such as Dagworth Station in western Queensland; weather reports; and a continuing conversation with an Australian who was undertaking a sort of spiritual journey. Similarly with the late Graham Middleton who swam the Murray and rang us every couple of weeks.

Some things have gained cult status, like the song 'I made a Hundred in the Backyard at Mum's' and feral shopping trolleys—both first observed on our program.

I have tried to ensure that the program remains relevant and up to date, but its popularity intimidates some, and attracts criticism. The fact that everybody gets a say is quite 'rad' too, not just politicians, industry leaders and media commentators.

The program relies on contributions made by you the listener. Maybe that's why it is such a popular program. You hear things and music that you just can't get anywhere else. It's not really about listeners' opinions, more about what they're doing. To me, the program connects up Australia rather than divides. The wisdom, strength, honesty and humour of the people take a front seat on Sunday morning. The thing

I like most, I think, are the things people say, like Andrew Derwent: 'And isn't it interesting how we just accept it (river pollution) and say, Oh well, we've ruined that, we'll just turn our back on it.' Simple truths.

I have met so many wonderful Australians over the years and you'll meet some of them in this book. As for me, I've taken a leaf out of Gilbert's book and I'm practising contentment. I'm not achieving it yet: it takes a bit of practice, apparently!

If you could have been at our outside broadcast in the park on a very cold Brisbane morning last year and seen Laura, age six, and her sister Emily, age three, in their duffle coats with hoods and coloured gummies, like little dolls, who marched up and presented me with a batch of jam drops, then you'd know why I love this program. What about Letty Katts, who wrote the song 'A Town Like Alice'. When I invited her on stage to play (which she did) she said, 'I always thought composers should be heard and not seen.' What about the bloke driving a cane harvester who explained, 'I'm getting married on the 11th of November (Remembrance Day) so all me mates can observe a minute's silence every year.' What about Luciano from Mittagong who rang on Australia Day to say 'I'm getting Aussie today!' It proves that some people do get through on the phone on Sunday, even though Jan from Toowoomba wrote, 'It's like trying to get an audience with the Pope' and Bruce from Bathurst, 'It's easier to get a date with Elle Macpherson!' A million wonderful people. Like Robert K. Morgan 'the hospital chaplain bloke' from the Prince Charles Hospital in Brisbane who noted down many humorous calls and conversations from the program over the last three years. Robert kindly made his excellent collection available for this book.

My Mum Lorna is a great woman, a great Australian, and it's really thanks to her too that you have had such a unique program. Her advice and encouragement have kept me on the straight and narrow most times. She's the same lady who often wrote essays for me at Uni on subjects as diverse as psychology and economics while I was . . . I forget. 'Mum, can you just write me a bit on this . . . here's the topic, I've got to go now . . . ' Some Saturdays I'll say, 'We haven't got much stuff' and she'll say, 'Oh, the people will help you.' And she's always right.

I appreciate listeners' encouragement, like the woman who phoned the program and said, 'Don't let them cross you out.' I've had literally hundreds of people say the same thing. It's often the first thing they say when I meet them at outside broadcasts or concerts.— 'They're not going to cut you, Macca, are they? There'd be a revolution!' My answer is, 'Talk to you Sunday.'

# *It never ceases to amaze me!*

from
LYN
WODONGA
VICTORIA

**M**Y HUSBAND, born and bred in the country, used to visit a brother who lived along a creek on the next property. On the darkest of nights as he walked along the creek he heard this call close to him. He said each time it was chilling.

My own experience was with him in 1950. We were driving home in the horse and gig late one night when out of a paddock to the left came the most blood-curdling scream imaginable. It was like a woman being strangled, giving off shrilling, gurgling shrieks. (You had to hear it to believe!) Even our pony was affected and gave a big leap forward—the gig lifting too, and we did the last half-mile in record time.

from
RAY
LILYDALE
VICTORIA

**I**N THE EARLY '30s I worked for a farmer near Gulgong in New South Wales. I had been to a dance at Mudgee riding on horseback and returning home about two am, it was a bright moonlit night and as I approached the homestead there was this awful screaming noise. My pony would not go any further so I tied him up at a tank-stand not far from the house, removed the saddle and bridle and let him go, then carried the gear over to the woolshed where the noise came from. Several times the noise like a shrieking woman erupted and my hair stood on end. Eventually I plucked up courage and opened the door of the woolshed. It was bright moonlight, but I couldn't see anything. I went to my bunk and in the morning I asked the boss what it could have been. He said it was a screaming owl and he had heard them a number of times.

MARGARET
GLENDENNING
EVERTON UPPER
VICTORIA

## BILL DANIELS' COO-EE-IN' WOMAN

Bill Daniels heard the story when he was just a lad
Shrugged his shoulders, laughed a bit, and called the locals mad,
He was familiar with the bush, he knew the beasts that prowled
Dismissed as dreams the whispered tales of nights a woman howled.

Cecil Connors shook with fright remembering how he rode
Down through Upper Everton along the Beechworth Road,
A dreadful scream filled the air, his very blood ran cold,
The frantic pony fought the bit and bolted uncontrolled.

'Twas white,' he said, 'with trailing gown, pale arms that reached for me,
Flew right behind my horse's heels, wailing eerily.'
There were some believed his tale, others knew him well
Suspected that he'd had a few at the old Railway Hotel!

Years passed by, the story was forgotten then until
One night Bill Daniels set up camp somewhere near Kelty's Hill,
His peaceful slumber shattered when a strange, tormented shriek
Echoed through the tree-tops along the Yellow Creek!

Ghastly moaning rose and fell, it came from every side
A woman sobbed in agony—Bill stood petrified,
His curly coated dog backed up and cringed against his thigh,
Whimpering and whining as the darkest hours crept by.

Bill never did discover what had made that nightmare sound
Squirrel glider or a powerful owl were theories bandied round
'I don't know what I heard out there,' he'd ruefully relate,
'But the poor dog was so terrified its curly hair stayed straight!'

It is rumoured that in recent times a haunting cry's been heard
Mysteriously unexplained by animal or bird,
If some sad ghost is wandering here, may she soon find peace
Her spirit know tranquillity, her restless searching cease.

from
ROSEMARY THOMSON
NERANG
QUEENSLAND

**W**HAT PROMPTED ME TO write were the calls about the 'screaming woman birds'. I hope these quotes from my father Dr David Fleay's definitive book on the Australian owls titled *Nightwatchmen of Bush and Plain* may help to settle the age-old question once and for all. Father's great love for the owls of Australia led him to study them both in captivity and the wild for over seventy years. He bred the elusive powerful owl in captivity and after forty-two years of trying and deduced in early days that most reports of the so-called 'screaming woman bird' came from open plains country of Victoria's Wimmera and Murray River districts; typical haunts of the barking owl as opposed to dark secluded gullies and dense timber environments suited to the much larger powerful owl, the bird being blamed early this century for the blood-curdling shrieks.

These quotes from *Nightwatchmen of Bush and Plain* give definite proof that the personable little barking owl is totally responsible and it is the hen bird that does the shrieking.

One dark night in March 1939, during a prowl along Healesville Sanctuary tracks in armed search of marauding cats and foxes, I heard a loud, startling, tremulous scream repeated three or four times, at intervals of perhaps ten seconds. It came from away down in the barking owl aviary vicinity and suggested a woman's voice calling 'h-e-l-p'; it was both weird, urgent and hair raising. At long last strong conviction grew that the barking owl was indeed the 'screaming woman' of the long years of mystery. That was indeed a memorable and exciting evening. The fact that these screams are only heard occasionally, and during the months of March and April (late autumn), is interesting in bearing out the mysterious nature and rare use of this particular call note. Uttered with open beak, it is exactly what one imagines a girl or woman would utter on perceiving some object inspiring abject terror. It is single, loud and forcefully given, and may be repeated eight or nine times at intervals of about ten seconds, or, on some occasions with minutes between each performance. In case it may be thought that either the powerful owl, barn owl, the masked owl in its various forms, or the sooty owl could be responsible, we have had each and all of them under close observation for year after year. The results are entirely negative as far as this special scream is concerned. Why, it may be asked, do they scream? Certainly it is a feature of the fall of the year and the exciting courting time when the birds may be temporarily afield from one another, for it is a cry that carries further than the 'wook-wook' notes. With variations it is employed to intimidate trespassers at the nesting site and is a well-calculated deterrent to creatures possibly menacing new-fledged young.

## GALAH

from
David Berman
East Greenmount
Queensland

I was a little pink galah
Just sitting on the highway tar
Just sitting, eating on the road
Wheat that spilt from someone's load
Fighting for the finest seed
Disgusted with my partner's greed
Then flying high to miss the cars
Which often flatten slow galahs
Then landing on the road once more
To get the wheat we'd missed before.

Just when I found a lovely grain
It made the other wheat look plain
It was big and rounded but
It had fallen in a rut.
My friends are squawking, 'There's a car
Get off the road ya mad galah!'
I didn't fly I'd just about
Got that delicious seed dug out.
My friends were making quite a fuss
Squawking that 'The car's a bus!'

I got the seed an' flew but splat
And now I'm feeling rather flat,
A very sore and sorry bird,
The driver hadn't even heard
And here I am stuck on the grill
Feeling like a dopey dill,
But not everyone can poach
A ride upon a tourist coach
And as I drive about today
I see the world a different way.

Life's not only piles of grain
Sprinkled there like golden rain
There's other things along the road,
A dead wombat and flattened toad,

12

And there's a mangled kangaroo
A victim of the highway too.
A blue-tongued lizard thought it great
To lie and thermoregulate
In the middle of the road
But he's squashed there like the toad.

The wombat with his tiny stride
Ran but found the road too wide,
The roo had some grass to munch,
Saw the lights, hopped then crunch.
Now eating them's some hawks and crows,
There's never any dead of those
And up here on the grill with me
There's moths and hoppers and a bee,
A butter and a dragon fly,
The highway caused them all to die.

So all of you who use the road,
Drive a car or spill a load,
Or fly towards bright headlights
Or hop across the road at nights
Or lie there baking in the sun
Or run across the road for fun
Or eat the grass along the side
Just think of all of us who've died.

I LIVED WITH A FRIEND who kept fine, show-quality fowls. The pens were devoid of grass and other nutrients. We rarely got any eggs from these birds and the house in which we lived was riddled with cockroaches. I put a lot of cockroach traps around the house, the jars with a bait and slippery sides. At regular intervals I would collect all the cockroaches into a large single container and take them down to the chooks. The chooks would see me coming, become very excited and quickly polish off all the cockroaches. After this, they supplied us with an overabundance of eggs, such that we gave a lot away.

from
NORM WILLIAMS
NEW FARM
QUEENSLAND

*Mary-Anne of Kallangur, Queensland was interviewed by Macca at Southbank:*
MARY-ANNE: 'My husband's blind and he's just got a new guide-dog. It's a Double-doodle.'
MACCA: 'That's a worry.'
MARY-ANNE: 'They crossed a Labrador with a Poodle and got a Labra-doodle — well, they couldn't call it a Poo-a-door — and then they crossed it back with another Poodle and got a Double-doodle.'

from
JOAN MARSHALL
MOORABBIN
VCTORIA

YOUR FEARS THAT OUR platypuses may be in danger during the drought brought back memories of a delightful interlude I was privileged to share with a platypus some years ago. While travelling north, I had booked into a motel a few minutes off the Hume Highway bridge where it spans the river between Wodonga and Albury. Towards sunset while walking across the bridge I stopped to admire the view, and there was a platypus frolicking in the river. As a steady stream of heavy traffic roared across the bridge, the drivers were unaware of the kaleidoscope of nature below. The platypus played for more than an hour, circling an area close to its burrow. It was a delightful sight. As a child in the country I had seen platypuses on isolated stretches of the Moorabool River bordering our property in Victoria, but never envisaged seeing one of these fascinating creatures so completely at home in such a heavily populated, noisy area.

• • • • • • • • • • • • • • • • • •

from
DR PETER HORNSBY
UNIVERSITY OF
ADELAIDE

I DO NOT KNOW A great deal about wombats—just sufficient to distinguish the sharp from the blunt end—and in my experience each can be equally nasty! My own area of interest is with rock wallabies, particularly those found in South Australia.

My wife and I came to Australia from the UK in 1969 and I'd never heard of rock wallabies (or wombats for that matter). My first acquaintance with wallabies came in 1971, and I started working in earnest with them in 1972. In those days, there was only one scientific paper on South Australia's most numerous rock wallaby, the yellow-footed rock wallaby—written in the 1850s about animals held in the London Zoo. I could not believe nothing else had been written, and in the ensuing months I scoured every newspaper and magazine published in northern South Australia in the last century. I didn't find much on rock wallabies, but the message coming through loud and clear was that opening up the inland was pure grit and hard work with no spare time for such erudite topics as rock wallabies. If there was any interest in them at all, it was as a welcome alternative for the pot, or a few extra bob for the pelts—or just getting rid of them as vermin attacking the crops.

Things have changed a great deal since then, with concern about how many are left and conservation being the key word today. My main work is conducted from a research unit in the North Flinders Ranges. It is located at the top of a cliff that is home to a large colony of yellow-footed rock wallabies. The dunny is near the unit and I reckon that apart from the goats the view from the seat is one of the best in Australia!

• • • • • • • • • • • • • • • • • •

from
NEIL & GWEN McLEOD
FOREST HILL
QUEENSLAND

PIE IS THE SON of Kamakazi and Mum Magpie who lived on our farm for many years. Kamakazi was always friendly except at nesting time, when his diving skills came to the fore. From his lookout atop a tall silky oak tree, he would dive like a dart only shearing off at the last moment with his wings squeaking like an F111. Hence his name Kamakazi Pie. He was never known to strike anyone.

In September 1995 Kamakazi and Mum Magpie gave birth to two babies. That weekend we went away and on arriving home on Monday Kamakazi didn't come to greet us as usual. Next morning we went looking for him and sure

enough some idiot had shot Mum and Dad Pie leaving two starving babies in their nest atop a gum tree about one hundred feet up. As we couldn't climb up the tree, a decision was made to shoot the nest down. So getting my trusty little .22 calibre rifle I kept hacking away at the three large limbs that the nest was built around.

After about fifty rounds the nest finally tilted. My wife who had been standing at the base of the tree with a large padded hat caught the first pie, but the second wasn't so lucky and landed a bit hard. We took the two little bodies into the house and fed and watered them. They were at this stage five days old. They had no feathers and their eyes weren't yet opened. Sadly the second pie died the next day.

However, Pie No. 1 is now about four months old and a real chip off the old block, darting and diving like his dad. His territory is our home and its surroundings. He sleeps on his perch with his poop tray beside our bed.

from
JACQUIE STUDHERN
SWIFTS CREEK
VICTORIA

• • • • • • • • • • • • • • • •

**I** WANTED TO TELL YOU about our wedge-tailed eagle Clarence or Charlotte, we don't know which.

It was found in our paddock in a dazed state by my husband Tom. He was able to pick it up and has continued to handle it for a fortnight with no sign of aggression. It has a beautiful golden head, which we are told proclaims its youth, and its wing span is about six feet. For the first few days we fed it gravy beef and chicken with tongs. We made a cage from a large tank with a branch for a perch, and wire front.

We had reason to be away overnight, only to return and find our eagle hopping around our vegie patch much to the delight of our dog Ralph.

We felt it was much improved after a week and put it out on a back gate to get its bearings. We hoped to do this in a quiet way but it was like a circus. The chickens and roosters formed a background choir of clucking and crowing, Ralph whined and wagged, afraid the eagle was getting more attention than he was, and to top it off our two geese, Dave and Mabel, rushed over with wings outstretched honking loudly in greeting, but our eagle despite all the commotion stayed put. It preened itself in the sunshine, remained all night and allowed Tom to put it back in its cage next morning with a freshly shot rabbit for breakfast—what a life! We consider it a privilege to get this truly magnificent creature strong enough to once more fly above our mountains.

• • • • • • • • • • • • • • • • •

**A**S A FRIEND OF COOLART, a conservation reserve at Somers, on Victoria's Westernport Bay, I first heard about a pair of the reserve's resident wild swans from the wardens who were onlookers to the incident.

These swans had nested on a little man-made island at Coolart for a number of years. One spring, after they had hatched eight cygnets, one of the wardens was horrified to see a fox attacking the female swan. Whether it was due to his shouts from the bank, or the bird's skill, she managed to escape. Then, to everyone's surprise, the cob drove his mate away from the nest, and from her cygnets. She languished alone, a forlorn and miserable swan, for over three weeks. Then

from
JOAN MARSHALL
MOORABBIN
VICTORIA

she began cautiously approaching her family. The wardens then noticed the pair gathering nesting material. They say this is often a pair-bonding exercise, but in this case it heralded a new nest and the start of a second family!

The Coolart people think the cob drove his mate away from their family because he feared the cygnets would have become accustomed to the smell of fox on their mother, and of course would then have had no fear of an arch enemy. Happily, the pair raised several more families at Coolart before seeking newer pastures.

---

*Brian from the Department of Primary Industry on a bad outbreak of blue-green algae on the Darling:*

MACCA: 'This blue-green algae — it's pretty toxic?'

BRIAN: 'Mate, it's more toxic than a bite from a tiger snake — it can knock a cow at thirty yards.'

---

| from |
| :---: |
| JOHN BLAY |
| MILLERS POINT |
| NEW SOUTH WALES |

THERE'S A LITTLE PLACE on the far south coast of New South Wales called Bermagui which, apart from its fishing and gorgeous landscape, is pretty close to being the home of the spotted gum. Even though they occur along the east coast from Victoria all the way up to Maryborough, they seem to grow bigger and more beautiful in Bermagui than just about anywhere else in the world.

Over the past few nights the spotties have become like a kind of bush Kings Cross with constant activity. By day there are squadrons of shrieking parrots, all sorts of species, darting from one lot of trees to another. The hum of bees is just about worse than traffic noise at peak hour. By night, the noise is even more incredible. It even blocks out the sound of the surf. The treetops are full of flying foxes squabbling and shrieking. The possums have become more aggressive too, grunting and bellowing against territorial invaders. Then you notice the air is thick with the scent of nectar, and that fine stamens have just started falling everywhere to make a white carpet.

Round the edges of the forests, bee hives have arrived on just about every flat clear place available. And you can see, from a distance, the top of the forest isn't its usual green or reddish from the new growth. It's been painted a thick creamy white with blossom.

Those creatures, like the flying foxes and the parrots, must have some kind of built-in charts that tell them exactly when the trees will be in blossom because they are not commonly found in the region otherwise.

The beekeepers will tell you that the spotties come into flower on 15 April every three years after twenty-three months elapse between bud and flowering. They're reluctant to give you spotted gum honey, some even say that it would burn the back of your throat. In fact, one time I did manage to wrest a jar of the pure stuff and found it to be very strong, but tasty and interesting even though it wasn't the sort of honey I'd want to eat from day to day. They treasure it because they use it for blending. It gives the milder honeys some real flavour.

The bloodwoods have been in flower, masses and masses of it, for a few months now. But the very volume of the spotted gum flower overwhelms the district. From the coast, right up into the hills, it's the blossoming of a very special and beautiful place.

• • • • • • • • • • • • • • • • • • •

**I** HAVE HEARD MANY a good poem or a little story that tells how life used to be and the hardships that our forebears faced, but I consider this poem will prove it all totally correct. I believe it was credited to a clergyman in the Riverina during the 1902 drought. At the time a decent piece of mutton or beef was a rarity. Rabbits, of which there were many thousands, were always on the menu wherever the parson called. Finally the drought broke and at one farmhouse he visited the parson was delighted when a plate of roast beef was put before him at dinner. Asked to say grace, he intoned:

from
ROBERT M. BAUER

Rabbits hot, rabbits cold;
Rabbits young, rabbits old;
Rabbits fat, rabbits lean;
Rabbits dirty, rabbits clean;
Rabbits big, rabbits small;
Rabbits short, rabbits tall;
Rabbits black, rabbits white;
Rabbits for breakfast, rabbits at night;
Rabbits stewed, rabbits roast;
Rabbits on gravy, rabbits on toast;
Rabbits by the dozen, rabbits by the score;
Rabbits by the hundreds, and still some more;
Rabbits tender, rabbits tough;
Lord spare me from rabbits, for I've had enough!

• • • • • • • • • • • • • • • • • •

## THE EMU

from
WINSOME SMITH
WOY WOY
NEW SOUTH WALES

I saw this bloke on the telly,
American he was,
talking about the emu farm
he was starting in the States.
He happened to mention, as if he'd know,
that emus are ugly birds.

Well I'm here to tell you, mate,
There's nothing ugly about an emu.

Do you know that when emus run
their soft tail feathers
waft up and down like a tutu?
There's nothing ugly about that.

Do you know that the father emu
hatches the eggs and nurtures the babies
and wears a grin as wide as any proud dad?
There's nothing ugly about that.

Do you know that baby emus wear stripes
as bright as an old-fashioned blazer,
and they follow their dad everywhere
like a class of Victorian schoolboys?
There's nothing ugly about that.

Do you know that an emu
will come up behind you
and look over your shoulder
to gaze into your face
with round eyes full of curiosity?
There's nothing ugly about that.

Do you know that when an emu
makes its dignified way through the brown grass
its steps are almost as stately as a brolga's?
There's nothing ugly about that.

Do you know that an emu
can peck the tiniest morsel of food
out of your palm,
and all you will feel
is a touch softer than a kiss.
There's nothing ugly about that.

Do you know
that out here where it doesn't rain
we breed 'em nine feet tall
and an emu can give you a kick
that will send you to Kansas,
or even further—to buggery and back?
and if you want to insult an emu, mate,
get yourself out here
and try telling him to his face,
then we'll see who's ugly.

* * * * * * * * * * * * * * * * * * * * * * * * * * * * * * * * * * * * * * * * * * * * * * * * * * * * * * * * * * * * * * * * * * * * * * * *

*Bert had a cowbell on his front gate and when it rang his two Great Danes would race down to fend off the visitor. Macca got a recording of the bell and played it on the program. Bert phoned the following week to tell of the events: 'The dogs heard the bell on the radio in the bedroom and looked puzzled. Then they went for the radio and wrecked it.'*

* * * * * * * * * * * * * * * * * * * * * * * * * * * * * * * * * * * * * * * * * * * * * * * * * * * * * * * * * * * * * * * * * * * * * * * *

LISTENING TO YOUR PROGRAM I heard about the killer whales attacking the whales. It reminded me of a similar sight my late husband and I saw on our honeymoon. In 1937 we were travelling by ship from Brisbane to Melbourne (there were interstate ships in those days). The captain said that as we were running early and he didn't want to arrive in Sydney on Sunday and incur double docking fees, he was going to stop the ship for several hours and we would all be issued fishing lines. A lot of fish were caught, but the highlight was whales being attacked by killer whales only a few hundred yards from the ship. The killers came right out of the water and onto the whales. It was a terrible sight. The captain said we only saw it because the engines were stopped, or the noise would have kept them away.

from
ALLIE EVANS
SWAN HILL
VICTORIA

• • • • • • • • • • • • • • • • • • • •

OUR HOUSE IS SITUATED twelve miles north of Forbes, New South Wales. It is located in a closed-off area of natural woodland and is surrounded by an extended native garden. This setting is a sheltered place and provides a peace that one can only experience in the bush.

from
GREGORY CANNON
FORBES
NEW SOUTH WALES

There has been an influx of wildlife into the area; accordingly a colony of spiny echidnas has taken up residence under the house and breeds there. The little ones are cute and my wife refers to them as 'walking teapot covers'. We have some lovely snapshots of them parading in solemn order along the garden path.

A number of small yellow sand goannas have moved in as well. They love the garden sprinkler and prey on the many smaller pests to be found in the area. It was a rare sight, on one occasion, to observe the ritual of a mating pair. They were standing upright, forearms outstretched embracing like two young lovers before going to ground and getting on with the job. Of course, we have the inevitable snakes and have on camera a mating couple entwined in the form of a catherine wheel.

There has been as well a proliferation of birds—honey eaters and parrots of every description along with many other varieties of the feathered population. For these we have set up a number of bird baths and there is much competition and quarrelling for a drink and a splash.

The pool section of one of the baths has broken away, leaving exposed a small hole in the top of the column. A pair of blue bonnets nest here each year. It's a comical affair watching the efforts of the parent bird trying to squeeze down the hole, the tail feathers sticking high in the air and gradually disappearing.

• • • • • • • • • • • • • • • • • • • •

WHEN I LEFT SCHOOL in 1926 I got myself a job helping a plumber in the Blue Mountains, west of Sydney. One day, while helping to dig a trench for water piping, I came across a two-inch green frog in a cavity about six inches below the surface. The frog seemed happy enough to be released and hopped away. The cavity itself was several times the size of the frog, and it was smooth and had a glazed surface. How did the frog get there, and how long was it there? An explanation of sorts came in more recent times when I heard a fellow on the radio, during a science session, say that in drought conditions some frogs bur-

from
WALTER FROYLAND
MACKAY
QUEENSLAND

row into the ground and have the ability to encase themselves in a thin plastic-like cocoon, and can live in it without water for up to three years.

Many years later in north Queensland, after several years drought without any wet seasons, we received a tropical downpour of rain, which produced a knee-deep pond about fifteen yards across, in a hollow in sandy soil about thirty yards from our house. Later that evening the noise that came from croaking frogs in the pond was almost deafening. There must have been dozens of bullfrogs all croaking their little hearts out, apparently happy to be released from their tombs by the rain. This seems to back up the theory mentioned by the fellow on radio about the earlier incident. I don't think we need to worry about frogs becoming extinct. The human race will go first!

• • • • • • • • • • • • • • • • • • • •

from
PENNY MURPHY
MEANDARRA
QUEENSLAND

**I** THOUGHT I SHOULD reassure all those people who think green frogs are in short supply. Not so. In the Meandarra district where I live most of us seem to be inundated with them and would happily give some away. Don't get me wrong. I like frogs, but not everyone enjoys them jumping on their face when asleep or having to brush them off the toilet seat. We have lived here since 1968 and although we have always had green frogs even through the drought, there have never been as many as in the last two years.

They live in my ceiling, those that aren't residing in the house with us, and at the back where the eaves are not lined. They come out every night and line up in their hundreds, single- double- and even triple-decked before marching across the piping to the nearest tree or crawling down the walls to the ground to trip you up or ambush you if you should walk into the laundry. Those living in the house wander around at night as if they own the place and I must admit we haven't had many insects all summer. Actually, I have found that the ones in the lounge wait around until I turn off the light and when I come back a short while later they are all either lined up at the door or on their way there waiting for me to open it, which I do so our cat can go in and out during the night. The frogs all go out then but make sure they are all back inside and nearly hidden away before morning. Last night fifteen were waiting to be let out!

They have attracted the snakes as well and one big red-belly black coiled himself up in the bottom of a self-watering pot-plant pot and used it as a self feeder. I feel a bit like I am living in a zoo. In the last fifteen months I have caught over seventy large rats in my ceiling, we have the usual number of mice around and the geckoes are multiplying nicely.

Some of my friends and relations refuse to visit me these days, but we are doing our best, with some success, to train our grandchildren to love frogs!

• • • • • • • • • • • • • • • • • • • •

from
RAY DWYER
BERKELEY VALE
NEW SOUTH WALES

**A** FEW WEEKS AGO I heard you or a caller mention how cicadas spray liquid on those below. A few years back I was sunbaking in my backyard clad only in swim shorts. There was a light breeze blowing and even though I was cool I distinctly felt that someone was spraying me with the lightest of sprays. I got my binoculars, and focused them on a branch high above in a gum tree and was surprised to see a cicada directly above. I was more surprised to note that it was ejecting a fine jet sideways about ninety degrees to its body. This happened about every forty seconds. I guessed that as it was sucking the juice from the sap it was taking what it needed and rejecting the rest. I was surprised that the light breeze didn't disperse it elsewhere than on to me.

*Rory after being three days out from Birdsville crossing the Simpson Desert:*
*'Simpson Desert flies are the industrial strength version of their urban counterparts.'*

A LISTENER TOLD OF SEEING trees squirting water. I have seen a similar incident which I found on close examination to be caused (in my case) by young cicadas. I was so fascinated I took a series of close-up photographs of the event. You probably know that adult cicadas drop their eggs from the trees to the ground where the young burrow underground and can remain there for many years. An entomologist explained to me that when young cicadas emerge from the ground they climb trees where they squirt off excess moisture and wait while their soft bodies harden.

from
HOWARD HUGHES
TOORMINA
NEW SOUTH WALES

WHEN I WAS A kid in Scone we lived on a farm five miles out of town. Our house had a huge yard, some lawn, some vegies and flowers and an area of long grass. My dad got us a pet lamb to keep the long grass down, and we had a push mower for the lawn area. One day we were in town doing the shopping when a salesman my dad knew bailed us up wanting to sell us a new Victa lawn-mower. The salesman knew we had lots of long grass and the Victa would save us heaps of time and energy.

My dad pushed his hat back on his head and listened intently to his spiel. He let him go for about five minutes then said, 'We got a new lawnmower last week.' The salesman was taken aback and replied, 'You should have come and seen me. I could have done you a great deal.' He then enquired about the make and model. Dad said, 'I don't know, but it cuts the grass off neatly, rolls it up in little balls and throws it out the back.' The salesman said he didn't know of such a lawnmower and enquired again about the make. 'Pet lamb,' Dad said as we walked away!

from
JOHN HAYNE
TOWNSVILLE
QUEENSLAND

A CHICKEN WHO WENT INTO a library, walked up to the desk and said, 'BOOK, BOOK, BOOK.' The librarian said, 'I beg your pardon,' to which the chicken again replied, 'BOOK, BOOK, BOOK.' The librarian, impressed by the chicken's request, picked out what she felt were three appropriate books, and the chicken nodded and left.

The next day the chicken was back, returning the three books, and repeating its call of 'BOOK BOOK BOOK.' Again the librarian assisted and the chicken nodded and left.

On the third day, when the same thing happened, the librarian decided she

from
GWEN ELLIOT
HEATHMONT
VICTORIA

must follow the chicken to see where it went. They went along the road and down a path to a lovely quiet pool. As they got nearer the librarian noticed a frog sitting on a log near the edge of the pool. The chicken gave the books to the frog and the frog said, 'READ-IT, READ-IT, READ-IT!' (i.e. past-tense, pronounced RED-IT!)

*Coral rang from Streaky Bay, South Australia:*
MACCA: 'What can you tell us about sharks?'
Coral: 'Nothing. I never go near the water — it's too cold and it's too wet. I breed slow racehorses . . .'

from
GEOFF TELFER
CORDEAUX HEIGHTS
NEW SOUTH WALES

I HAVE JUST COME BACK from Western Queensland where I saw an amazing adaption of Nature to prolonged drought.

Late one afternoon I stopped on the banks of what should have been the Darr River just out of Morella, between Longreach and Winton. I went over and had a close look at a magnetic termites' nest. These termites have a very complex social structure and are the ones that build the tall narrow nests, the edges of which point north and south. Bushmen find direction by them as did pilots in World War Two.

The magnetic termite is soft bodied and lacks pigmentation. Consequently, it cannot tolerate strong light and dehydrates quickly. In order to maintain an even temperature and high humidity, the nests are constructed with thick walls and extensive passages and galleries. But because this drought has been so long, the termites in the nest I was looking at must have been threatened by dehydration because of falling humidity.

As I watched, a long line of termites marched from the nest to one of the few remaining puddles in the Darr River. When the first termite reached the water the line halted so that there was a single file of termites from the nest to the water. Then a second line of termites emerged and took up a position opposite the first line, so there were two straight lines of termites stretching from the nest to the puddle. When both ranks were in position, workers still in the nest started passing buckets down the first rank, which were filled when they reached the puddle and then passed up the second rank where they disappeared into the nest. The buckets were apparently emptied in the nest and the water increased the humidity. I would like to know if other listeners have seen this phenomenon. If the practice is widespread, it could explain why some of the water released from dams has not reached the farmers for whom it was intended!

from
ANNE COLVILLE
HABERFIELD
NEW SOUTH WALES

I ENJOYED THE TALE OF 'cracking' a snake on your program and was reminded of one of the very earliest memories from my childhood.

Outside our house we had a gravel path lined with stones. One night my mother was walking along the path when she saw a large snake disappearing down a hole under one of the stones. She decided that since it was mostly down the hole it couldn't turn around and bite her, so she bravely grabbed its tail and shouted for my father. I came running out as well, of course.

My father took over holding the snake, saying 'Stand back! Stand back! I'm going to crack it.' Mother picked me up and retreated to what she thought was a safe distance and Dad swung the snake around his head. As he brought his arm down for the 'crack' the snake slipped from his hand, flew through the air, and wrapped itself around Mother and me.

I don't know whether we or the snake were the more shocked! It dropped to the ground, took off into the bush and we never saw it again. I can't have been more than about three at the time, but I can still feel the panic in my stomach after more than forty years.

## G'day, this is Macca

TOM: It's Tom from Nyngan here. I just wanted to tell you that all the echidnas haven't been cooked and eaten!

MACCA: Tom's referring to a letter I read from a lady who said that some years ago her parents cooked an echidna and it tasted like a cross between pig and something else. I was hoping they hadn't shot it and that it had just dropped dead on the back porch or something.

TOM: Well, a fortnight ago we'd left a light burning on our concrete verandah where my wife keeps a lot of pot plants, and when we heard a noise we went out and there were seven echidnas on the verandah.

MACCA: That must be some sort of sign. A bloke rang me once to say he'd seen a carpet snake and it was a sign of rain.

TOM: Well, as soon as they saw us most of them froze. A couple of them went over the edge on their noses and froze there, but one little bloke about the size of a small pumpkin didn't stop at all; he came over and checked on this pot and that pot and smelled our slippers, and when I put my hand down he poked his nose into the palm of my hand and he didn't know what to think about that. We just waited there and they messed around until we got tired of it and left them there, but it was lovely to see them. We often see one or two because one of them camps under a shed near here, but we've never seen seven.

MACCA: Gee, seven echidnas. I wish I'd been there.

TOM: Yes, it was a real joy.

Macca: I've only ever seen one. They don't usually stay around for long, do they. They dig a little hole and disappear in the ground. Well, that's a lovely story. I'd watch leaving the shoes out, there might be a bit of a problem there!

I HAVE BEEN REALLY FASCINATED by the 'in-depth' scientific discussions about the Australian Hoop Snake. It is of course better known among herpetologists as *Hoopus australis*.

Did you know that *Hoopus australis* has a large cousin in South America called the giant hoop snake, or *Hoopus maximus*? This snake uses the same form of locomotion as *Hoopus australis*. By adopting the hoop shape it is able to roll at

from
KIM KNIGHT
YORK
WESTERN AUSTRALIA

quite high speed, especially when pursuing its prey. In ancient times the diet of *Hoopus maximus* consisted entirely of the South American mammoth (*Pachydermus humungous*). According to South American folklore, the snake would prop itself up against a tall tree in the fully hooped position and watch the valley below for the mammoth. When it saw the mammoth, it would give a quick flick away from the tree, and commence hurtling down the slope. On reaching its unsuspecting victim it would, in a single action, unhoop and then rehoop around the midriff of the beast, which would be stunned, winded and knocked over all in an instant.

So successful was this hunting method that *Pachydermus humungous* is now extinct.

Fortunately for *Hoopus maximus* there was other similar prey available in the form of local wild pigs (*Porcus familiarus*). Because the giant hoop snake is so much bigger than the pig, during the rehooping action it actually wraps itself several times around the pig, but the end result is still the same. The snake seems to prey on the male pig only, apparently because of its similar (albeit smaller) appearance to the mammoth (they both have tusks and a long snout). As the diet of *Hoopus maximus* is now narrowed down to the male pig, it is often described as being 'boar restricted', or in the local language, boa constrictor.

I do hope that this information can be used to further enlighten your listeners.

• • • • • • • • • • • • • • • • • •

from
ROD MALDMENT
VAUCLUSE
NEW SOUTH WALES

**A**NOTHER SNAKE STORY FOR YOU. Years ago I knew a tram conductor named Alec Holmes who used to catch snakes for Sir Edward Hallstrom and Taronga Park Zoo.

One day I caught his tram and there he was on the footboard and asked if I would like to see 'The beaut red-bellied black I caught this morning.' 'Yep,' I replied and Alec put his hand inside the blouse-type jacket that trammies used to wear and produced about two foot of red-bellied black snake for all and sundry to see. The other passengers were horrified and made a hasty retreat to the far side of the compartment. Anyway, after a minute or so Alec calmly fed this snake back into the darkness and warmth of his jacket, collected my penny fare to Bondi, then off he went to the next compartment along the footboard with a cheery 'fezpleeze!'

• • • • • • • • • • • • • • • • • •

from
MAX L. TAYLOR
ARMIDALE
NEW SOUTH WALES

**W**HILE INSPECTING A RABBIT-PROOF fence from horseback I came upon two dead brown snakes. Being on opposite sides of the fence and approximately seven feet long my assumption was that an abortive mating had taken place; each snake stuck in the netting about a foot back from the head. Moral to this story: attempted matings through wire netting fences can lead to a painful death.

• • • • • • • • • • • • • • • • • •

from
DOROTHY KNOTT
UMINA BEACH
NEW SOUTH WALES

**T**HE DROUGHT OF THE 1980s brought snakes close to the house looking for water. One day my husband was in our shop and heard a rustling noise. When he turned to investigate there was a brown snake curling its way out of the till! My husband jumped the counter and went into my son's house next door and my son came down with a gun. The snake had gone! There was no sign of it, so into the garage workshop alongside they went. Graham and Dad gingerly looked and yes, Graham spotted it. Bang! But there was movement again. Bang! After three shots and no dead snake they slowly moved everything. They had shot the hose! They eventually killed the snake.

• • • • • • • • • • • • • • • • • • •

A TEAM FROM BREWARRINA WENT out to play a social match against Tarcoon—an outlying station. The pitch was set in the middle of a small claypan with only small patches of grass out near the boundaries.

Tarcoon batted first and were 6 for 52 when one batsman skied a ball high over midwicket towards the boundary. Although the fieldsman had some distance to run, it looked like he could make the catch. It soon became apparent, however, that the ball was about to land on a spot occupied by a very large brown snake. Being terrified of snakes, he propped and turned with great agility, leaving the snake to catch the ball if it wanted to.

It was never quite clear whether the ball hit the snake but sufficient to say it reared a couple of feet in the air to defend itself. The batsmen, who were taking an easy single, saw the predicament of the fieldsman, and being the only ones with weapons in hand forsook the run in favour of disposing of the snake. While they were doing this, one enterprising fieldsman (unafraid of snakes) threw the ball back to the keeper who stumped one batsman, then ran out the other. The umpires conferred, and in the true spirit of the game in those days (1936), gave both batsmen 'not out'. They also chastised the fieldsman who returned the ball and the wicketkeeper for such a low-down 'snake-in-the-grass' act.

from
RALPH ROBINSON
FORBES
NEW SOUTH WALES

• • • • • • • • • • • • • • • • • • •

I KNOW THAT WHAT I am about to tell you sounds like a shaggy dog story but it's absolutely true.

The game was 'fetch the bark' during an autumnal clean-up in the back garden. I'd throw the bark and my spaniel would fetch it. However, the game came to an abrupt end when turning around on one occasion I noticed the bark seemed thinner than her usual offering. As I bent closer towards it, I noticed it had eyes at one end! The realisation that it was a brown snake was instant and I yelled at the spaniel to: 'Drop it!' followed by 'Don't drop it' and then, with desperation in my voice, pleaded: 'Go away.' The more I shouted, the more excited she became and the snake's head swung to and fro in the air, narrowly missing my kneecaps. I decided there was only one course of action and made a mad dash to the house, slamming the door behind me. (Bear in mind I had two children to gather up, too!) The faithful spaniel followed screeching to a halt at the sight of the slammed door. I settled the kids and then peered out of the window, feeling somewhat anxious for the spaniel! I'll never forget the sight that beheld me, one bemused patient spaniel, head between paws, waiting for the game to be resumed and one poor mangled snake, its eyes bulging and practically meeting each other (not unlike a flounder's), with a frozen expression on its face begging for mercy. I know the feeling! Learnt from the experience? Yes, I went straight out and bought a rubber ball.

from
ANNE
'IN THE MOUNTAINS'

from
SYD & OLIVE
MCCREDDEN
LEONAY
NEW SOUTH WALES

OUR REASON FOR WRITING this letter is in regard to your snake story in this morning's broadcast. The story of the snake eating its way up that person's arm is believable. I spent eighteen months in the war years with the RAAF stationed on an aircraft strip in a place named Iron Range on Cape York. We had an occasion when one of the civil construction corps workers retired for the night 'under the weather' and went to sleep with his arm hanging out of his cot. He woke the camp with his screams and a python gulping his arm down its throat. Our medical orderly rescued him by pulling the arm from the snake's gaping mouth. It was badly lacerated and the poor man was a complete write-off. The incident is true and was witnessed by quite a number of onlookers.

● ● ● ● ● ● ● ● ● ● ● ● ● ● ● ● ● ●

from
CATHY
ROLLESTON
QUEENSLAND

CATHY HAS HER OWN 'snake highway'! She's shot over one hundred and fifty brown snakes in the six years she's been there. Her record is six in twenty-four hours. Before resorting to drastic measures she tried garlic and geese deterrents. No luck!

● ● ● ● ● ● ● ● ● ● ● ● ● ● ● ● ● ●

from
JOHNE BOURNE
THANGOOL
QUEENSLAND

A COUPLE OF MONTHS BACK there was a reasonable spot of rain around Taroom which put a bit of a fresh in the Dawson, so a mate, who I'll call Kevin and I decided we'd spend a night fishing a hole we know, a few miles from Moura. Was just after dark. Moon was a couple of days past full and was just high enough to throw shadows, but not much light. We both make our own lures most of the time, but Kev had recently bought this particularly spectacular plastic imitation frog and was working it along the edge of a half-sunken log where we'd picked up nice yellowbelly on previous trips. He'd made a few casts without any action. Then there was a swirl, a splash, and a really powerful strike. The fish fought on the surface, with a fair bit of splashing and thrashing, so I assumed it was a Dawson barra (saratoga), but when he finally got it alongside into the light there was a good lump of a king brown snake.

'Better cut the line, mate,' I suggested.

'No way! I'm not doing fifteen bucks worth of lure to a stupid overgrown earthworm. He's not even hooked, just hanging on. Pass the net. I'll belt him with the handle.' A rapid search of the dinghy revealed no landing net.

'Pass your rod then. I'll hit him with that.'

'Not pygmalion likely, son. I've just replaced the tip you caught in the car door last trip.'

'Jeez, some people are fusspots. All right, slip us the rum bottle, then.'

I fished the bottle out of the bow locker and passed it to him, keeping a very wary eye on the side of the boat. Kev grabbed the bottle by the neck, looked as though he was going to use it as a club, then changed his mind, unscrewed the top, and poured a couple of glugs over the snake. The first one splashed on top of its head. As it lifted it to see what was happening, the second one went straight down its throat.

I should digress slightly here to explain about Kev's rum. He gets it by the demijohn, uncut, through some business contact in Bundaberg. When it arrives, it is truly fearsome, but he cuts it down a bit—with battery acid and Tordon, I think—and this sort of rounds the corners off, and gives it a bit of a palate, but is still worthy of respect. Anyway, the effect on the snake was most satisfactory. It spat the frog out, looped the loop a couple of times, then headed for the bank, leaving a track like a torpedo.

We needed a couple of glugs ourselves after that and had just got our lines back in the water when there was a bump on the side of the boat. We assumed it was just a stick carried in the current. But it was repeated, louder. It was on Kevin's side, so I passed him the torch to see what was going on.

'Looks like it's the snake back again, mate.'

'Ah yair, what's it on about?'

'Dunno, but it's holding its head up, and has two frogs in its mouth!'

### G'day, this is Macca

GEOFF (from Goonalda, Queensland): I'm interested in snake talk and in particular Sir Joseph Stoeppel and the discovery of the 'Stoeppel Adder'.

MACCA: Can you throw any light on it?

GEOFF: Yes, there's been another development. Sir Joseph had a nephew who was also very interested in herpetology. His name was Vincent Crean, although typically it was shortened to Vince, and so the first snake he observed was known as the 'Vince Crean Viper'!

MACCA: Geoff, what do you do when you're not taking the tablets?

GEOFF: I've got a four-hundred-tree mango farm here, thirty kilometres north of Gympie. Not a bad way of life.

LIKE MOST COASTAL TOWNS these days there's been quite a lot of development in this area, including a housing estate about three kilometres from our place and a golf course. Since then we've had a huge influx of snakes (mostly red-bellied black snakes) and also some kangaroos and wallabies. I see the snakes every two or three days and they're very timid and frightened. One hot day as I was lying in our hammock near the dam a snake went right underneath and I just lay there absolutely frozen!

> from
> ARYLYSS
> TEA GARDENS
> NEW SOUTH WALES

I'VE SEEN COOPER CREEK under flood and every tree full of browns and king browns and rats—it's a fantastic sight! When the floodwaters hit us we were stuck for about six weeks and were reduced to eating snakes and anything else that floated by.

> from
> RIC SHINE
> HERPETOLOGIST

I USED TO SELL ICE-CREAMS for Streets, driving a van from Wagga up through Tumut, Gundagai, Gaylong, Binalong, Cootamundra, Junee and back. One day, on the road between Tumut and Gundagai, I came across a dead red-bellied black snake nearly eight feet long. I put it into an empty five-gallon ice-cream can on the truck, and drove back to Wagga, arriving quite late. The other drivers and the boss (I didn't know he was terrified of snakes) were counting their money

> from
> ROBERT
> SYDNEY
> NEW SOUTH WALES

in the office. I opened the door, threw in the can saying, 'Here's a present for you blokes,' and the next second the boss is leaping out of the window at a hundred miles an hour. The other drivers are yelling at me and I'm trying to tell them the snake's dead. But they grabbed me and threw me into the office where I was confronted by a very much alive and angry snake! I followed the boss out of the window, and later we had to re-kill the snake.

*Robin came on the line from Sydney.*
MACCA: 'Robin, you got any messages?'
ROBIN: 'Yes, Ian, Frank rang up — his dog has tinea and he's tried everything, and he wants to know has anyone got a remedy.'
*A bloke in the crowd yelled out something.*
ROBIN: 'I didn't quite get that, Ian.'
MACCA: He says "Shoot it!"'

---

> from
> JANE
> WEST PENNANT HILLS
> NEW SOUTH WALES

WE WERE BUSHWALKING AT The Basin in Pittwater when a ranger showed us a diamond python devouring a recently caught kookaburra. Apparently the snake was up a tree and grabbed the bird when it landed. It crushed the bird and then over a period of about three hours, beak first, consumed it. One of the funniest sights was the ferry driver who popped by each hour to check its progress!

---

### G'day, this is Macca

TESS (from West Chermside, Brisbane): I have a snake story for you.
MACCA: Go, Tess.
TESS: We had a motel and an old couple parked their car under a tree in the shade. After they got into it to go to town, they're driving along and she said, 'Dad, snake!' and he said, 'Where?' The bloomin' thing had come along the back seat, down the neck of the loose shift she had on, through the dress and out into the shopping bag on the floor. Dad pulled the car over, ran around and opened the passenger door and killed both the snake and the shopping bag.
MACCA: I thought you were going to say her!

---

*Going north for a week, Macca reported that at Queens Beach, Bowen, the water was so inviting he ignored the warning about stingers and went swimming. A lady from Bowen wrote: 'If you insist on swimming with the stingers, you'd better wear pantihose, and as for the crocodiles, they're not fussy about what you wear.'*

# 2

# *T*ogether under the Southern Cross

from
JIM DONALDSON
FORSTER
NEW SOUTH WALES

IN FEBRUARY 1942 I was a young soldier aged twenty years and when the Japanese overran Malaya and Singapore I was taken prisoner. On 12 May 1942, just twelve weeks after being taken prisoner, I was among 3,000 Australian prisoners who were taken by Hell Ship from Singapore to Burma to commence building the railway line from Burma to Thailand. The Railway of Death.

I spent the remainder of 1942 and the whole of 1943 in Burma and was taken out in April 1944. For part of this time I was in a prison camp on top of the high mountain range which separates Burma from Thailand. The nights in Burma are pitch-black as there is no reflection of any lights from cities hundreds of miles away. Because the nights are so black the stars are brilliant and seem very close in the heavens. One dark night I spent some hours squatting at the latrines, I had dysentery and it was not worth staggering back to my hut only to have to retrace my steps. So I just sat there. I was staring into space and admiring the stars when, to my amazement, I saw the Southern Cross low in the southern sky and some distance above the horizon. The next day I told some of my mates that I had seen the Southern Cross. They would not believe me and said I was delirious. I told them I would show them, and so late that night went to the latrines with three or four of my mates. The skies were crystal clear, and there, well to the south and clear of the horizon, was the beautiful Southern Cross. One of the boys, who was very sick at the time, broke down and cried at the sight of the Cross which was also shining on our dear homeland thousands of miles away.

I am not ashamed to say that I shed a few quiet tears myself as the sight of the Southern Cross brought memories of our loved ones. The young man who broke down did not make it home to see his beloved Southern Cross. He died some months later in Thailand.

• • • • • • • • • • • • • • • • • • •

from
J. A. D. BLACKBURN
ESSENDON
VICTORIA

THIS MORNING I HEARD the moving story of the POW who saw the Southern Cross while working on the Burma Railway. As an army surveyor in New Guinea in 1942–44 I carried out star observations as part of our topographical mapping program. Your item set me wondering exactly how far north the Southern Cross could be seen. I did a little bit of rough calculation and came up with the following:

The Cross never sets south of latitude S.33.05' near Newcastle, New South Wales (S.32.56') but, of course, is invisible to the naked eye in the daylight hours. In the Northern Hemisphere the complete cross can be seen at favourable locations and times, as far north as latitude N.27.06', some 300 nautical miles north of Hong Kong (N.22.11'). At latitude N.33.06', near Nagasaki, Japan (N.32.47'), only the uppermost star in the Cross may be seen due south, right on the horizon. At the end of March it rises at the same time as the sun and so cannot be seen except in the southern latitudes where it appears upside down during the night. At other times it may be observed before sunrise or after sunset depending on the location and date.

When the Cross is standing vertically it is due south of the observer. At other times you must extend the long axis of the Cross by four and one half times its length downwards. This brings you to the point in the sky about which all of the stars appear to rotate. It is known as the South Celestial Pole and marks true south. Its angular height above the horizon is equal to the latitude of the place.

Some years ago an advertisement was widely published which showed the Southern Cross shining above an oil rig which purported to be in Bass Strait. The length of the cross, its orientation, and its distance above the horizon clearly indicated that the location was well into the northern hemisphere. So much for truth in advertising!

• • • • • • • • • • • • • • • • • • •

I SERVED AS A BOMB AIMER on 215 squadron based at Digri, north of Calcutta in India. It is my great pleasure to confirm that the Southern Cross can be seen from parts of the Northern Hemisphere as the following anecdote reveals. At the time of this incident I was flying with 359 squadron, to which I was temporarily attached, and based nearby.

On the night of 7/8 May 1944 after laying magnetic mines in the mouth of the Salween River at Moulmein in south-eastern Burma I had an experience which possibly saved the crew and Liberator bomber EV971 from a very watery grave. After releasing the mines from a height of 200 feet amid some mild gunfire from the river banks, I went to sleep. It was about midnight. Our course home was westerly to a point west of the Burmese coast and then northerly to our base near Calcutta in India. Fortunately the bomber in which we were flying was not fitted with a front gun turret, and so the front was glass. When I awoke some time later I saw the Southern Cross in front of us. I pointed this out to the navigator, a New Zealander, who immediately contacted the pilot, an Australian, on the intercom to ascertain the course he was flying. His reply was 220°, but he should have been flying 320°! The navigator, who was excellent at taking star shots, soon determined our position and the pilot altered course. We arrived at our base with a little petrol to spare. Course 220° was taking us out into the middle of the Bay of Bengal and the petrol would have been exhausted long before the sight of any land.

from
RAYMOND SOUTH
WAGIN
WESTERN AUSTRALIA

• • • • • • • • • • • • • • • • • • •

YOU WERE TALKING ABOUT the Southern Cross and places from where it can be seen.

The Southern Cross can be seen on most days in Chicago—during daylight—which is not surprising since we can only see it at night! But it will be about one minute late in Chicago!

We spent a sabbatical year in Canada in 1967 and visited the planetarium in Chicago. After an interesting display my young son piped up in an Aussie voice, 'Where's the Southern Cross?' Silence from the crowd. Most of them did not know what it was, but the demonstrator laboriously turned the machine around and one minute later educated the audience about that remarkable cross.

from
JOHN I. TINDALL
MATRAVILLE
NEW SOUTH WALES

• • • • • • • • • • • • • • • • • • •

I HAVE LIVED IN CANBERRA since 1956 and have always loved it. It has been a wonderful place to bring up children. Canberra was small in the 1950s and the skies at night very clear. It was wonderful to be able to drive to the bush in about half an hour. These days it takes a little longer, but it's still a beautiful garden city.

from
OLGA STEELE
RED HILL
ACT

In March this year, near the end of summer time, I happened to be awake several times one night. It was full moon and this is what happened. I have a dog called Solomon, a black miniature poodle, who is now fourteen years old. Cataracts dim his eyes, and his back legs sometimes give away, but he has been my companion and friend all these years. I had to get up and let him in and as I opened the door and walked outside I noticed the brilliance of the stars. The brightest in my line of vision was the Southern Cross and the two Pointer stars. And then very early one Sunday morning shortly after this I walked outside and the garden was clothed in moonlight. I seemed to be in my own private heaven. I wandered around and thought how beautiful it all was. Later that morning on 'Australia All Over' I listened to those who were away from home—the lady from Cairns who wished she was back in Wagga, the Captain of the oil tanker somewhere at sea, the truckies on their long-distance hauls—and I knew we have something to keep us all together, close to the land and its people: we all live under the Southern Cross.

*Jack Eston, owner of the Gilgandra, New South Wales, observatory said to Macca:*
*'I think we lost the ability to tell the stars the day they took the backyard toilet away and put it in the house.'*

## G'day, this is Macca

ANDREW PORTEOUS: (Perth, Western Australia): A couple of weeks ago you took a call from a listener who expressed confusion at the Southern Cross being what he called 'upside down' when he got up in the morning. The answer's simply that the stars rise and set daily, as does the sun, the only difference being that they do it approximately four minutes earlier each day which means that they catch up one full day in each year. So if the listener got up at the same time in six months the Southern Cross would be exactly one hundred and eighty degrees different from where he saw it before.

MACCA: Do you see the Southern Cross in the northern skies?

ANDREW: You can see from some of the Asian countries.

MACCA: You sound as though you know this pretty well.

ANDREW: Well, I'm a surveyor, and astronomy is part of our training because of the position and direction fixings we use. However, it's being used much less now because we have the GPS constellation of satellites, and surveyors here are doing the control of their metropolitan subdivisions using the GPS satellites. Nobody here seems particularly worried, but other countries worry that it's completely controlled by the US military, and if they decided to switch it off for some security reason a lot of people would be in a lot of trouble.

MACCA: Does it mean that young trainee surveyors don't learn how to use the stars now?

ANDREW: It's one of those things being debated. Because there's more and more new knowledge, if everything was left in courses they'd take seven or eight years. At a conference in Malaysia a couple of years ago it was quite an issue. I think the people there, partly because they're Muslims, feel very close to the stars. An old gentleman got up and said, 'The GPS constellation belongs to a foreign power, but the sun, moon and stars belong to God.'

# 3

# There's a lot of weather about

*At the end of May, South Australia had bad dust-storms — a big smudge from Kangaroo Island to Mount Gambier, going over Victoria and Bass Strait. Dennis rang in and Macca asked about the dust.*
DENNIS: 'Victoria pinched the Grand Prix from us, so we thought we'd give 'em the dirt to go with it.'

from
LEON & JANE ASHBY
ARAMAC
QUEENSLAND

WE'VE HAD SIX CONSECUTIVELY dry years here on our 36,000 acres until this last week. We are supposed to average eighteen to twenty inches and for the year prior to last week the total was five inches. I was working the dozer in our dry lake last week and noticed an oil leak. Leaving the dozer in the dry lake bed, I took off the offending pipe and headed home to repair it. On my return storm clouds were brewing so I left things as they were. That night one and a half inches fell, the next evening another two inches fell and after four days eight and a half inches had fallen. The creeks were absolutely 'bankers' and the dozer was in five feet of water. It will have to stay there for maybe a year until the lake level falls through evaporation.

I thought you might like to know that folklore has it the best way to make it rain is to leave a vehicle in a dry dam or lake.

*An Australian surf champion went to Bali for a competition. While there an earthquake set up a big tidal wave which swept inland, taking everything with it. Our surf champ survived:*
'I told them, that's the way we surf in Australia — in a hut through a jungle.'

from
COL WHITE
INNISFAIL
QUEENSLAND

THIS MORNING WE HAD some friends over for breakfast. It looked like being a beautiful morning so I set up the tables in the backyard. The bright red tablecloths were set off superbly by the freshly mown thick emerald grass. Even the weeds in the garden looked bright and cheerful as they became part of the atmosphere. A couple of kookaburras, a butcher bird, two willy wagtails and the inevitable myna birds were hopping around in anticipation of being able to pick up some crumbs. The politicians were safely locked away in Canberra and there was a feeling of peace and serenity about our backyard that needs to be experienced. Simply describing it is inadequate.

Then you played the Innisfail Rain song.

Within five minutes the sky turned from blue to grey and a languid sort of Innisfail shower swept across the yard. You could almost sense the smirk on the face of the raindrops as they observed the flurry of activity entailed in transferring everything to under the house. You should never trust the weather in Innisfail at this time of the year. I think the important point to note is that it is not only at outside broadcasts that you can produce rain.

DURING THE DROUGHT IN the 1930s my swaggie Uncle Bob always carried a handful of dust in his first-aid kit while travelling (on foot), toting his swag, looking for jobs in the outback.

He said that people got so used to living in drought conditions that sometimes, if the drought broke, the raindrops could send them into a state of shock and the only way to revive them was to throw a handful of dust in their face.

from
PEGGY BALFOUR
MULLUMBIMBY
NEW SOUTH WALES

• • • • • • • • • • • • • • • • • • •

WEEK BY WEEK I hear you speak of drought and listen to its effects. Last week I went to see for myself. I was in Condobolin a few days before you.

As I drove west from Orange I cried for the dying earth. This is my country and it is wasting! Even the trees, grey-green in the overall view, are brown and drooping. Dead kangaroos by the score alongside the roads and sheep pulling at bare soil where no more nourishment lies.

And then I went to the 42nd West Milby Rodeo and Gymkhana. West Milby is not even a hamlet, just a couple of sheds and a generator, transformed by a team of local young men into a sports ground for the day. The merry-go-round was eight forty-gallon drums on a converted clothes hoist, and the operator spent the whole day providing rides for children. Another stalwart drove a tractor with small carts attached throughout the day, and a crop duster dropped dozens of ping pong balls with 5c, 10c, etc. written on them, to be redeemed for a bag of sweets. The adults enjoyed all manner of events like nail driving and dog leaping (the dogs doing the leaping, not the people!) and the most fun came from a drum full of lizards, bogeye variety, with numbers painted on them, which raced out of an upturned drum to the edge of a dusty circle. Everyone had a wonderful time.

from
MARGARET MOLLOY
CHURCH POINT
NEW SOUTH WALES

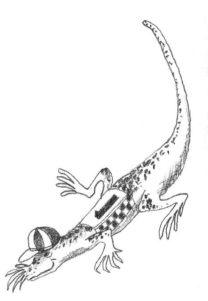

The purpose of the day—and here's my tribute to the great Aussie spirit—was to raise funds for local charities. People paid for the right to race their lizards, then bought them again later to boost the charity funds further. How can we city people do anything but be grateful and proud that the real Australian spirit survives and revives. Let it revive us all while we pray for rain. If there are tears out there, they don't make a public appearance. One man, when asked how he was going, said 'Chickens this year, feathers next year!'

• • • • • • • • • • • • • • • • • • • • • • • • • • • • • • • • • • • • • • • • • • • • • • • • • • • • • • • • • • • • • • • • •

*A jackaroo from Darwin in June:*
MACCA: 'Give us a weather report.'
JACKAROO: 'It was so cold last night I had to switch the fan off and pull up a sheet.'

• • • • • • • • • • • • • • • • • • • • • • • • • • • • • • • • • • • • • • • • • • • • • • • • • • • • • • • • • • • • • • • • •

I CAN'T STAND IT any longer—I had to turn you off again last week because for the second time I couldn't bear to listen to everyone raving on about all the rain when we've had next to none! I'm pleased for them but when you're the only area missing out again and again, it gets harder to smile, especially when everyone takes it for granted that the drought's over everywhere.

We are two elderly people who walked off our land after forty-five years last year and gave it to our son. Believe me we did him no favours. Because we gave the land away we are deemed by the government to have sold it for hundreds

from
AURIEL HARTWIG
MONTO
QUEENSLAND

of thousands of dollars, so we get no pension. We used what we had saved to buy our house in Monto and are reduced to living on practically nothing. This is no isolated case. It's happening everywhere where families are trying to hold on to their land.

The drought and the fact that the 98 per cent of Australians who live on the coast expect to get their food cheaper than anywhere else in the world, has quickly reduced us to a peasant class and it's likely to stay. Hence the excuse for a poem I wrote in one of my more bitter moments. I'm not alone, believe me. I know you can't help it, but please spare a thought for those of us who are still in dire straits and likely to be till God knows when.

What good is freedom when you have no food,
The air smells sweet and the birds sound good—
But your head hangs down and your steps are slow
What good is freedom when you've nowhere to go?

You once owned land like you're walking through
But the clouds blew away and the skies stayed blue
You fought the good fight—never counted the cost—
What good is freedom when the cause is lost?

The poets write of our wide brown land
The pollies bury their heads in the sand
'It's a lovely fine day,' they say on the coast—
They care not about what matters most.

They sing the anthem 'We're young and free',
I hope they're not singing of such as we,
We're old and tired, all our work was in vain,
What good is freedom without the rain?

*Jim from Mount Gambier, South Australia on the weather:*
'Mate, it rains for three hundred and sixty days and drips off the trees for the other five.'

from
LEIGH HARKNESS
QUEANBEYAN
NEW SOUTH WALES

ONE OF THE BEST COMMENTS on the government's budget I have heard came from a farmer friend. He told me that the government is acting like a farmer that had ten paddocks. This farmer was doing very well until a drought hit him. Things were so bad that he decided to sell off a paddock and use the proceeds to keep going.

When the drought broke, the farmer did well, but with only nine paddocks he did not do as well as he did before. So, when a drought struck again, he was in a worse state than before and had to sell two paddocks.

When that drought broke, the farmer could survive, but with only seven paddocks he could not put away any savings or fodder for the next drought. The next drought was disastrous for him. He had to sell three paddocks.

When the drought broke this time, he could not even survive on his four paddocks. He had to sell one just to keep going. When the next drought came, he had to sell the rest of his farm just to pay his debts. He then took a job as a labourer on his old farm.

• • • • • • • • • • • • • • • • • • • •

WHY DOESN'T IT HAIL during the night? The question has been asked several times on the ABC. I have to tell you of my experience with one hail storm. Woken in the early hours of the morning with a sharp bang on the roof, like a gun going off with increasing regularity, I leapt out of bed. At that moment there was a huge roar like a jet plane getting louder. Doors started banging, curtains blowing up to the ceiling, then it came, hailstones the size of golf balls, absolutely no exaggeration. As the hail was being blown horizontally by the ferocious wind untold damage occurred, windows smashing, flywire being ripped off doors and windows, cement sheeting walls pitted with holes, dents in the galvanised iron roof, garden hoses perforated. It lasted about twelve minutes, then there was quietness—very eerie. I went to check the dogs in their forty-four gallon drum kennels and they were very pleased to see me. No stock loss occurred, but unfortunately many birds were killed.

It was a terrifying experience in the dark of the night.

from
MARY DIXON
ALBURY
NEW SOUTH WALES

• • • • • • • • • • • • • • • • • • • •

I have been away fixing fences, dragging dead stock out of dams,
There has not been a 'Wet', for four long years . . .
The wife is not complaining, she has seen it all before,
But often now, is very close to tears.
Her smile is always cheerful, she has never yet demurred,
Yet I know, she sometimes suffers more than I.
At dawn, I often find her, in her night gown, in the yard,
Searching, for a raincloud, in the sky.

The tank is nearly empty, though the windmill is pumping still,
Another month, shall probably see us out.
Stock are dying daily, the creeks have all run dry,
Some say, we have a never-ending drought.
We knew the risks we were taking, when we chose this way of life,
Chose to make a living on the land,
Chose to raise a family, build a place to call our own,
Probably, there are those who understand.

There was no work available in the town when we were schooled,
Our only other option was the dole . . .
So, regardless of the hardships, the sweat, the dust, the heat,
Hopefully, we shall achieve our goal.
Farming is not easy . . . but we enjoy it, just the same,
We have many friends, who share our way of life;
Many friends, who suffer, yet never say a word . . .
But always there to help, in times of strife.

from
SKIP FARLEY
CAIRNS
QUEENSLAND

Tonight smells somehow different, there's something in the air.
A something, which I cannot quite define…
Flying ants in thousands, now blotting out the lights,
Falling on the table, as we dine…
I peer thru' open windows …to the paddocks out beyond,
See darkness, rent by lightning, on the plain,
The distant roll of thunder … a coolness in the air…
That 'Smell', now well remembered…the 'Smell' of coming rain.

from
EILEEN CUMMINGS
LEGANA
TASMANIA

NIGEL RINGING FROM THE Gobi Desert and mentioning my son Nick's involvement with the Ash Wednesday fires has inspired me to write. It has refreshed my memory of something wonderful that happened at that sad time. I think this is a beautiful example of human thought and compassion. The sad part, which I will not dwell on, was that Nick lost his home, his possessions and his Dalmatian dog in the Adelaide Hills. The next-door house was spared so he went to stay there for a while as he pieced his life together and decided to rebuild. One evening he returned from work to find a notice on the door: 'Beware of the dog'. Inside was a beautiful Dalmatian pup. This is the wonderful part. The CFS (Country Fire Service) knew of his loss and had heard that the CFS in Victoria had saved a litter of Dalmatian pups when some kennels were burnt out at Cockatoo. The owners had offered them to replace dogs lost in the fires and the firemen in the Adelaide Hills arranged to have a pup delivered to Nick. It was a bright spot in a tragic time. Australians are terrific, aren't they.

*Adrian the weather man in Port Hedland phoned:*
MACCA: 'Give us a weather report for Port Hedland.'
ADRIAN: 'Probably hot and dry, but perhaps a late storm.'
MACCA: 'You speak like all these meteorological blokes!'
ADRIAN: 'Yes, we're highly skilled in the use of words like "perhaps" and "probability"…'

from
'GRANDMA'
KARUMBA
QUEENSLAND

WE ARE FAMOUS FOR our prawning, being one of the biggest exporters in Australia. However I would like Australians who have not visited here to know about the spectacular phenomenon of the 'Morning Glory'. The Morning Glory is a sausage-shaped cloud formation that passes over usually in the morning at sunrise, although occasionally during the night, during August and September.

One moment the skies are clear, but within a few minutes one can see and hear the wind (which turns very cold) associated with the approach of this formation. It stretches from horizon to horizon, rolling over and over into itself; and moves so fast that it's all over within a few minutes. It is a glorious sight and one is left with a feeling of great exhilaration in its wake.

*Macca asked a bloke in Western Australia the name of his property.*
BLOKE: 'Elsewhere.'
MACCA: 'Why did you call it that?'
BLOKE: 'Well, when I hear the weather they say, "Rain and showers in the south, elsewhere dry", so I reckon they're talking about my place.'

Your tiny hand is frozen,
As also are your feet.
Please turn around so that
Our extremities don't meet.

In the tenderness of first love
We bought a double bed.
With all my heart I wish
We'd bought twin beds instead.

Although I love you dearly
I really get the fidgets
When from the warmth of slumber
I encounter your cold digits.

Please buy yourself some mittens
And woolly bootees, or
With frozen hands and ice-cold feet
You're sleeping *on the floor!*

from
PAT EISLER
TRARALGON
VICTORIA

## MACCA MAINTENANCE

A two-minute shower only twice in a week
Will freshen you up, keep you fragrant and sleek.
Make the 'bird-in-the-bird-bath' your daily routine
On the shower-less days, to ensure you're clean;
And, in any case Macca, your listeners won't know
Because smells don't transmit on a radio show.

from
DOROTHY B. WATT
BRIAGOLONG
VICTORIA

I HAVE A WEE STORY about 'showers' or, in my case, washing children. I am the eldest of seven little Australians and our mother would supervise washing us when water was scarce. She'd say she would wash us 'down as far as possible, then up as far as possible and then she'd wash "possible".'

In the case of two-minute showers I think it might be wise to wash 'possible' first just in case you ran out of minutes!

from
CORALIE STREATFIELD
VASSE
WESTERN AUSTRALIA

from
DAVID BEARUP
GUYRA
NEW SOUTH WALES

## THE ADJACENT RANGES

There is a cockies paradise, a perfect place to farm,
It knows not drought nor bushfire, free from nature's harm.
Within my mind I picture it, God's chosen little spot,
But just to tell you where it is, I find that I cannot.
The weatherman he knows the site, promotes its virtues well,
Yet where it is he's talking of, I'm blowed if I can tell.
The forecast says, 'Raining on the Coast—Extending to the Adjacent Ranges,'
And there it is, the elusive spot, that's free from pastoral dangers.
Logic tells me this paradise, is east of the Great Divide,
How can a place so often mentioned, be so easy to hide.
I've wandered down the atlas, from Cape York to Bermagui,
I reckon it's a secret hideaway, of the supreme rainmaker 'Huey'.
The first place that came to mind, was Queensland's dampish Tully,
It seems to cop a drop or two, bereft of a dryish gully.
Lots and lots of mountain names, but 'ADJACENT' wasn't one,
So I looked further southward, for my search had just begun.
My finger lingered at the easterly point, Murwillumbah's 'Mt Warning',
Is it in a maze of Sun's first rays, that awaken Australia each morning.
I continued to roam closer to home, Guyra, where the little boy was lost,
Perhaps each peak I was anxious to seek, was covered in winter frost.
On and on to Oberon, west of the mountains called 'blue',
I had a look in each cranny and nook, it never yielded a clue.
I've searched in vain for this mountain chain, as far as I can go,
I am indeed a man in need, for a mate to give me a blow.
So I'm begging all drovers, other rovers, or any blokes who knock around,
Can someone kindly direct me to, this favoured piece of ground.

*Don, an auctioneer in Cairns, was driving from Mackay, and he had a nice turn of phrase:*
'I've just come over the Farleigh hill,' he said, 'and the valleys are all cloaked in a doona of mist.'

from
JENNETTE BISHOP
MELROSE
SOUTH AUSTRALIA

## ELSEWHERE NEAR THE ADJACENT RANGES

So you wonder where the Adjacent Ranges could be,
Well there's a place that's always puzzled me.
It's a place that is spoken of every day,
When hearing the weather report, they say,
'It's raining there in the Adjacent Ranges
But Elsewhere is fine no forecast for changes.'

It's true these places are hard to find,
They're not on a map of any kind.
They appear to be in the state where I live
As through the place names I carefully sieve.
But of these two names there is no trace,
Yet the weather is told in either place.

When in other states for a visit short,
Up pop these names in the weather report.
Once again to the map I turn my attention,
But in these other states there is still no mention.

Elsewhere's the place I'd like to be
As it's always fine and warm you see.
I fancy it must be a Camelot sight,
Good weather by day and raining by night.
Everything pleasant and green and lush,
For the weather seems always in spring's first flush.

Perhaps Elsewhere and the Ranges have been,
All the while in a hidden land unseen.
Established and firm in an interesting place,
In only the mind in the reporter's case.

So what a shame we shall never get together
In those places that could give us so much pleasure.

## G'day, this is Macca

MACCA: Cyclone Olivia has been wreaking havoc on the coast of Western Australia, and on the line I've got Andrea Menzies from Balmoral Station, which is about eighty kilometres from Pannawonica. Andrea, tell us what it's been like, when it started, and what's happened at Balmoral Station.

ANDREA: Well, it came through about 7.30 at night with very bad winds. We were very close to the eye because we definitely experienced the calm. The eye went through at about 8.30 and it was calm for about twenty minutes and then we had another couple of hours of very strong winds which completely took my roof off. I had ceilings and things coming in, so it was a very terrifying experience.

MACCA: I'll bet. Have you experienced cyclones before?

ANDREA: Yes, I have, but I've never experienced anything like this one.

MACCA: What did you do?

ANDREA: Well, obviously, I was inside, and I had to think of my own protection because once the roof and ceiling in the kitchen went I didn't know what other ceilings would go. I was huddled under a mattress under a table, watching a wall flex. I'd packed the lounge chairs up to try to give myself some protection if anything else was going to come in around me.

MACCA: Did it dump a lot of water over the landscape?

ANDREA: No, with this one there wasn't as much rain as we normally get out of a cyclone. We measured approximately ninety millimetres of rain, but we'd lost the lid off the rain gauge so I don't know how accurate the reading was. With the kind of winds we were getting I think the rain would have been horizontal and a lot of it actually missed the gauge.

• • • • • • • • • • • • • • • • • • • • • • • • • • • • • • • • • • • • • • • • • • • • • • • • • • • • • • • • • • • • •

JACK THE CABBIE: 'I work three am to three pm.'

MACCA: 'What passengers do you get at three am?'

JACK: 'We pick up all the drunks.'

MACCA: 'That must be a great job.'

JACK: 'It gets harder as you get older—after the sun comes up we get a better class of passenger.'

• • • • • • • • • • • • • • • • • • • • • • • • • • • • • • • • • • • • • • • • • • • • • • • • • • • • • • • • • • • • •

# 4

# *L*ittle possums

## G'day, this is Macca

AARON: Hello, it's Aaron Maloney from Broadford. I'm ringing up because I haven't said hello to you for ages. Last time I spoke to you was down in Melbourne and I was only in grade 5 and now I'm in year 8.

MACCA: That's right, you and your brother have cystic fibrosis and you spoke to us in about '93. How are you?

AARON: Good, thank you.

MACCA: That's good, and how's Gerard, your brother?

AARON: Oh, he's pretty well. He's very tired because last night we were in an amateur production for our school and we got home at eleven o'clock so it was a bit of a late night. I'm ringing up to tell you about cystic fibrosis week next week. My school is selling roses and we're planting roses in the garden, sixty-five of them, because a young boy said to his sister, 'What disease have you got?' and she said, 'Cystic fibrosis,' and he said 'Sixty-five roses?' and that's how it came about.

MACCA: So you're planting sixty-five roses. What school is that?

AARON: Broadford Secondary College in Victoria, and it's on next week. If anyone sees people selling the roses, which are little pins, they could buy them for a few dollars and that would really help the research.

MACCA: I'm sure. I hope I see them because I'm going to buy one. How are things in Broadford otherwise?

AARON: Oh, school's pretty good, and Broadford's a really nice place to live. Recently I've really got into school productions. I've always wanted to be an actor, and I've finally got my chance. The producer for the Broadford Amateur Group came up to me and said 'You're very good, son, you're needed for our production next year,' so I'm really pleased about that.

MACCA: Good on you, Aaron. That'll be great: lots of things to do and lots of things to learn. And cystic fibrosis week is on in the coming week and people should buy a little rose wherever they see one for sale.

AARON: That'd be very nice, yes, because a lot of lives are lost—young children—and it's very sad.

· · · · · · · · · · · · · · · · · · ·

from
VICKIE SORENSEN
CLYDE
VICTORIA

MY NAME IS VICKIE SORENSEN. I am eleven years old. We are doing a project on a famous Australian and I picked you because my dad listens to you all the time, well every Sunday.

Could you please send me a picture of yourself. Can you tell me a bit about yourself? I will tell you about me. I have a dog called Misty, two birds, one fish, two water snails and I had fourteen crabs but they're dead.

· · · · · · · · · · · · · · · · · · ·

from
ANNABELLE COPPIN
(AGE 10)
WESTERN AUSTRALIA

MY NAME IS ANNABELLE COPPIN. I'm ten years old and live on a cattle station in the Pilbara in Western Australia. I do Port Hedland School of the Air. I love the bush. I listen to your show quite a bit. Yes, South Australia and New South Wales had a terrible drought but please don't forget about us. We had a terrible terrible drought for four long dry years. We watched cattle die of hunger and thirst, our wells started to dry up. We had thirty poddy calves (calves with dead mothers). It was awful. Please don't forget us.

## CLEAN UP DAY

Our name is Australia Fair,
We are good, we have flair.
We're asking you to lend a hand,
To help us clean up our land.
If we keep it clean
It will be a great scheme to keep Australia looking like a dream!
No more rubbish to ruin our land
Because everyone gave a helping hand.

from
EMMA COCKS
(AGE 11)

I woke up on a Sunday morning
When the rooster
Cock-a-doodle-do's
To hear Mum and Dad's radio
Giving out good news
Macca's gonna be in Lincoln
And did the news spread fast
from Mrs Thelma Rodgers
To all the kids in the class
The great day had arrived
And people from all over town
were there to meet Macca
And listen to his program right out loud
Macca played his songs
And sang along with them too
I think Macca's great don't you!
So switch on your radio on Sundays
And listen for the news
Is Macca coming your way?
For if he is that's great news.

from
CRISTY SCHRAMM
(AGE 12)
PORT LINCOLN
SOUTH AUSTRALIA

I LIKE TO LISTEN TO your program every Sunday morning and my teacher at Whorouly Primary School made this section on your program an English and SOSE lesson.

Well, to start off I live in Bowman's Forest about thirty-one kilometres from Wangaratta, fourteen kilometres from Myrtleford and seven kilometres from Whorouly (War-ow-lee). The area is known for the wine, high country, and the famous bushranger 'Ned Kelly'.

There are seventy-nine children at our school and four class teachers. I like our school because everybody knows each other and we all work together as a team; be it a concert or a sports day. There are eight children in grade six which is my grade. We usually have an end-of-year concert, a sports day and a ball game day.

I like living in the area because there are lots of waterways, the bush and

from
LINDEN HEYWOOD
BOWMAN'S FOREST
VICTORIA

heaps of clean air. We have a river paddock. We swim there just about every day of the summer and walk down around the lagoons every week. There is abundant bird life and we think there are bandicoots hidden in the sprayed blackberries. We go rapids riding on a tractor inner-tube. In the river we go boating and fishing. I can only remember one major flood which was in October 1993. Another great example of teamwork. One house on a hill had taken in about fifteen people. Whorouly in Aboriginal means underwater so I guess it lives up to its name.

I like living on a farm because there's lots of room to run around, kick the football and play cricket. In the spring, when the grass is long, we make tunnels through the grass. I like feeding the poddy lambs and playing basketball in the shed on rainy days. We ride our horses down to the river and canter up the hills. We all own our own cows and sell their sons as bullocks to the abattoir. My dad is mad keen on merino sheep.

• • • • • • • • • • • • • • • • • • •

from
KRISTY FRANCIS, YEAR 8
PARNDANA AREA
SCHOOL
KANGAROO ISLAND

**M**Y NAME IS KRISTY FRANCIS and I live on Kangaroo Island. Kangaroo Island is regarded as the birthplace of South Australia because it was the first place Matthew Flinders found in South Australia. Kangaroo Island got its name because when Matthew Flinders was sailing past he saw a brown lump and as he got closer he realised it was a kangaroo. They had not eaten fresh meat for such a long time that when they landed they killed lots of kangaroos and had a big feast.

The only way you can travel to and from Kangaroo Island is by boat or plane as it is approximately twenty kilometres to the nearest point of the mainland which is Cape Jervois. The population consists of approximately 4,000 people and due to the isolation of the island you know most of the people around you. There are three schools on the island, Parndana Area, Kingscote Area and Penneshaw Area. I go to Parndana Area along with about 250 others from the ages of five to eighteen.

I love living on Kangaroo Island for many reasons. I live in the town centre of Parndana and only have to walk up the road to go to school. I like living in Parndana because I am close to friends, close to the shops, close to school and it is safe. You can walk down the street at night and not have to worry a bit about crime or something happening to you. I also like living where I do for the simple reason that you don't have to worry about locking your car doors when you go into the shop because Parndana has a generally good community, it is not polluted and is just across the road from wildlife that you would only be able to see on the mainland in a zoo.

I have visited other parts of Australia but I think that if I do end up moving I will still come back here as it is where I was born and is and always will be my home.

• • • • • • • • • • • • • • • • • • •

from
LERA GRIBAKINA (AGE 14)
RANDWICK
NEW SOUTH WALES

On your program you were talking about the wattle. Well, I have some interesting information about the Australian emblem. In Russia, where I lived for most of my life, wattles were given to women on International Women's Day, 8 March, and I think that no women had any idea that this golden flower could come from a place so isolated as Australia. I even wonder if they knew that Australia existed. Only after coming here I found out that the wattle was an Australian native plant and an emblem.

I really enjoy your program, and after hearing about the budget cuts to the ABC I keep hoping that it will not hit 'Australia All Over' strongly or, even better, not at all.

P.S. Just one more thing. In a camp during year 7 we had a trivia night, and one of the questions was, 'Name the Russian ballerina whose name is a dessert that is purely Australian.' What do you think they said? Sarah Lee! Well, I don't know all the Russian history, but I don't there was a Russian ballerina named Sarah Lee. It was actually Pavlova.

## G'day, this is Macca

HENRY: Hello, it's Henry Crawford from Devonborough Downs sheep station, just west of Olary, South Australia.

MACCA: That's where you've had all the rain. How old are you, Henry?

HENRY: I'm twelve. We've had about nine-and-a-half inches of rain, that's quite a bit, although I know that a station just west of Olary has had about thirteen-and-a-half inches.

MACCA: I'll bet that's the most rain you've seen ever, Henry. What has it been like? Have you been flooded at your place?

HENRY: No, our house in on a hill so it all just runs past, but some of our friends' houses were washed away.

MACCA: Really! Does it look as though you're going to get more rain?

HENRY: They're forecasting it for this afternoon but everything looks nice and green now. It rained for about two days.

MACCA: Tell me about Devonborough Downs.

HENRY: It's about eighty thousand acres and we run about five and half thousand sheep. It's pretty good to live here: no noise of city streets, but now we've got the noise of frogs from all the rain.

MACCA: The train line got washed away near Olary, didn't it? Have you been down to have a look at it? Is it far from you?

HENRY: It's about thirty-odd kilometres, but we can't go anywhere because you walk out the front gate and you just sink down in mud.

MACCA: Nine-and-a-half inches of rain is a lot. Have you got brothers and sisters?

HENRY: I've got two brothers who are at boarding school in Adelaide at the moment. They've been wanting to come home to see it all. My mum says it's a once in a lifetime experience.

MACCA: Can I talk to Mum?

GLENYS CRAWFORD: How are you?

MACCA: I've been talking to Henry, who's full of information.

GLENYS: He certainly is, but there's a lot to tell, I guess. In 1989 we had huge floods here: some places recorded between five and nine inches overnight but everyone is saying that this rain has been the biggest ever recorded. We've had two rescues by Rescue One helicopter in this area, people who were floodbound; their lives were really in danger.

MACCA: It's nice to talk to you. Henry's a nice little kid, isn't he? Do you teach him by correspondence?

GLENYS: I certainly do.

MACCA: I'd love to come and see you sometime when things dry out a bit, eh? Thank Henry for calling me.

* * * * * * * * * * * * * * * * * * * * * * * * * * * * * * * * * * * * * * * * * * *

from
STACEY COLE
MACKAY
QUEENSLAND

**HI**! MY NAME IS STACEY and I'm sixteen from Eton in Mackay, Queensland. I was listening to 'Why I Live Where I Live' and heard a letter from a man who said that there was cultural imperialism in Australia from the Americans. Well, I tend to agree with him. I go to Whitsunday Anglican School in Mackay and I'm in Year 11 and my Modern History teacher always says there has been the 'Coca Colavisation' and 'Mcdonaldarisation' of Australia. Just look at teenage fashion today — the baggy 'homey' fashions from the US of A.

I want to know what happened to the Aussie. The true blue, dinky di, can't give a damn Aussie? Recently I represented Australia in my sport, roller skating, in a Junior Pacific Competition in New Zealand (for those who are wondering, I came 2nd!). Anyway, it seems half the team were skating for America 'cause they wore 'Chicago Bulls', 'San Francisco 49ers', etc. clothes. Are they ashamed of the country? Well, call me a nationalist, but I love my country and I'm proud to show it. I hope our country doesn't turn into a baby of America. That's all.

* * * * * * * * * * * * * * * * * *

from
NORMA MORTIMER

**I** RECENTLY DID A bit of volunteer work for a man called Bill Crews who is minister for Ashfield (NSW) Parish Mission and chairman of the Exodus Foundation. In the five hours I was there I saw approximately 150 people get a more than wholesome lunch, and saw Sister Helen, who is from the nearby Catholic church, load up her car with food to take to young families who can't get to the hall for lunch. These people are men and women with shattered lives, people who have been set free from mental institutions—none of them know how to cope with the outside world so they all come to Bill and Sister Helen.

Worst of all was seeing the young homeless kids—kids who really don't choose to be homeless. As one kid I interviewed said to me once: 'On the street I have a 50/50 chance of being bashed or molested, at home it was a sure thing every night. Once my father finished with Mum, it was me and my sister's turn.'

Ian, Bill Crews needs help from Australia and I know your program can get the word to people who might like to help.

P.S. I know it is not nice to mess up people's Sunday morning with a tragic story or request such as this, but I want to do everything that is possible to salvage young lives. Winter is the worst time of all for them.

* * * * * * * * * * * * * * * * * *

## G'day, this is Macca

WADE: Macca, it's Wade here from Bli Bli. I'm eleven, nearly twelve, and I've just been to Ayers Rock on our first big holiday with my brother, Lee, and Mum and Dad.

MACCA: Did you have a good time?

WADE: Yes. We climbed Ayers Rock, Dad and Lee and I, and Mum walked around it with us. It was really good fun.

MACCA: I've never climbed Ayers Rock. What's it like—is it scary?

WADE: Yes. The chain's really low and it's very steep and narrow in some parts.

MACCA: How long did it take you to climb up?

WADE: It took us an hour to go up and an hour to come back down.

MACCA: You took it steady, that's the best way to do it, isn't it?

WADE: Yes, we had plenty of rests, and then we went around to the Olgas and we walked around those. They're very beautiful, the Olgas. And we went to the Valley of the Winds, which is a big walk, I think it's about six kilometres. We saw a little wallaby there.

MACCA: So was this a trip to the Centre in the school holidays?

WADE: Yes. And we went down to Coober Pedy. It's quite fascinating. We went to the underground motel, which is big; we really enjoyed Coober Pedy.

MACCA: So you'd never been to the Northern Territory before?

WADE: No. We came up the Birdsville Track and we saw lots of big wedge-tailed eagles, and all the wildflowers had come out because they've had lots of rain and it was really pretty. A tyre fell off the truck on the Birdsville Track and as we were getting it fixed this cow jumped up on Dad's chest and tried to give him a cuddle. He had to push it off his chest because it nearly knocked him over. He said it was so funny, but he was a bit scared because it just kept following him around.

MACCA: Wade, a lot of people listening to this program this morning wouldn't have done half the things that you've done. You've been on the Birdsville Track, you've climbed Ayers Rock, you've seen the Olgas, you saw a wallaby—you've done it all!

WADE: We've got our didgeridoos so Lee and I are playing them. We'd love to start a little band with Mum on the music sticks.

MACCA: Well, don't forget me: I play the guitar and I'm learning the trombone, so you learn the didge with Lee and I'll play guitar and Mum can play the music sticks. Wade, tell us about Bli Bli. Have you got a farm there?

WADE: No, we haven't got a farm, but we've got quite a big house. We have a swimming pool in the front which we let the kids in the street use, and we have a half tennis court up the back so we have great games.

MACCA: Yes, all roads lead to Wade's place, I'd say, with a half tennis court and a swimming pool. It's been lovely to talk to you, Wade; we'll talk again, I reckon. You ring me any time something's happening. You can be our reporter in Bli Bli.

WADE: Okay. Thanks a lot, Macca. It's nice talking to you, too.

IN 1994 I HEARD you reading a letter from a chap in Western Australia suggesting what is wrong with the country and how he felt it could be righted, e.g. National Service, mothers staying home with children and generally going back to how things were in the 1950s when life was much simpler. Up until twelve months

from
PAMELA RULE
LATHAM
ACT

ago that is exactly the way I felt, but I was brought back to the 1990s with a jolt when I had to face the fact that drugs did not just happen to other people and their children, but were actually in my family right under my nose and I had not seen it. I had to wake up to the fact that life is not the same for my children as it was for me.

I had what I thought was a normal family, two children, a boy and a girl, and a stable home life. So how could it be that my child turned to drugs? Unbelievable. My husband, who is ex-military, and I had nowhere to turn for help for our son, until my husband, by chance, went to a lecture by Ken Dyers at the AIS in Canberra. How often in life a chance encounter or meeting offers the answers you are looking for. We learnt to take responsibility and stop applying the rules of the 1950s and the changes in all of our lives is amazing. Our son has turned his life around and our relationship with him is better than it has ever been. There is an honesty and openness that was hidden before.

What I really wanted to say was that there is hope, but we all have to take responsibility for our own lives and not keep putting that responsibility onto others.

. . . . . . . . . . . . . . . . . . . . . . . . . . . . . . . . . . . . . . . . . . . . . . . . . . . . .

### G'day, this is Macca

ROHINI: Hello, Ian. I'm Rohini from Newcastle, New South Wales. Happy Mother's Day.
MACCA: Well, thanks very much Rohini.
ROHINI: Actually, I have been trying since last week. I wanted to talk about how I like this program and how it is good for people like us who are migrants here. So that we know more about Australian culture and the countryside. For example, I learned the word 'sheila' from this program.
MACCA: Oh dear.
ROHINI: I knew the word 'bloke', but I didn't know the word 'sheila' and one of my girl-friends mentioned it to me and the very next Sunday I heard it on this program. So that was good.
MACCA: Well, I reckon you're a top sheila, Rohini.
ROHINI: Thank you. I also wanted to share that we don't have in our Indian culture Mother's Day. It's good to have a Mother's Day and Father's Day. But we have one interesting day called 'Sister's Day' and 'Brother's Day'. We celebrate it twice a year, once around our new year time in November, and another I think March or April. We express a feeling how sisters love their brothers and brothers love their sisters.
MACCA: Isn't that nice.

. . . . . . . . . . . . . . . . . . . . . . . . . . . . . . . . . . . . . . . . . . . . . . . . . . . . .

# *T*hat's us in those films!

*We were on the plane back from Perth. I'd flown over to attend a luncheon for the launch of the SAS Resources Trust (which, by the way, is still looking for donations) and to do the program at 6WF. You can't escape watching the TV on planes —it's in your face—but I was just looking, no sound, and this bloke is driving a Zephyr. Then a Bondi beach scene, and a young girl pushing a stroller, and I thought, Hey that's an Australian film. (How unusual.) I reached for the headset and so began another saga.*

*'Mr Reliable' is in my top ten of best films. And it's ours. Sadly, because of inadequate promotion and the stranglehold Hollywood has on the world, 'Mr Reliable' died a quick box office death. But not before we were able to let thousands know what a good film it was.*

*I must admit the censored version I saw on the plane made it an even better film than the unedited version I later saw on the big screen at the Kogarah Mecca. As with most of its screenings the audience applauded spontaneously at the end of the film.*

*I see my role and indeed it's what the listeners expect, to present Australia to Australians. I hope to continue to do this wherever I am. I'm so proud to have been able to bring to the notice of Australians things of interest and value that are too often ignored by newspapers, radio, and especially television. 'Mr Reliable' is just one of hundreds of examples.*

• • • • • • • • • • • • • • • • • •

from
BEVERLEY BONAR
WESTMEADOWS
VICTORIA

SINCE HEARING THAT YOU support 'Mr Reliable' I intend to listen to you on Sunday mornings. The film was showing at a theatre complex at Tullamarine and I saw it twice knowing it wouldn't last long. (A few months ago an Aussie film 'Love Serenade' didn't make it to the local theatres. I found it at an independent theatre and it was a terrific film, so I was aware that some theatres don't support Aussie films.) 'Mr Reliable' is the best film I've seen, yet I was very disappointed that six or eight people max were in the theatre each time. People I speak to have never heard of 'Mr Reliable'. They prefer to go see those awful American films containing violence and with no real story. I rang the theatre to try and find out why the film was removed and the person answering the phone said they had 'other commitments'. I'm sure promotion has a lot to do with it. If it is re-shown, I'll certainly be there to see it again.

• • • • • • • • • • • • • • • • • •

from
ANNE BROOKSBANK/ELLIS
PALM BEACH
NEW SOUTH WALES

AS A FILM AND TELEVISION writer, I've listened with a lot of interest to your praise of 'Mr Reliable'. I too missed it when it came on so briefly, though I would certainly have seen it if I'd had the chance.

The problem, as I'm sure you're aware, applies not just to this one film, but to a number of other very good Australian films that were never given a real run on local screens. I've missed too many of them, but my husband, Bob Ellis, has always made a point of getting to such films (though even he too missed 'Mr Reliable') because he writes a column for *Encore*, the film magazine, and often reviews Australian films there. I think everyone in the film industry would tell you that Bob has consistently been a generous critic towards Australian work, where other local critics often seem more carping towards Australian films than the imported product. I know Bob recently gave much praise to 'Dead Heart', and it is good to see it rightly resuscitated by good publicity generated by Bryan Brown and Ernie Dingo when it was seriously flagging. As you correctly said this morning, films die without publicity and the distributors, mainly foreign-owned, seem reluctant to put any money into publicity for Australian films. The films are so often put into a small cinema in the big cinema complexes, and allowed to take their chance against the heavily publicised imports. It is almost inevitable that the Australian films, however good, will lose out, and will be pulled off after a few weeks, and be tagged, however unjustly, as failures.

• • • • • • • • • • • • • • • • • •

ON MY WAY HOME from Alice Springs 'Mr Reliable' was shown on the plane and I'd recommend it to anyone as I'm a movie buff and loved it. I'd love to see it on the large screen.

from
LOLA KEARNEY
CAMPANIA
TASMANIA

• • • • • • • • • • • • • • • • • •

I'M SO GLAD YOU have taken up the cause of 'Mr Reliable' and the graveyard ending for it and so many other fine Australian movies. I do hope that you will be able to effect some sort of Macca Miracle and resurrect poor Wally from his undoubtedly premature grave. As the director of photography and director of 'Mr Reliable' are my brother and sister-in-law, I watched first hand the unbelievable effort they put into this film over a couple of years and the most excruciatingly long hours to undergo the successful transition from the picture in the creators' eyes to the picture on the big screen—that tens of thousands can enjoy. It is terribly sad when all that effort is struck out in one fell swoop by people not directly involved in the making of the film but who have the say on marketing.

from
MARGARET CLANCY
ASHGROVE
QUEENSLAND

Up here in Brisbane where the film was made, there was no 'live' publicity at the time of the eventual release (six months after the gala opening night here in August). There was the Sydney-generated 'A Current Affair' which included great footage of the real-life siege, and the ABC's Anna Reynolds ran an excellent discussion on the film itself and life in the sixties — on the very day the film ended in Brisbane.

'Mr Reliable' had more than 400 extras so, for a start, they and their families and friends were very keen to see it, but the timing of its release was awful—a few days after school went back up here, when everyone was very busy at the start of term—and the entertainment budget had been blown during the holidays anyway. It would be interesting to know which other films the distributor was involved in pushing at the same time. Probably big American ones? Easier to do, with their huge overseas marketing machines and their slick ads.

My brother was also co-producer for 'Hotel de Love' another excellent movie released earlier, in January, which also bit the dust unexpectedly quickly. These movies are just not receiving the promotion they deserve—but also, the Australian public is not supporting this homegrown product. Buy Australian means cinema seats as well as other products.

• • • • • • • • • • • • • • • • • •

53

*During a discussion about the film 'Mr Reliable', Macca reminisced with Robin about the 1960s.*
MACCA: 'Remember Turf, Rob? I used to smoke it.'
ROBIN: '*Smoke it!* Isn't that what the horses run on?'

from
RODNEY FIELDER
OATLEY
NEW SOUTH WALES

YOU WERE ENQUIRING about people who were in the film 'Sons of Matthew'. It all seems such a long time ago now, but I played the part of Luke as a child. Luke as a man was played by Tommy Burns.

A few years ago I met up with John Ewart after a showing of the film at the Opera House and from the stories he was telling he had a lot more fun on location than I did, although my letters home to my mother said that I was having a good time. We children were carefully supervised all the time and had to keep up with our school studies with the tutor who was employed for this purpose. Even though I was only ten years old I can remember being very impressed with the beautiful Lamington Plateau area where the outdoor film was shot. Studio filming was done at Cinesound Studios at Bondi. In an era of 'short back and sides' I must have looked a bit odd with my longish and straggly hair and certainly had to put up with a lot of teasing from my school mates. I received a telegram from Charles Chauvel, dated 4 July 1947 which read 'Please do not cut hair and be ready for studio work within three weeks.'

It is nearly fifty years ago now but the memories remain. I am the proud owner of a copy of a very entertaining and well-made film.

from
PETER BROOKS
MALVERN
SOUTH AUSTRALIA

I WAS INTERESTED TO HEAR you discussing the film 'Jedda' today. The final scene was shot at Katherine Gorge, Northern Territory, where 'Jedda' jumped to her death. This film was then airfreighted via the ill-fated Comet jet which crashed into the sea near the island of Elba. Rather than return to the Northern Territory Charles Chauvel decided to retake the jump scene at Kanangra Walls, twenty kilometres south of Jenolan Caves, New South Wales. Kanangra Walls was the western most point reached by Ensign Francis Barraillier in 1802 during his attempt to cross the Blue Mountains. Ensign Barraillier is also credited with the first use of coo-ee in the bush!

from
JAN CARROLL
AVALON
NEW SOUTH WALES

I RECENTLY WATCHED A VIDEO of 'On Our Selection', with Leo McKern and Joan Sutherland. I thoroughly enjoyed it. The underplayed humour had me laughing till the tears rolled down my cheeks. It was brilliantly cast and simply a good story.

My grandfather, E. J. Carroll, produced the original silent version of 'On Our Selection' and many other early Australian movies: 'The Lure of the Bush' (the book being written by my maternal grandfather long before my parents met), 'Ginger Mick', 'The Man from Kangaroo', etc. E. J. Carroll placed Raymond Longford in charge of his Palmerston studio where he successfully produced Rudd's 'New Selection' and 'The Blue Mountains Mystery', but after that Carroll ceased regular production. This action was a serious blow to the industry. At the

Royal Commission, Longford reported that Carroll as an exhibitor had been told that unless he left the production field Australasian Films would terminate his overseas film supplies. Longford stated: 'As part owner of some Queensland theatres E. J. Carroll depended on the combine for his supply of film and, as they were opposed to local production, it would be impossible for him to continue should they cease supplies.' A more ironic discovery, made some years later, was that not only had 'The Blue Mountains Mystery' enjoyed success in America, but all the Carroll–Baker films earned substantial profits in both the American and European markets. By means of some shady accounting, the Chicago corporation handling overseas distribution had sent the Carrolls only the smallest returns. By the time this was realised, it was years too late! The same old movie mafia!

In July 1920 it had been EJ's intention 'to send film footage out of Australia as against the foreign film mileage which now comes in.' I still think that is what Australian film makers should aim to do. We should not attempt to appeal to overseas markets. A good story is a good story in anybody's language.

· · · · · · · · · · · · · · · · · · · ·

Macca, it's a tragedy. I mean there should be a local film industry in Tamworth. There should be a whole genre of country and western films. There's no reason why not: the market is there, the audience is huge and loyal. Also, there's never been an adequate marriage of Australian music and cinema. There should be three poker machines in the RSL club in Lismore which fund local, country-town movies. I mean there's no reason why not! I mean it's only money and we're probably spending the money on parking stations that we could actually spend investing in a film that could bring a lot back out of a mere Australian audience and a careful trickling through the country cinemas.

from
BOB ELLIS
(FILM-MAKER)
SYDNEY
NEW SOUTH WALES

## G'day, this is Macca

OWEN: It's Owen Stickles from Perth. I'm not in Perth at the moment I'm travelling down to Melbourne from Sydney in my car. About sixteen hours ago I got off an aeroplane from Lima in Peru. I'm writing a screenplay for a film and part of the screenplay was to travel, if possible, on what I thought was going to be a passenger train out of Lima which climbs over the highest standard gauge railway in the world. The passenger train is no longer running but I managed to get permission from the chief of operations there and they stuck me up the front so I travelled the railway up in the Andes with the driver and the co-driver.

MACCA: Oh, mate, we'd die to do that! Are you going back—can we come? Is it dangerous over there? I don't mean the train ride, but the terrain. Aren't there bandits and things?

OWEN: Yes, the Shining Path and all that sort of stuff. From time to time you have to keep in touch with your embassy—Australians are looked after by the Canadian Embassy there—and they publish lists of where you should not go. I wasn't travelling up in the northern part of Peru where there is some bandit activity, but it's interesting because they're carrying ore back over the top of the mountain twice a day and the trains have these open wagons with three or four guards sitting in them.

MACCA: With guns?

OWEN: No, they don't have guns, although there are plenty of guns in Lima. There's a policeman on every corner with a sub-machine gun. It's a very strange place to be when you're used to the free and easy atmosphere we have in this country.

MACCA: How long did the trip take?

OWEN: Ten hours. It's even interesting how it happened. I was to pick up the train at three o'clock in the morning and I got myself out of bed and dressed about two o'clock and went to the front door of the hotel, which was bolted and locked. Suddenly the owner of the hotel came out and said, 'I'll take you down across the bridge because there are bad men there. They'll rob you" and he went away for a moment and came back with a pistol and live ammunition in his pocket!

MACCA: What's the film you're making, Owen? Is it a doco?

OWEN: No, it's a screenplay for an adventure–romance movie and it'll start off in the cotton fields of New South Wales and wind up in Peru.

MACCA: Is there a place for me in it? Have you finished the casting?

OWEN: No, Macca, I'm writing it, I'm not casting it.

MACCA: Oh well, write me in. I can be this Australian soldier of fortune who's on holidays and who's driving trains! Where was that train in Peru going to?

OWEN: Up over the Galera tunnel, which is 15,681 feet. The roof of the world, Macca.

MACCA: Oh, what a train ride!

*A caller talking about a bloke who took up painting in gaol and used to paint rotten fruit:*
'He was a great artist. They make a fuss about Michelangelo, but this bloke was brilliant on putrid.'

56

# *T*he Bell Show

There were plenty of smiling faces at the Bell Show, Queensland, and the showgirls wore great hats. I was tempted to get behind the wheel of a B model Mack, and the John Bourne AAO Perpetual Jam Drop Trophy was on display.

# *B*irds, Tree and Sky

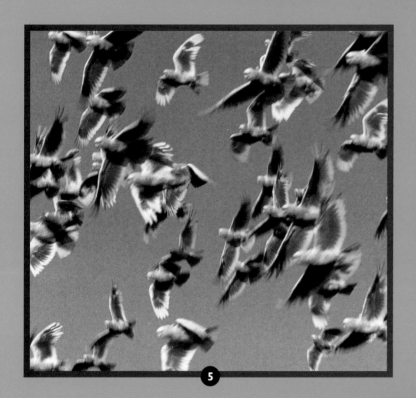

5

6

7

8

Major Mitchell cockatoos, a mackerel sky, a crow's ash (*Flindersia australis*), and a female glossy-black cockatoo — just a few examples of our unique bird life, sky and landscape.

# *T*oads, Dog, Snake and Joey

9

10

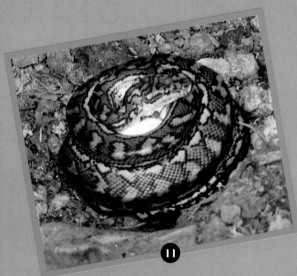

11

As well as marvellous letters and poems, listeners
send in interesting and amazing pictures. Here we have
backyard cane toads, a 'reindeer' daschshund, a carpet
snake and eggs, and a joey on the bottle listening to a
ghetto blaster.

12

# *P*lane, Train and other Travel

13

Here are some travel styles from around Australia.
The replica Vickers Vimy over Allora, Queensland 1994; the
locomotive 1770, *James Cook*, working the Kuranda scenic
railway; and eight-cents-a-day ABC travel for Kel and me in
Melbourne.

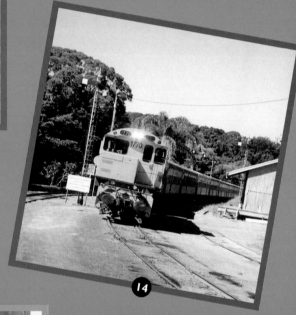

14

15

# *I*t's the national pastime!

from
JOHN McKECHNIE
THARGOMINDAH
QUEENSLAND

# KIHEE STATION

West of Thargomindah
On the Eromanga Track
I once worked Kihee Station
But I won't be going back.

Was summer when we got there
In the year of '92
Me and the missus
And a cattle dog named 'Blue'.

We worked Kihee together
The missus and me
But she hated every moment
Wanting to be free.

She dreamt of city living
A place I'd never be
She wanted shops and people
And picnics by the sea.

She said Kihee's no place for a woman
With heat, dust and flies
At night we sat on the verandah
Watching empty starlit skies.

For Kihee is a dusty place
Where rains don't often come
With stunted Gidgee and Mulga
Red dust and relentless sun.

Now the missus has gone to the city
The dog has left me too
He wouldn't work the mickeys
And he hated kangaroos

But I had to continue
To do the things I do
Riding fences, moving stock
And chasing brumbies too.

Well the muster is finally over
And all the work is done
The ringers have departed
For the boss's other run.

Alone I sat and pondered
What life meant to me
So it's goodbye lonely Kihee
With the missus I'll soon be.

## GHOST GUM

from
MINA MEUCKE
CRAFERS
SOUTH AUSTRALIA

Earth road from Hermannsburg 19 K
Meanders Finke River dry creek bed in May.
'Four-wheel drive only,' firm hands on the wheel,
Tyres bouncing and lurching on outcrops to feel
Passage through gravel or slithering sand.
'No collection of firewood beyond this point' mark
That nature's ecology lies in tree, root and bark
Being preserved for the animals, insects and life
Too small to compete with man's squandering hearth.
The jolting, the grinding, the loose boulders breached,
The green of Palm Valley, the oasis, is reached . . . and
We linger, we ponder the marvels of time.

Slow leaving, back tracking in dust corrugation,
Suddenly there in its utter perfection
Alone stands the Ghost Gum
Between earth and time:
The trunk velvet smooth and leaves vibrant green
Nature preserved in Eternity's dream

## ODE TO ROBIN

from
COL WHITE
INNISFAIL
QUEENSLAND

.

There's someone on the show noted for her cheeky grin
She's the charming, eloquent, mellifluous Robin.
The sweetest voice on the radio
Her appearances, probably best described as a cameo.

Answering the phone or making cups of tea
Tasks efficiently done with much glee.
Placid and composed and never under duress
I think Rob is the unofficial manageress.

She trots in and out bringing us news
Relaying many of the listeners' views.
Sometimes serious, sometimes funny
Alway delivered in a voice full of sunshine and honey.

Oh yes, our Rob has poise, grace and charm
In any situation she's in control and always calm.
She plays the accordion, but one thing we haven't heard yet
Is her, and Macca's trombone, playing a duet.

Have a chat to her on the phone, she's always so cheery
Never negative and never dreary.
She's somewhat loquacious and rather pert
But is it true that she wears a leather skirt?

*Rob rang Macca from the Sydney studio:*
'Ray called from Dubbo and said it was so windy he had to tie his truck to the phone box to keep it stable.'
Macca: 'Rob, how many times do I have to tell you, *I* tell the jokes on this program.'

from
COL WHITE
INNISFAIL
QUEENSLAND

## ODE TO LEE

I wonder how many listeners are just like me
And appreciate the contribution made to the program by Lee.
She's the one on the show whom Macca calls Kel
The one who does her job so well.

Over the years her reputation has grown
As she spends Sunday mornings on the phone.
And I can picture just what she looks like
As she works so hard away from the mike.

She's elegant and charming and full of grace
A petite little chin and a lovely sweet face.
She's vivacious, efficient, with a temperament that is sublime
She toils away trying to keep Macca in line.

I reckon she likes watching cricket and reading good books
Wherever she goes, she attracts admiring looks.
She works very hard, is always on the go
She's an integral part of our favourite show.

In a few lines of some pretty ordinary elocution
I say, thanks Lee, for your contribution.
One day, no matter where the place
I'd like to say g'day, not on the phone, but to your face.

## TALL POPPIES

from
ANNETTE WARNER
WARRNAMBOOL
VICTORIA

Tall poppies are lovely.
They wave their coloured heads,
Take chances with their future,
And sometimes pay the price of loneliness.

Tall poppies are vulnerable.
The crowded field floor
Finds ways to keep them tied there,
In the open space—of loneliness.

Tall poppies are the ones that pride
Themselves on their achievements.
Not ones for courting failure in themselves,
Or to wallow—in their loneliness.

So tall poppy, lift your head.
Be proud of what you do!
Stand tall, and know that in the end,
You'll prosper—through the courage of your loneliness.

## HINCHINBROOK NIGHTMARE

from
'MACUSHLA'
TOWNSVILLE
QUEENSLAND

As I was going to Hinchinbrook
I met a man with mega-bucks,
Mega-bucks spawned mega-plans
For shaking up this quiet land.
Mega-plans for mega-yachts
Crowding out the fishing spots,
Mega-harm to dugong, turtle
Where the mega-speedboats hurtle.
Mega-crowds and mega-noise
Obliterating peaceful joys,
Mega-jet skis on the bay,
On land, Mega-rates to pay.
Mega-sewage to discharge,
Mega-buses, planes and cars.
Mega-people, glitz and 'fun'
(With the sandflies in the sun),
Mega-walkers on the tracks,
Ghetto-blasters on their backs.
Mega-sand loss from the shore
Where the mangroves are no more,

Channel crammed with Mega-boats,
While on the water garbage floats—
Plastic, bottles, cans and oil,
Soon there's nothing left to spoil.
Stop! Let's take a second look!
Keep MEGA out of Hinchinbrook!

## THE YACKANDANDAH PANDA

from
ALBY BAILEY

It was up in Yackandandah that I came across the panda
Sittin' quietly by the river, eatin' grass.
So I got down on me belly 'cause I'd seen them on the telly
And I knew that they were big but not too fast.
And as I watched him eating, I thought for just one fleeting moment
I could catch and take him home,
And I'd revel in the glory of the never ending story
How I had a giant panda of me own.

But how to catch a panda that's turned up in Yackandandah,
And must have walked at least ten thousand miles.
And then I had the notion that he must have swum in the ocean
And must be close to bein' pretty stuffed.
So I quickly rushed up to him with a headlock,
then I threw him flat on his back and tied his legs up tight.
And I took him back to Yacka, on the back of me Alpaca,
But it took the day and nearly half the night.

So I've got his panda, in a cage, on me verandah.
But all me mates just think it's one big lie.
So me and me old panda we'll just sit on me verandah
And watch the rest of Yacka—passin' by.

## AUNTIE'S VISIT

from
BILL GLASSON

CLIFTON

QUEENSLAND

This long drought has been a killer, not a hoof left on the place,
And we haven't had a good crop since Columbo lost a case.
All the Downs are like a desert, nearly everybody broke;
I'd clear out but can't see fifty yards, with all the dust and smoke.

I went into town this morning, looking for a few days' work;
Everybody there was smiling, Clifton's mayor gave me a smirk.
All my girlfriends from the Senior Cits. were giving me 'the eye'
And the local bowlers looked as if they'd played—and won—Jack High.

I asked teacup reader, Nancy, 'Is the whole town going mad?'
'Macca's coming up to Allora,' she said, 'and we're so glad.
He's going to break the drought, you'll see cows bucking off their brand.
—It's in the tea-leaves—rain will follow McNamara's Band.'

Her prediction will be right, the rain will follow, we'll survive.
Though we're not sure how much later it will be till rains arrive.
But you've cheered a lot of people and you've brightened up the towns,
Just by telling us you're coming, to the droughty Darling Downs.

## THE FENCER

from
PAULINE SMART
PORT AUGUSTA
SOUTH AUSTRALIA

He'd spent his life on the big station runs
Raising dripping mirages with wires.
He'd fenced the horizon on days when the sun's
Touch alone could take hold of the pliers.

He built the dog-fence on the desert's red flank,
And watched the wild camels tear it down.
He flood-gated the Cooper from bank to bank;
Dug post-holes in iron-hard ground.

His were the hands that cradled the fleece,
Keeping the wild dogs at bay;
His was the sweat on the squatter's lease,
Though he never saw half of their pay.

He put the lines on dozens of maps,
Yet never read one in his life.
His ways were not always from textbooks perhaps,
But his fences were straight as a knife.

He'd saved enough money by age twenty-four
To spend a few months in the town.
And married the girl in the Four Square Store,
All proper, with a veil and a gown.

And his wife loved the bush, as she knew she must,
For theirs was a rough sort of life.
Her linen was hessian, her lace was the dust;
She was more of a mate than a wife.

Their home was always the edge of an empire,
Where the bush became graced with a name.
But they always chose to build their campfire
On the bush side of the fence, just the same.

But he sits alone now, on his verandah in town;
His mate's been gone more than a year.
And each evening he watches the sun going down
On their campsites, and water-holes clear.

He checks on the last fence he's ever to make,
Where his yard and the rest of the world meet;
The measures the council demanded he take
To keep his old dog off the street.

He's never spent time doing nothing before,
But now he can sit and just wait
'Til he makes his camp on the fence-line once more,
And rolls out his swag with his mate

## MARY HAD A LITTLE SHARK

from
Ross Henry
New Norfolk
Tasmania

Mary had a little shark
Its skin was darkly grey
And everywhere that Mary swam
The shark swam all the way.

It followed her along the coast
From Bondi beach to Noosa
Always swimming close behind
It didn't want to lose her.

Let's have a rest, young Mary gasped
And give ourselves a break
It was then she noticed something strange
About her friendly flake.

Its eyes were blank, its teeth grown large
It smiled like Phyllis Diller
And Mary knew immediately
Her pet could be a killer.

Then they heard the shark alarm
The shark cried 'Strewth! That's me!'
Mary shot through for the beach
The shark swam out to sea.

Mary often tells this tale
How she escaped from harm
Because she knew at all times
To obey the shark alarm.

And how when she got home again
She didn't give a damn
For any other kind of pet
Except a little lamb.

## MARY HAD A LITTLE LAMB

from
ROSS HENRY
NEW NORFOLK
TASMANIA

Mary had a little lamb
Its fleece was rosy red
But when she sang 'Click Go the Shears'
The lamb shot through in dread.

'Touch not my bonzer coloured coat'
The lamb was heard to cry
'Who the hell do you think you are?
Flash Jack from Gundagai?'

'For ages now I've wished I could
Get mockered up like this
And now you want to whip it off!
...You're a flamin' heartless miss.'

'Come back cross bred,' Mary called
'Your coat will be all right
'Cause I'll restrict my shearing
To fleece that's snowy white.'

So, back the red lamb gambolled
But waiting for him there
Were snow-white lambs all bleating
'Jeez mate . . . you're a liar.'

## AUSTRALIAN NAMES

from
ED BALTHROP
USA

I am in love with Australian names,
With Illawarra and Woolloomooloo,
With Broken Hill, lost mining claims,
With Yanko and Dubbo and Kakadu.

I am in love with Darling Downs,
With Wagga Wagga and Coongoola,
With a town called Alice, with outback towns,
With Bateman's Bay and Merimbula.

I am in love with Australian names,
Their vowels dripping wet from the tongue,
With consonants closely confining as hames*
Controlling, patrolling where dreamtime has sung.

I am in love with wide-open spaces,
Cape York, the Atherton Tablelands,
With Ayers Rock, Coolgardie, such spaces
Where solitude sets silent demands.

I am in love with Murra Murra,
Rockhampton, Yeppoon, and Harbour Bridge,
With Bennelong Point, and Kununurra,
Culburra, Kalgoorlie, and Opal Ridge.

I am in love with Springs called Helen,
Callala Bay and the Margaret River,
With a long-limbed Aussie girl named Ellen,
And Bomaderry and the Shoalhaven River.

I am in love with Parramatta,
With Wollongong and Carrington,
With Geelong, Queenscliff, and Wangaratta
With Caringbah and Paddington.

I am in love with Australian names,
Those paperbark gunyas that never collapse.
Words tripping the tongue to two-up games
Like kangaroo mobs. They cluster the maps.

I have sung you my song of the Down bloody Under,
Where sheilas are shapely and the blokes plurry strong,
Where kookaburras call and galahs raucous thunder.
Chant cockatoo. Bless billabong.

*hames: a buggy shaft

from
CARMEL RANDLE
PRESTON
QUEENSLAND

## JUST A WOMAN OF THE WEST

Hello there! I'm Jess. Frank's wife. You'd like a look around?
Hop up here beside me in the front.
The dog can ride the load behind—he's getting rather spoiled!
Don't mind the mess. I'm sure that knife is blunt!

I've just a few small jobs to do—Check the turkey nest—
The pump's been playing up too much of late—
Take a message to the shooters; pick up the weekly Mail;
Feed some starving stock…You'll do the gate?

Read the rain gauge by the creek—(We think we saw a scud . . .)
Check the boundary fenceline by the bore;
Estimate how many cows by now have dropped their calves
In the paddock that we know as 'Mangalore'.

I'll have to clean the quarters 'cause the shearing starts next week—
Still that task might have to wait another day
'Cause there's jobs that Frank needs doing, and there's only me to help
Now the children have all chose to go away . . .

And there always is the housework—that includes the washing-up
And the washing . . . and the ironing . . . and the books . . .
And since there is recession, and a downturn, and a drought,
There is no staff—of course it's me that cooks!

You think I need a holiday? Frank would never go!
I'd love the coast! Build castles in the sand!
Feel the moisture of an ocean breeze! But what I'd love the most
Would be time to walk together hand in hand.

But the land is an obsession that has claimed his very soul!
A monster to be kidded, coaxed, and tamed!
It's his source of inspiration, and his never-ending goal
Where his every waking moment's thought is aimed.

For life upon this distant run is not all that it seems.
I sometimes wonder whereabouts I stand . . .
I produce his sons and daughters—but I don't produce his dreams.
He loves me—but he's married to the land!

## MY DREAMBOAT

from
MAUREEN TAYLOR
IRYMPLE
VICTORIA

I've got an Aussie bloke
one of the gentleman folk.
A fine specimen of a male
a sex symbol without fail.
He has a cute beer pot belly
hanging over his belt like jelly.
His jeans he wears with aplomb
showing just a bit of bom.
My heart for him just longs
as I glance at him in his thongs.
His cowboy hat looks real neat
and his navy singlet is so sweet.

I never ever get snooty
if he wants to fish or go to footy.
At a match he likes to have a beer
and he's always got the loudest cheer.
Some people say he's a loud-mouth drunk
but me, I reckon he's my spunk.
A real snazzy hunk of beef
especially when he wears his teef.

Sometimes after a bit of booze
he has a little snooze.
I watch admiringly from the door
and listen to that familiar snore.
With mouth wide open he looks a treat
from the tip of his head to his smelly feet.
The top of his head is a little bare
but under his arms there's still lots of hair.
Do you know the part of him I like the best?
His warm, dark, furry, curly hairy chest.
Oh he's such a spunk—a cuddly bear,
we really make a wonderful pair.
He calls me his little moo
I call him my dream come true.

He lets me use his axe and shovel
and he even has a brand new mower
and when he takes me fishing
I'm allowed to be the rower.
I don't get flowers—of course I don't mind
no romantic notes or anything silly of that kind.
But on Mothers' Day
I hear him say
(especially for me)
'Hey kids, get her a cup of tea!'

Oh, I just hope all the girls upon this shore
find a dreamboat like mine they can adore.

· · · · · · · · · · · · · · · · · · · ·

from
MURIEL COURTENAY

BUNDABERG

QUEENSLAND

## OUR SCHOOL OF ARTS

The weatherboards are twisted,
the paint looks pretty thin,
Weeds are growing round the stumps—
the roof, more rust than tin.

It has never heard a symphony,
nor seen Old Masters up on show.
No smash hit plays on the stage;
those things it wouldn't know.

But our faithful School of Arts
has served us day and night.
The library books are housed there.
A refuge for those in plight.

It has seen a lot of baby shows
and deb balls by the score.
Housed meeting long and fiery
when politicians held the floor.

It's the venue for local weddings,
farewells when folks leave town.
We used it when we had no church
and when the school burned down.

Four walls, a roof, a creaking floor,
it holds a warm place in our hearts.
There's our past, present and future
enshrined in our School of Arts.

## BONDI

from
CHRIS DODDS
CHISWICK
NEW SOUTH WALES

We set our alarms for an early 5.30
Wait for a surf check unshowered and dirty
Watch the sun rise as the day has begun
For some it means work—for us it means fun.

We trek through the city with traffic and smog
Down George Street to Wynyard with 'yuppies' who jog
We hurry up Pitt, see Hyde Park on the rise
Two businessmen rush past us downing meat pies.

With boards catch the Bondi Express just in time
380 it leads to the beach so sublime
We travel down Oxford Street cafes in sun
Selling croissants and coffee to those on the run.

The water's in view now the surf's going off
The bell's rung, the doors open 'Grab all your stuff'
We cruise down the headland and onto the sand
The 'posers' are baking great bodies all tanned.

We both paddle out to the farthest clean break
A set comes on through, there's a wave I must take
The swell picks me up and I fly down the face
The wave is my Master but I am the pace.

A 'bottom turn' comes with a cutback and snap
I set myself up and I slice through a gap
The barrel is forming and caves on my head
I fall in the pit 'ugh' the drop feels like lead.

The pipeline then breaks and I'm left deep inside
The shore's heading quickly—but oh what a ride!
I pop out the end, try a spinner and drop
Pull out from the whitewash and come to a stop.

I turn round and paddle, stop, tighten my fin
After four hours of beating decide to give in
For a cold shower we stagger all gee'd and excited
Hungry, exhausted, McDonald's is sighted.

The trip home's a breeze back to Circular Quay
Our gear's twice as heavy for Peter and me
Say 'Bye' to my friend, yell 'I'll call you at ten'
When me and my mate rush old Bondi again.

● ● ● ● ● ● ● ● ● ● ● ● ● ● ● ● ● ●

## AUTUMN IN TENTERFIELD

from
MURIEL COURTENAY

BUNDABERG

QUEENSLAND

Come to Tenterfield in April
When the air is crisp and clear
And the trees in multi colours
Loudly proclaim that autumn's here.

Scarlet, orange, wine and saffron
Flame liquidambars in the street
Where tumbling leaves are gathering
In brown drifts around their feet.

Poplars rise in golden columns,
From chimneys, wood smoke curls.
Claret ashes glint and gently quiver
In the breeze that twirls and skirls.

Vermilion berries, weeping willows
Touched gold by Midas' hand supreme
Bring colour to the hills and valleys
Clothed in bush of sombre green.

70

Dewdrops from the misty morning
Jewel cobwebs strung along the fence.
In the air the cattle's breathing
Hangs suspended, white and dense.

Russet, umber, maroon and crimson
To the colour dazzled eye revealed.
A rich feast of nature's soul food
When autumn comes to Tenterfield.

## PLASTIC MONEY

from
HELEN BRUMBY
ROSE BAY
TASMANIA

They're making plastic plates now,
They're making plastic forks,
They're making plastic spoons, too,
And even plastic corks;
They're making plastic wrapper,
And plastic Christmas stars;
And I've heard a rumour
They're making plastic cars!
But now the latest thing is —
(And I don't think it's funny)
The powers that be are making
Plastic (plastic!) money!
The plastic doesn't feel right,
It doesn't like to fold,
So we're supposed to keep it flat,
At least that's what I'm told.
They're making plastic money now,
I do wish that they'd stop;
It's like children's play money,
For when they're playing 'Shop'.
I don't mind plastic plates,
Though I don't like plastic forks;
I quite like the plastic spoons,
And cope with plastic corks;
But surely they are joking,
Though I don't think it's funny,
They don't make paper notes now,
They're making plastic money!

from
PEARL SMITH
ORMISTON
QUEENSLAND

## WHY DON'T I FLY

I'd miss the great Australian plains,
the space, the scent of hay,
those roads that struggle on and on
when night engulfs the day.
I'd miss the smell of morning,
the gum trees floating free in shimmering heat,
Mirages—with waterholes complete.

I needs must sit by the McIntyre,
watch the caravans come through
and gaze at the sculptured, snow white clouds
in the Goondiwindi Blue.
Will the road to Boggabilla still be lined with white
where tufts of snow white cotton
are blown from the loads at night?

Flying in an aeroplane, I could never gauge the pain
of dying hopes and endless toil
as farmers pray for rain.
When I'm chasing semis down the highway
seeking room to pass
I can watch the rising costs of fuel
while I'm stepping on the gas.

When I see the sheep spread thinly
on the white-gold bleaching plains,
where time has etched a sameness on the scene
I'll know this is Australia, unique and quite unreal,
A vast, brown land where Burke and Wills have been.

Out where the highways meet and go their separate ways
a thousand starving cattle graze the road.
In an aeroplane, you'd never know
If they were travelling fast or slow
or if the drover has a mate to share the load.

Why don't I fly?
I'd never see the pink galahs, in densely moving clouds,
do arabesques with swirling grace across the evening sky;
or count the poor, dead bodies of the wandering kangaroos
who'd ventured forth across the road
and never really knew,
what hit them.
I'd never share the heartache

of those battlers in the West,
who plough and plant their paddocks
still hoping for the best.

By the time I cross the Murray down Yarrawonga way
I'll half expect a bunyip to appear.
Perchance, if I should miss him, 'cos he's wandered off, elsewhere,
I'll be back again to greet him, when I pass this way, next year.

## JUDY'S LOO BLUES

from
JUDY MCALISTER
QUANDIALLA
NEW SOUTH WALES

When I was married in '73,
We lived in a farmhouse, my Kenny and me.
House had seen better days, that was for sure,
The windows would stick, and so would the door.
There was a gap in the lounge between the floor and the wall,
The chimney was leaning and threatening to fall.
But the worst part of all, I'm telling you,
Was the trip down the path to the outside loo.
'Twas a hole in the ground with an old wooden seat
And a crack in the floor where you planted your feet.
There were spiders and hornets and sometimes some bees,
Buzzing around you, with pants round your knees.
Sometimes you'd find there, the old friendly dog.
Once, even a snake, who was chasing a frog.
I ranted and raved and cursed that old loo,
Then in '74, just out of the blue
We moved to 'Pineleigh', the place Ken called home,
To share with his mother, who was now all alone.
It was an old-fashioned homestead with verandahs all round,
With a big country garden and the chimneys were sound.
A much better place than our humble first shack
But wouldn't you know it, the loo was outback.
A fibro shed with a floor of cement
And a deep, dark hole where your penny was spent.
The end of the next year, our first baby was due
And we finally achieved it, our first inside loo.
That baby's at Uni now, out having fun,
We have two teenage daughters and a twelve-year-old son.
The old house has gone, a transportable instead,
And the old outside loo is a small garden shed.
But horror of horrors, in 1994,
The drought hit our farm, much worse than before.
Our water is rationed. We have two-minute showers,
My garden is wilting, my poor trees and flowers.

There's no place like home
(when there's an indoor loo.)

73

We skimp and we save, what more can we do?
Give up the use of our inside loo!
The old loo's been swept, there's a new seat in there,
That my Kenny has fashioned from an old dining chair.
The girls are depressed. Their scowls are in vain
But we're stuck with this loo, till God sends us rain!

## G'day, this is Macca

IAN: Hello, Macca, it's Ian Brown from Melbourne, calling from the Amazon. I'm on a trip to the Amazon Basin and I just thought I'd give you a few figures on what it's like over here. This is an enormous river; it's 5,500 kilometres long, although it changes its name here and there along the way. I've just been on a cruise boat from Manaus to Belem, five days downstream, and I'm only about 220 km from the Atlantic Ocean. The river averages 2.5 kilometres wide for all the distance from Manaus to Belem, which is 2,000 kilometres. The amount of water here is just amazing. This river redefines the word 'river' for me: I think in Australia we really only have streams. One important thing is that this river contributes one-sixth of all the run-off from the land onto the planet's oceans. Isn't that an amazing figure, Ian?

MACCA: It certainly is. Can you tell me what you're doing there?

IAN: I'm actually on a holiday. I'm in between jobs from Melbourne University and I love rivers so I made a trip over here to see the Amazon, and I thought I'd ring up and say hello. I enjoy your program, Macca, so I thought I'd contribute to it.

MACCA: Good on you. So you're amazed by the amount of water in the Amazon. I suppose it's a sort of winter there, is it?

IAN: Not really. The wet season is just beginning and the temperature here is about thirty-five degrees and the humidity is about eighty-five per cent. It rains at about five o'clock in the afternoon nearly every day. I'm not sure of the figures exactly but the rainfall over here is enormous, and the figures for the Amazon Basin are just huge. There are 1,100 tributaries that run into the Amazon River and seventeen of those are over 1,000 kilometres long. It's just amazing the amount of water and moisture that's in this area, and of course the Amazonia region has one-third of the world's forest area and one-third of the planet's living creatures, so it has got to be looked after because this is where our oxygen supply comes from. This is the key to the lungs of the planet and if we don't look after it we're really in trouble.

MACCA: It's nice to talk to you this morning. You're obviously not in a public phone box on the banks of the Amazon, are you?

IAN: No, I'm on a cruise boat. The guys here with their Portuguese language have got me through to you, which I think is amazing.

MACCA: Thanks for your statistics, Ian, and especially thanks for your call from the Amazon. You have a good time, and look us up when you get back to Australia.

# 7

# Champions

from

IAN RECHTMAN

ST KILDA

VICTORIA

Greta Grossman (my mother-in-law) and Lily Prince are twins who turned ninety on Australia Day 1997. Greta arrived in Australia in the mid-1930s with a younger sister (Mini) for a holiday and to visit her uncle in Murwillumbah, New South Wales. Her twin (Lily) survived the Holocaust and arrived in Australia on one of the first migrant ships after the war.

The three sisters have had six daughters, seventeen grandchildren and eight great-grandchildren.

•••••••••••••••••••••

from

ANNE PIETSCH

POMONAL

VICTORIA

I thought you might like to know about my aunt Irene Plowman who died aged eighty-five. In 1938 Irene (then Irene Pyle), aged twenty-six, cycled from Sydney to Melbourne forty-one minutes behind Sir Hubert Opperman's record time. It took one day, sixteen hours and twenty-three minutes to complete the distance, ten hours twenty-four minutes ahead of the previous women's record. Her record remained unbeaten for twenty-eight years.

Irene owned a dress shop in Wangaratta and would close Friday night, ride to Melbourne (a distance of 230 miles) in less than ten hours, shop for material on the Saturday and return home on the Sunday. This was part of her training in preparation for the ride.

It is almost impossible for cyclists of the 1990s to imagine the standard of cycling equipment that existed in 1938, not to mention the road conditions. At the time of Irene's attempt the distance from Sydney to Melbourne was 570 miles (970 km). She completed the journey on two hours sleep and averaged 22 km/h. Her diet consisted of honey sandwiches washed down with milk and supplemented by raw eggs which to save time she would crack on her handlebars.

•••••••••••••••••••••

from

JAMES SELLINGS

(AGE 70)

MOUNT VERNON

NEW SOUTH WALES

## THE TRAIN RIDER

You have seen the bush by moonlight, from the train while speeding by
You have seen the bright red sand dunes, underneath that clear blue sky
You have heard the Ghan a-calling, and have answered with your heart
You have sent your love to Uluru, and I know that we must part

I have taken you this morning, with your swag for all to see
And seen you safely seated, on the Melbourne XPT
There's an Overlander waiting, with your bed all nicely made
And overnight while lulled to sleep then you're in Adelaide

The mighty Ghan is standing there, with a throbbing restless air
Your heart is near to bursting as you walk up to the stair
And I know that I have lost you, to a thousand tonnes of steel
Two thousand rearing horses, and a host of iron wheels

For you've seen the bush by moonlight, from the train while speeding by
And you've seen the bright red sand dunes, underneath that clear blue sky

You've said that you are coming back, in a fortnight's time or so
But the Gulflander is calling and I know that you will go

And once you get to Queensland, there's a new train runs out west
You will ride the rails to Longreach, in your ceaseless railways quest
There's a Cockatoo in New South Wales and an Indian in Perth
An Explorer down to Canberra and all will see you berth

You will ride the old Sunlander and the Tea and Sugar too
The railways of Australia, are the dearest things to you
For you've seen the bush by moonlight, from the train while speeding by
And you've seen the bright red sand dunes, underneath that clear blue sky

Perhaps one day we two might meet, at a level crossing track
I know that is my only chance, to try to win you back
For I must ride the bitumen and the red dirt roads I feel
While you must ride the railroads, with their shiny tracks of steel.

. . . . . . . . . . . . . . . . . . . . .

## PEDAL PUSHERS

from
JAN HODGE
TORRENS CREEK
QUEENSLAND

*Jan Hodge congratulates Jack Griffin (age 72) from Geelong, Victoria and Eric Doughty (age 76)
from Wollongong, New South Wales as they set out on their epic ride around Australia*

Congratulations Jack and Eric
Why you do it I'm not sure,
But 'tis a mighty effort
For two veterans of the war.

You choose to ride around Australia
For a very worthy cause,
Though every fifty K or so
you take a little pause.

Every day you push those pedals
And the wheels go round and round,
Seems to me I'll guarantee
That you're not wheelchair bound.

With the sponsorship of BP
And your front team, Des and Brett,
Behind you comes the van with spares
In case a puncture you may get.

Some folks may think you're crazy
Or short of a brain or two,
But you have my admiration
For the gutsy thing you do.

It seems that age is no real barrier
When your heart is feeling young,
Now me I know my 'use-by' date
Has very nearly come!

Around Australia on a pushbike
In about one hundred days,
May the good Lord travel with you
And keep you safe always.

Total distance 13,684 km to be ridden in 96 days. Due to a few small changes the total distance will now be around 14,500 km.

To date only 17 riders have ridden 'continuously' around Australia.
1900: Arthur Richardson
1900: David Mackay
1985: Jack Griffin (61), Don Lattrel (50), Norm McDonnagh (49), Ben Pederson (50)
1985: Danish team of four riders
1985: Ian Hay (56)
1987: Graeme Millbourne (56)
1989: Rod Evans (33) set record
1989: German rider (40) set new record
1992: Jack Griffin (68), Tony Spark (51), Alf Ewins (50), Bryan Stephens (56)
As you can see Jack and Eric are the two oldest riders to attempt this feat.
On several occasions the riders covered 190 km in the day. On one occasion they averaged 33 km/h for a distance of 184 km.

* * * * * * * * * * * * * * * * * * * * * * * * * * * * * * * * * * * * * * * * * * *

*It's a red-letter day when Gilbert of Tweed Heads rings up as he did when he turned ninety-eight.*
MACCA: 'How are you, Gilbert?'
GILBERT: 'I'm very humble about it, but I keep excellent health. My sister's a nurse and she showed me how to jiggle the solar plexus, and it keeps you in wonderful shape. Y'know, it's your laughing muscle, and I like to think I've laughed myself into old age.'

* * * * * * * * * * * * * * * * * * * * * * * * * * * * * * * * * * * * * * * * * * *

| from |
|---|
| LEILA HATHAWAY |
| MANLY |
| QUEENSLAND |

## ODE FOR EDIE ON HER HUNDREDTH BIRTHDAY

*Chorus:*
A Queensland, wild colonial girl,
Ede Daley is her name.
She is her family's pride and joy
Let's celebrate her fame.

A Warwick, wild colonial girl, Ede Eastwell was her name,
Was born in eighteen ninety six. Let's celebrate her fame.
A likely lass, she charmed them all. The lads to Warwick sped.
From far and wide they courted her, but Ede just shook her head.

Then Herb Daley came to call. He swept her off her feet.
She wrapped him round her fingers, for upon her he was sweet
December seventeenth they wed, in nineteen seventeen.
He was a blacksmith full of fire—our Ede became his queen.

And after that for many a year, they Daley kids did raise.
They wander'd wide and far afield thro' Queensland's outback haze.
She gave 'em hell and made them toe the line that she had made
And Herbie often felt her tongue when he in error strayed!

When he brought home a bottl' of rum 'n fell sleeping on his bed,
Our Ede with water topped it up. 'There's more for him,' she said.
Another time with horse and trap across the tracks she ambled.
A train went thro, the horse it fled. Ede, trap and eggs were scrambled.

Ede managed all with strength and skill, though funds were often few.
She stretched things here and fixed 'em there 'till was good as new.
We'd need a hundred years to sing her exploits and her joys.
Her tricks, her jokes, her way to cope with Daley girls and boys!

And now those kids have bred their own 'till they are quite a crowd.
(At last count 'twas One O Eight!) Our Ede's done Queensland proud!
She's granny, mother, aunt and friend, to all now gathered here.
Let's toast our own colonial girl our Queensland pioneer.

*Words by Una Way*
(with a lot of help from *The Wild Colonial Boy*!)

• • • • • • • • • • • • • • • • • • • •

**I** WROTE TO YOU LAST year asking if you would kindly send my 103-year-old grand-mother Myrtle Wheaton a cheerio call on your show which she listens to reli-giously—you kindly obliged. It was a very special moment for her. Living in the New England Tableland region for all of her life, my grandmother is no stranger to the radio and nowadays being confined to her bed, the ABC and especially cricket broadcasts are her companion. She turns 104 years on 18 August. I saw grandmother ('Ma' as I refer to her) just six weeks ago and at almost 104 years she still has a very alert mind.

from
PETER DOGGETT

ROBINA

QUEENSLAND

*Father Brian rang from Perth:*
'Yesterday I did a wedding. He was ninety and she was eighty-four. It was just lovely, but I must admit the bridal waltz was a bit ordinary.'

*Macca was talking to a golden oldie who had married for the third time when he was ninety-three.*
MACCA: 'How old is your wife?'
CHAP: 'I dunno — you'll have to ask her.'
MACCA: 'And this is the third time! They say once bitten twice shy.'
CHAP: 'Yes — I'm very shy.'

| from |
| --- |
| LES |
| KINCUMBER |
| NEW SOUTH WALES |

TOMORROW IS OUR WEDDING anniversary. Though being a 'bit past it' I wanted to join my wife—who is a Macca addict—in her bed to give her body a warm cuddle and to show that I love her more than any other person. She agreed as long as I did it without talking, 'So I can still hear Macca!' One usually doesn't chatter when in a cuddle-huddle—or do they today? What have you got, Macca, that induces a woman to prefer your chatter to a little bit of marital nonsense?

| from |
| --- |
| M. M. HALL |
| BATHURST |
| NEW SOUTH WALES |

## VISITING THE GIRLFRIEND

He's just in from working on the farm
All sweaty and hot and dusty
A bath will do no harm.
The water is a'boilin'
In a drum above the fire
Pull out the old tin bath tub
Hidden under coils of wire.
See the rats a'scatter
As he drags the old tub free
But 'Blue' will keep them busy
As he chases them with glee.
A little hut with verandah
Has always been his home
He sings a little song now
As he settles in the foam.
Sixty years he's been around
No girl has won his heart
Until he met sweet Sally
He loved her from the start.
It's for sweet Sally now
He's settled in the tub
A man don't bath too often
When he's livin' in the scrub.
He dreams of bonny Sally
And dries himself with care
A dab of metho 'tween the toes
Some powder here and there.

Out from 'neath the mattress
Comes a pair of denim blues
A red checked shirt is handy
And a pair of dusty shoes.
Visions of his Sally
Come floating into view
He sparks the old Land Rover up
And waves goodbye to 'Blue'.
Soon he is with Sally
The love light of his life
And if she will have him
He will take her for his wife.

## AFTER VISITING. . .

Well 'Blue' old mate I'm home again
Sal gave me scones and tea
But now my heart is filled with pain
For she said 'No' to me.
'Jim,' she said 'You're my best friend
I'll treasure you like gold
Our friendship lasts until the end
But marriage leaves me cold.'
Well I'll get over it old 'Blue'
She'll always be around
Teas and scones and a meal or two
And I've still got you old hound.
Just you and me and carefree days
When the magpies sing a song
The breezes blow and the cattle graze
It's true we both belong.

• • • • • • • • • • • • • • • • • • •

## HARMONICA HOMECOMING

from
LEN MULLIN

*(For Mal Rabe)*

Last night in my dreams,
somehow it seems
I died and was sent down below.
And there on the stand,
the Harmonica Band
was preparing to put on a show.

But Satan in rage,
Yelled 'Get off the stage
have none of you blokes got a brain?
I'm here to torment,
those who didn't repent
we bloody well don't entertain.'

Then myself and my mates,
tried the Heavenly Gates
and received Peter's welcoming hand.
He said 'We have harps,
playing flats and sharps
we don't need a Harmonica Band.'

That's when I woke,
I was still a live bloke
Not visiting Heaven or Hell.
So I'll start a new day,
to come here and play
with you blokes at our RSL.

•••••••••••••••••••••••••••••••••••••••••••••••••••••••••••

### G'day, this is Macca

ALEX: Good morning. This is Alex. I'm in the Java Sea on an oil rig about a hundred miles from Bali. We left Singapore last week and we're under tow towards the West Australian coast to drill a well off Barrow Island. We're quietly trucking along at six knots towards the coast.

MACCA: Alex, it's amazing to think of you out there pottering along at sea. Is it light, what's the sea like. Tell us all about it.

ALEX: Right now it's about twenty-five degrees. During the day we get a few thunderstorms. It's dark—pitch black dark—there's nothing around us, the radar's not showing a thing, but occasionally we get a small fishing boat or coastal freighter going past and have had to change direction a couple of times.

MACCA: Where are you from, where do you call home?

ALEX: I live in Perth but I'm a Tassie Devil!

MACCA: Right! Tell us about the rig and the barge tug.

ALEX: We're being towed by a large oil rig support vessel which has got two 4,000 kilowatt engines and is pulling us on a cable that's 750 metres long. We've got two thrusters which provide power as well—they're 1,400 horsepower—and we're burning about 70–80,000 litres of diesel fuel each day to get along. The rig's 370 feet long, and the weight at the moment is around 30,000 long tons.

MACCA: That's an amazing story. What phone are you calling on? Usually if it's a satellite phone there's a delay, so you're not going up to 240,000 kilometres and coming back down are you?

ALEX: Yes I am. It's quite a good phone.

MACCA: It's a ripper! A hundred miles out from Bali in the middle of the sea. I wish we were there—we could have a cup of tea. I'd love to come for a trip sometime—we could do the program from the rig.

ALEX: You never know what we can organise. All I need now is a jar of vegemite—there's none on board!

# 8

## **W**hy I live where I live

from
LAUREL NEWTON

ROBINVALE

VICTORIA

**I** WAS DRAGGED, KICKING AND screaming, to Robinvale in December 1950. When the war ended and my husband returned from a Japanese POW camp, his health ruined, his first thought when his discharge came through was to apply for land under the soldier settlement scheme. I said 'No' and continued to say no for four years, but was eventually forced to give in!

We drove across the bridge from Euston, past the big windmill, and through the Robinvale of 1950. A scattering of derelict galvanised shops with a pub on the corner behind a straggly row of date palms. If my spirits dropped as we drove through this shabby town, they hit rock bottom when, two miles further on, we arrived at our future home—two canvas tents on a sandy, wind-swept hill, carpeted with dried saffron thistles.

For two months we endured life under canvas, cooking over a fire in a hole in the ground. We slept on mattresses thrown on the tent floor and we went to bed with the birds because our only light was a kerosene lantern. But we knew, when we 'burnt our boats', we were there for the long haul and things could only get better.

Our second home was fondly called 'the hut'. This was a galvanised iron building with a concrete floor which we were allowed to use as temporary living quarters. Some of our furniture came out of storage and we slept in proper beds. We had a wood stove, a water tank and a kerosene fridge. Tilley lamps were a great improvement on the hurricane lantern and we felt we had moved into the lap of luxury.

Work on the vines progressed, children settled down at school, and we watched our future home take shape before our eyes. The big day, moving in, eventually arrived, followed shortly by an even bigger day, the extension of electricity throughout the settlement. But the biggest day of all was when my husband signed the purchase lease on the property which would become our home for the next thirty years.

My home is now a cottage in the township. Forty-seven years have passed, I am now eighty-five years old and I still live in Robinvale. Why? Because I love the area I now call home, and would be as reluctant to go as I was to come.

• • • • • • • • • • • • • • • • • • • •

from
JOAN MCPHERSON

BUNBURY

WESTERN AUSTRALIA

**I** WAS BORN IN HAMILTON in the Western District of Victoria. Where the hills roll away from the foot of the Grampians and the scent of the pines clings to the gullies. Where you can stand on the cemetery hill and look over the whole valley.

I went rabbiting with my aunty and uncles as a youngster. When life was hard and free—a different hard to nowadays. I grew up in Warracknabeal and I think I am rather lucky as I have seen life change. I have seen dust storms leave dirt two inches thick through the house because of one open window. I have felt the mice run over me in bed through a mice plague. I have worked as a shed hand on sheep. I have hand-milked cows and taught calves to drink from a bucket. I have learnt to drive tractor, truck, bulldozer and motorbike. Seen lambs die in gistment. Have lost a young son in a farm accident and seen others lose loved ones.

Through one and all we have always been able to get by. We probably will again. The one thing that seems to be missing is the time we take to spend with each other. I am so fortunate to live in a part of the country where I can put my feet up and watch the tide roll in and out, or watch the sun come up over the estuary as the birds and dolphins feed. I can spend time with pen and paper, and give an ear to a friend when needed. I always have time to sit and wait for the kettle to boil. This is a timeless land and I sometimes have the feeling that people move through and don't really see what we have around us.

● ● ● ● ● ● ● ● ● ● ● ● ● ● ● ● ● ● ●

**I** LIVE HERE BECAUSE I have to live in the city for my job. But to live in The Rocks is a bonus. I'm originally from Deepwater, a small town situated between Tenterfield and Glen Innes. Growing up there was magic. Being snap frozen during the long, harsh winters and keeping fit in the summertime swatting blowflies as big as the merinos that dotted the paddocks. My childhood put me in good stead to dodge some hardened city slickers as big as the blowflies at home!

Living at Lower Fort Street, under the shadow of the mighty coathanger, the Harbour Bridge, is like a slice of Deepwater. The shopkeeper is a friendly bloke and he's always good for a yarn, as is the local butcher in Millers Point. The butcher has done us proud at many of the neighbourhood barbies with his A1 cuts of meat. The local watering holes are plenty. Dangerous really! However, the 'Hero of Waterloo' is my oasis. I can wander in any time, say g'day to Glen the barman and know I'll see a few local characters who have spent many years working on the waterfront, at Pyrmont, Balmain and Garden Island. The history that I have learned from these wharfies and sailors is terrific. The warmness that oozes from this neighbourhood is as vast as the Harbour itself. However, give me the bush any day! I steal home as often as I can to smell the eucalypts and see the multitude of magpies in Mum's backyard. To be able to catch the horses and for Mum and I to ride up through the bush on a moonlit night along the river — it's the best!

from
ALISON LOCKWOOD
THE ROCKS
SYDNEY
NEW SOUTH WALES

● ● ● ● ● ● ● ● ● ● ● ● ● ● ● ● ● ● ●

**T**HE CASSETTE BLARED AND the passengers sang along while I drove the bus through a dusty track homeward. Both adults and children sang the choruses, certain of the words. Words that were lost on me, a white Australian, who could not understand their Aboriginal language. The tune was bright and gay, the voices happy, so the words didn't matter. I found myself tapping along with the rhythm.

A dingo crossed the road in front of us and immediately the cry went out 'dingo' followed by numerous echoes as each child spotted the wild dog. We flew past trees, leaving behind a trail of dust as the miles melted away. The sign at the gate welcomed us home to Manyalluluk—English translation, Frog Dreaming.

Topping the last rise, all singing ceased as we took in the scene before us. Tall gum trees dotted upon green grass that sloped gently towards a rocky billabong. Pandanus palms and paperbark trees lined a winding creek, flowing constantly into the billabong. Small children played, splashing each other in the water, their brown bodies glistening in the sunlight. The sounds of a didgeridoo playing reached us as we slowed and came to a stop. A few children jumped off the bus and ran to join the old man making the sounds. This ancient musical instrument brought images to me of an era of long ago, a culture nearly lost. The boys

from
LORI MARTIN
KATHERINE
NORTHERN TERRITORY

gathered round their elder as he and the other men instructed them how to play. Stories of the Dreamtime were told as they decorated the didgeridoos using a blade of grass. Paint was taken from rocks, mixed with water and gum from the trees under which they sat.

The girls had joined the women sitting on the ground a little way off. Here they would learn the art of weaving and basket-making. Earlier the women had walked barefoot into the thickest parts of the surrounding bush. Seeds, roots and flowers had been collected to dye the leaves gathered for their craft. One woman grinned broadly as she held up a goanna she'd caught to supplement her family's diet. All those who live at Manyalluluk hunt and fish for traditional foods. She takes the children on those excursions so they can learn about bush tucker.

All who live in the community contribute. They are running a business. A tourist venture. The Aboriginal people at Manyalluluk have a strong sense of purpose and self respect. I came to live here and to be employed as their bus driver. What I didn't count on was the enormous social benefits; the warmth of their friendship has to be felt to be understood. They live under laws relating to understanding and accepting of one another. Unconcerned with unnecessary materialism, theirs is a sharing community of love, trust and forgiveness. Not to be mistaken as a sign of weakness or apathy, they possess a strong, independent spirit.

• • • • • • • • • • • • • • • • • • • •

from
JOANNE GAUDION
ROSEBANK
NEW SOUTH WALES

**W**HEN I WAS LIVING in Melbourne—as a university student—your program was an escape from the confinement and confusion of all that happens around you. I have since moved to the North Coast of New South Wales and taken up work as a fruit picker, and it's my latest residence I want to tell you about.

My home is a cabin made from flitches and the hessian-lined walls give it a very natural, homely feel. It is situated in the bottom of a valley, down a very steep descent, so steep I must leave my car at the top and make the trek home by foot. There is a creek which flows around the front, about ten metres from my front door. And since all the rain we have had in the past week—which washed my bridge away—the only way through is to take off the boots, roll up the pants, and wade through. This reminds me of all the good times spent as a child playing in the flood-water on our dairy farm at Traralgon in Victoria. I have no electricity or phone, but don't feel I am doing without anything.

I have a combustion stove for hot water and cooking, a gas fridge and 12-volt lights. This morning I am in luck! The small trannie I have (AM and SW frequency only) is letting me just listen to your program over all the static. This lifestyle enables me to live a life full of appreciation for all I have instead of being constantly reminded—by commercial television and the like—of everything I don't have, don't care to have and, more importantly, don't need!

• • • • • • • • • • • • • • • • • • • •

from
EDITH KERR
LAUNCESTON
TASMANIA

**I** LIVE IN LAUNCESTON, Tasmania. I love it because it is a beautiful city with many parks and gardens and has some large bush areas that extend into the city in an area known as the gorge, which has swimming pools and a lake that you can swim in if you can swim well. This area including the swimming pool is still free and provides a lot of enjoyment particularly during the summer months. A large rock concert and several music festivals are also held there each year. There are many good walking areas not too far from the city and the beach is three-quarters of an hour's drive away.

But none of this has anything to do with why I live where I live. I live here because my husband has finally been able to put down his roots and they are now so firmly implanted that I don't think anything could shift them.

My husband was brought up under the Victorian welfare system in boys' homes and institutions and during his childhood never knew a place of his own. When he was fourteen he went out to work on farms. We have been married for seventeen years. We bought this house ten years ago and have been paying it off since. He now feels that he has a place that he can call his own. This small house is much more than a castle to him. It represents an achievement—the fulfilment of the Australian Dream, something that cannot be taken from him by the whim of the welfare or an owner. That is why we live where we live and we won't be budged.

---

*Macca asked a bloke if he knew another bloke who came from the same district.*
BLOKE: 'I've never met him—I wouldn't know him if he stood up in my porridge.'

---

I HAVE ONLY BEEN living in Australia for the last three-and-a-half years, but during that time I've developed a real passion for the natural wonders of this beautiful country.

After travelling around almost the entire country during my first year here, I now try to see as much of Western Australia, my new-found home, as my spare time will allow. Every time I venture out into the bush, I feel just as awe-inspired as the first.

Take this weekend for example. My husband Dane and I visited Dryandra State Forest, the largest area of remnant vegetation/woodland in the Western Wheatbelt, and one of the last strongholds of the West Australian mammal emblem, the numbat. Sadly most of the numbat populations in Western Australia have been wiped out due to clearing of their natural habitat and predation by foxes. Imagine my delight, when after two hours of literally tiptoeing around the forest, I sighted one of these rare, exquisite creatures. My patience rewarded, I continued on and later came across my first ever echidna ambling along. What, with the flashes of beautiful colours as twenty-eight parrots darted among the trees and early wildflowers, I felt very privileged to be in such a place. Australia is one big treasure chest of unique natural wonders which none of us should ever take for granted.

from
SUSAN BARRATT
NORTH FREMANTLE
WESTERN AUSTRALIA

from
GEORGE ADAMS
(JACKEROO)
PALMERSTON, NT

• • • • • • • • • • • • • • • •

I LIKE TO GET UP early on a Sunday morning and tune into FM Triple D. I amble outside with the radio blaring (Well, I am awake so everybody else may be as well), light a fire and put the billy on. Of course it is still dark that hour of the morning, so can you imagine the cheery blaze of a billy boiling over fragrant Northern Territory pine logs, the fragrant smell filling the morning air? Because it is cold—around sixteen degrees—I wear a sleeveless coat. Being a man who loves his breakfast I cook over the open fire and savour it while I am engrossed in your program. Later I amble to the laundry where most times I have to scrub the dirty clothes before I place them in the washing machine. By this time I have lowered the radio's decibels on advice from my neighbours who have threatened to place the radio in a most uncomfortable place for myself. So, all in all I really enjoy Sunday morning, except for the neighbours' advice on what to do with my radio!

*Billy Kerr from Kalgoorlie, Western Australia:*
'Out here when "Australia's Most Wanted" comes on, half the pubs empty out.'

> from
> KATE TAPP
> YEPPOON
> QUEENSLAND

WE LIVE ON THE central coast of Queensland, actually opposite Great Keppel Island. It's dreadfully dry here at the moment, but when the rains do come it completely changes the countryside, and my opinion also. We came from Tasmania so do find it quite (to say the least) different.

Following is a poem written by a dear friend of mine, Kath Austin. It says how I feel about Tasmania. I do not enjoy living up here. I find it very difficult to cope with the heat, sand flies, mozzies, cockroaches, snakes, ants and fleas.

## TASSIE WOMAN

In winter, when my day begins,
the dew bejewels the grass;
cold beads of sweat adorn
the kitchen's gleaming brass.
I throw the kindling in the stove
first scraping ashes out,
and watch the first grey wreaths of smoke
go trembling up the spout.
The porridge-meal goes in the pot
I stir to get it right,
and glance outside the door to see
It's still as black as night!
Oh woe is me! I'd love to be
still snuggled up in bed,
but then I plonk my gumboots on
and go outside instead;
to feed the chooks and ducks and geese
and milk my gentle nans,

(rewarding each with lucerne chaff);
and scald the creaming pans.
A hearty go with axe and block
to split a pile of wood,
to get it under cover while
the weather stays so good.
I long to be in warmer climes
and miles from winter chill;
but see, above, the warming sun
rap dancing in the hill!
So you may keep your tropic heat
your mozzies and your flies,
I'll stay, and spend my mortal span
beneath the icy skies.

*Kath Austin*

* * * * * * * * * * * * * * * * * *

I'M SERIOUSLY ADDICTED TO your program and I even left the country to try to dry out!

This is why I live where I live. In 1987 I met a bloke from Mackay on his long-service leave in the UK. We had forty-one hours courtship and a week in between and married in March 1987. I gave up home with five children and five grandchildren for love of this man. I was fifty-nine! Sadly my husband died and I tried to settle back in the UK, but wept every time I played your tapes and saw Aussieland on the TV. It was all so crowded . . . why doesn't UK sink? So very claustrophobic and cold and everyone so depressed. I failed to forget the people of Queensland—so gregarious, so happy—the magic colours of this land, the blue of the mountain ranges, and most of all, Eimeo, this very spiritual place.

P.S. I'm not a POM but a FRAG—half Frog (French) and half Haggis (a Scot!).

*from*
*CHRISTINA NORTON*
*EIMEO*
*QUEENSLAND*

* * * * * * * * * * * * * * * * * *

LISTENING TO YOU A couple of weeks ago, I heard a beautiful poem about the horses from the Light Horse that had to stay behind after the war. How strongly I related to that lovely poem. All my life I longed to own my own horse. As a kid, if I was very good and waited patiently I could have a ride on someone else's at the end of the day. The wait was always well worthwhile.

Now I am the proud friend of my very own dappled grey called Duke, who whinnies and neighs to me as he comes up to the fence and I whinny and neigh back! I love it when I go into the laundry and reach up for the old stock saddle, carry the bridle and his rug (that smells so strongly of our last ride) and head down to the yards. Once saddled and talking all the while, it's a little jump and up into the creaking leather and down the drive. We ride through bush, open country and forest; along quiet, soft gravel roads inhaling that glorious early morning air fresh with eucalypt, and the sun on our backs makes it heaven on earth. He goes from a walk into a canter and we meet so many other animals who come to their fences out of curiosity. He loves a gallop along an open stretch and to crop the grass when we rest a while, tearing at the lush green—a

*from*
*MARGOT MARTYN*
*TYLDEN*
*VICTORIA*

lovely horsey sound. Then it's a 'Ye haa' up the drive, a wash, a bucket of feed, a hug and a smile you can't wipe off either face!

I then go into our old kitchen for a huge breakfast and plan the day's labour. Sometimes it's digging thistles or painting a shed, my cottage garden, the vegie patch, cleaning out the chook pens, stacking a bonfire or chainsawing up yet another fallen branch. At the end of the day my cup runneth over.

Are there greater joys than gathering the eggs out of the nest, having a drink in the orchard, stripping an old piece of furniture, listening to music by a cosy fire, snuggling into bed with wind roaring around the house or taking morning tea on the verandah with a friend? To go to bed at the end of the day bone weary but heart happy is a truly great feeling.

•••••••••••••••••••••

from
FRAN KENDALL
MOUNT GRAVATT
QUEENSLAND

THIS MORNING IN YOUR 'Why I Live Where I Live' segment one of your correspondents described the historical interest to be found living in suburbs of capital cities. It occurred to me that I, too, am representative of a large proportion of the Australian population—single female unit dwellers. I live in a very small unit made of bricks and cement that is not on a broad and winding river, does not look out over an Australian wilderness, and there isn't a kangaroo or koala in sight. My little nest is a real treasure trove of memories. When I first came to live here about two years ago, the walls and floors were dark and dismal and the furniture was old and very tired. In the following month my sisters and daughters and their husbands completely transformed the place. Pastel paints, frilly cushions, floral curtains and silk flowers (sorry about that) have been selected and arranged by others just for me. There are smiling photos of babies on the walls. To add to this wonderfully colourful and cheery gallery of memories, I have many of the simple treasures that lived in my parents' home for as long as I can remember. Just ordinary things like the plastic doormat my grandmother spent many long hours making and the hat my dad always wore is hanging jauntily on the hat stand at the front door. Sure, I can't wake up in the morning and look out at the trees but I can watch the sun spinning coloured rainbows through the prism hanging at my kitchen window.

When I close the doors and draw the curtains in the evening, there is a small sense of belonging as my eyes wander from one small, inexpensive but priceless object to another—each holding remembrance of a special person, a special time. Surrounded by all this, why would I live anywhere else?

•••••••••••••••••••••

from
GAYE MORRIS
REVESBY
NEW SOUTH WALES

I LIVE IN REVESBY. Now I know this does not sound very romantic or beautiful. In fact to the ordinary observer my home looks very boring and dowdy. My husband and I moved into this house thirteen years ago. (We had very little money, so it is an old ex-housing commission fibro-type.) It had one tree and an outside dunny.

During the last thirteen years we have grown to a family of four and one dog. We planted trees and gardens. Added bits and pieces there. It still looks like an old housing commission fibro-type, but now many birds visit the garden and I can sit in the dining room and watch the bull-bulls and doves playing in the bird bath and sparrows gossiping in the trees. I see the tiny wrens hopping in the grass and wattle birds in the grevilleas and every now and then a beautiful crimson rosella comes to eat the seed bell hanging in the jacaranda. We have flowers sparkling in the corners of the garden and I hear my children laughing in the backyard playing cricket. The kookaburras laugh at the kids.

It may not be that lovely old house by the ocean that I'm always dreaming about — but hey — it's better than a poke in the eye with a sharp stick. And I love it.

••••••••••••••••••••

I LOST MY ALL (a fruit property at Moorook) a few years ago and had to start all over again. I came into the bush to live for several reasons, and when I say bush I mean exactly that. I am about thirty-five kilometres from the nearest town (Waikerie) and surrounded by Mallee scrub, at a place called Boolgun, which at one time was both town and railway grain-loading and maintenance station. The line was closed about the end of the Second World War. When I first came here I had no power, used an old kero fridge (still do), kero lantern and wood stove, so was really back to basics. I still have to cart water in (about 15 kilometres). Although I live alone, with the exception of the wildlife (birds, snakes, lizards, rabbits) who always invade looking for water, I am never lonely. I am now trying to put together an emu farm, but the real reason for writing is to encourage others who have had to start again. I am in the over sixties bracket and the only resident of this 'town', but I am happy in the solitude, harmony and peace of the bush and would never wish to return to the towns to live.

from
SID CHUD
WAIKERIE
SOUTH AUSTRALIA

••••••••••••••••••••

I AM WRITING TO TELL you that your program reaches far and wide in both geographic and age terms. I am eighteen and studying at Melbourne University and come from the Riverina in New South Wales. Every Sunday I turn my radio to your program to listen to the people of Australia. I love hearing that familiar talk of points of rain, the drought and the country spirit. As many of your listeners have said numerous times, there is a sense of community, an unbelievable feeling of togetherness whether we are listeners in Melbourne or callers from Kalgoorlie. I do have one complaint, however—listening on a Sunday morning makes me horribly homesick. You certainly make us city town folk long for the serenity of country life, the smell of rain on dry grass and that clean-living feeling. The town I call home is Berrigan, population of 1,200, with a thriving CWA, four pubs, a footy team and a whole lot of character. What I enjoy most about country living is the intimate knowledge of everyone and everything whether it be a genuine community concern or old-fashioned town gossip, and that sense of security and safety unattainable in the cement world of the city.

from
ELIZABETH MCNAMARA
BERRIGAN
NEW SOUTH WALES

••••••••••••••••••••

WHEN I FIRST ARRIVED in Mount Isa I had no intention of making it my home. The scenery, the architecture and the climate had little to recommend them. The heat, the flies and the dust were a constant triple torment. And I was determined that as soon as I could afford it I would move on.

from
BRUCE JAMESON
MOUNT ISA
QUEENSLAND

Then I made a few friends, found a job and joined a club and the local Silver Band. My circle of friends expanded quickly, and I realised that they were all, without exception, the salt of the earth. There was not a 'quitter' among them, most likely because all the quitters had already quit and were living somewhere else.

I found myself living in a city where people still valued old-fashioned virtues like honesty and loyalty, tolerance and trust—a city where your worth was measured not on the basis of wealth, nor ancestry, nor of social background, but on your ability to do a good day's work, then to come back tomorrow and do it again.

The scenery is still uninspiring and the architecture downright depressing. But the people of Mount Isa are the best people in the world. And that is why, twenty-four years later, I still live where I live.

• • • • • • • • • • • • • • • • • • •

from
KATHERINE (14) & FAMILY
KARAMA
NORTHERN TERRITORY

**W**E CALL AUSTRALIA HOME because we live in an eighteen-foot caravan and where we park it is home and our backyard is Australia. We had to sell our house in Launceston because of that recession we didn't have, and have been on the wallaby for three years now. Although we lived for two years at Bidyadanga, south of Broome (where Dad was a builder) we spent a lot of our holidays travelling the west. Those two years at Bidyadanga were great. We met some wonderful people and learnt a lot about Aboriginal people and their culture.

Our favourite part of the trip (apart from travelling) is that we haven't been to school for three years. We do distance education from Tasmania and love it because our classroom is outside (when it's not raining).

We went on to Alice Springs and worked in Ntaria, Hermannsburg for a while then headed to Gem Tree where we got some garnets and met Ross, Ian and Jenny who taught us how to fossick and to spec, now we have the bug. Litchefield Park was beautiful, with its waterfalls and pools. Timothy's favourite part was going to Petherick Park, walking up Ford Hill and having a look at the Spitfire that crashed there in 1943. The machine gun is still embedded in the rock. We have been to most of the World War Two airfields and bases (our history lessons). We love going to museums and any other interesting spots we find on the way. But the thing we like best of all is the people we meet who become our neighbours in the places that become our backyard.

• • • • • • • • • • • • • • • • • • •

from
DIANA GILLATT
ALICE SPRINGS
NORTHERN TERRITORY

**A**LICE IS A VERY FRIENDLY town—big enough to have all the luxuries of restaurants, cinemas, sporting facilities, a good range of schools—and small enough that doing your supermarket shopping on a Saturday morning is a social event! Of course, having the backdrop of the spectacular MacDonnell Ranges reminds you even in town that you are in the centre of what I consider the best bushwalking country in Australia. Camping out under the clear starry skies of Central Australia, warm in your swag at night and exploring unexpectedly lush gorges and gullies during the day is my idea of a relaxing weekend. Like a lot of Territorians, I moved to the Centre for a job—but then like it so much I stayed.

I work for the Northern Territory Department of Health as a District Medical

Officer. A lot of people think of my job as being a Flying Doctor, but there is a lot more to it than that. There are six of us DMOs based in Alice Springs and between us we share emergency on-call (by telephone mainly these days but also by HF radio when needed) for everyone outside Alice Springs in Central Australia. That is, from the Pitjantjatjara lands in the north of South Australia, west to Kiwirrkurra and Tjukurla in Western Australia, east to Lake Nash on the Queensland border and up to Ali-Curung in the north. It is a big country!

People often ask me 'Is it like the television series?' I must admit that the night I attended a helicopter crash on a rocky hillside in the middle of a cattle station, with the local stockmen rigging up an IV pole for me out of mulga branches and waiting for the Airforce medical helicopter to take me and the two spinal patients back into Alice Springs—well, that could have been made into an interesting episode!

Most of the calls are less dramatic, but there is quite a variety, with the rugged station owners, the tourists from the cities and overseas, and the Aboriginal people out on communities all needing advice and help.

The other part of our job is spending two or three days a week doing medical clinics in remote Aboriginal communities. Some people like the excitement of doing emergency on-call with the Flying Doctors, but I must say I find it rewarding working with the nurses and Aboriginal Health Workers in the bush clinics. I really enjoy getting to know the Aboriginal people in the communities and being their GP. You should hear the delighted squeals of laughter as the patients and health workers try to teach me to speak Warlpiri!

There is a problem recruiting doctors to country areas all over Australia, and Alice Springs is no exception. Most people when I talk to them envy me the lifestyle of living in such a beautiful place and having such an interesting job. I think that if more city folk heard what life is like up here, they might think seriously of trying it out for a year or two.

· · · · · · · · · · · · · · · · · · · · · · · · · · · · · · · · · · · · · · · · · · · · · · · · · · · · · · · · · · · · · · · · · · · · · · · · · · · · · · · · · · · · · · · · · · · · ·

*A Tasmanian rang in about his state:*
'Tasmania is the testicle of Australia, infusing virility and strength into the mainland — it's a pity there's not two of them.'

· · · · · · · · · · · · · · · · · · · · · · · · · · · · · · · · · · · · · · · · · · · · · · · · · · · · · · · · · · · · · · · · · · · · · · · · · · · · · · · · · · · · · · · · · · · · ·

YOUR SHOW REMINDS MANY of us of our childhood, perhaps because it conjures up a time that seemed less sophisticated, more certain, and somehow more real. Growing up in the late fifties and early sixties, we kids would wander out of the streets and into the bush and the paddocks whenever we could.

We'd take our sandwiches and drinks and hike up nearby Red Hill. We felt a strange magic about that place, as though the hill knew all there was to know. We never talked about it then, but now I guess that it might have been an Aboriginal dreaming place.

In the paddocks, we collected cow dung to sell to our neighbours for their gardens. We learned to recognise a 'mixy' rabbit and to know the precarious still-ness of the blue-tongue. We learned to sense the coming storm and would gaze

from
CLIVE HAMILTON
DEAKIN WEST
ACT

across at the hills when the air filled ominously with the smell of rain.

Among the trees, we felt the damp closeness of the woods, the smell of the fungus, the silence of the breezes in the treetops. We experienced these things with the intensity that only children can.

The long sad cries of the ravens wheeling across the skies filled Sunday afternoons with that eerie melancholy of the Australian landscape. In a way, we little Aussies were closest to the land then; the timeless vastness and the disturbing pull of the bush seeped into our bones. We were not yet full of all the ideas and logic that rob adults of that direct connection with the country.

On summer mornings we'd walk on our leathery bare feet down to the river, across the grassland, watching for brown snakes, with the plovers fiercely calling and diving at us if we passed near their nests in the grass. As we sat waiting for the yabby to be enticed from its hole, the river slipped by taking our thoughts to who-knows-where. Down to the sea I suppose, where they merged with the great water.

The town I grew up in was Canberra. Australians like to criticise Canberra, confusing the politicians with the people. But the people—whether born here or in Melbourne or Albury or Townsville—are just like other Australians.

I've travelled the world since my dreamtime as a boy, but I'm back home now, in Canberra, where my roots sink deep into the earth. I'm one of the lucky ones—I know where my home is.

• • • • • • • • • • • • • • • • • • • •

from
BRIAN BULLIVANT
NUNGURNER
VICTORIA

EVERY SUNDAY MY WIFE and I are reminded of some of the reasons why we love to live where we live. The carolling of magpies from the radio echoes the same call from the birds in the large gum trees just outside our window, for me a more evocative sound of the Australian bush than even kookaburras (one that certainly helped to bring me back to Australia as a migrant two years after competing in the 1956 Olympic Games in Ballarat); the dry humour and laconic Aussie voices of many of your phone callers—so like some of my mates in our local CFA brigade and small rural community.

Even some of your contentious correspondents make us think about why we love being here. Take, for example, the complaints about small communities. True, small communities (and ours is very small, only about two hundred people) can be cliquey (they probably have to be to survive) but if you don't put on airs and graces, try to rally round in local events like fetes, family crises, and searches for missing kiddies, and show where your loyalties really lie you may be slowly accepted. You've got to give before you get something in return.

Even where we listen to your program reminds us of reasons why we love to live where we live—snug in bed during the sacred hours of six to ten on Sunday morning. Heaven help the dogs if they disturb us! Our bedroom window provides a view over one of the Gippsland Lakes and we watch wheeling pelicans and often the soaring flight of a majestic white-breasted sea eagle. In the summer the dawn sun pours straight into the room. Even if the windows are closed we can usually hear the sound of the surf pounding on the Ninety Mile Beach about three kilometres away as the eagle flies. Surely only a great country like Australia could give us such a paradise.

• • • • • • • • • • • • • • • • • • • •

## G'day, this is Macca

GARY: Hello, it's Gary Hill from Bundaberg. I just wanted to tell you that my missus is descended from the Yandruwandha tribe, around Innamincka, and her people had dealings with Burke and Wills and that mob, and I'm descended from the Garangarang tribe in Bundaberg.

MACCA: That's interesting. I read somewhere the other day that Australians could tell you ten American Red Indian tribes like the Sioux and the Comanches and the Apaches but I'll bet they couldn't name three Australian Aboriginal tribes.

GARY: I think you'd be pretty right there. My missus, Gloria, might be able to give you a little bit more on the Yandruwandha tribe. I'll put her on.

GLORIA: Hello, we've been trying to get on to you for the last twelve months! I look forward to the program every week. It was my grandfather's people that looked after King at the last. The word of mouth comes down, so we knew all that. My grandfather was from Innamincka and my grandmother's land was next door, Wangkumara. My son's doing a family tree; he's off to the archives in Adelaide next week to find out more. We know all about the Aboriginal side of it, but he wants the dates. We speak our language and I still say words to myself today but I have no-one to speak to except an uncle at Cunnamulla, so it's very difficult for me to hang on to the language. But we have tapes: a linguist was doing my granny and grandfather's language for about fifteen years before they passed away, so we were very fortunate. Although I was brought up with my people, when you're young you don't realise the importance of something like this.

MACCA: No, and it defines us so much. The thing that defines Australia—apart from our unique flora and fauna—is our Aboriginal people and their language and all the names— Oodnadatta and so on—all derived from the Aboriginal language and people.

GLORIA: I have a niece who's going to Adelaide University next year to take up the language, and my son who's doing our family tree is thinking about going to University to do that as well. We should have more emphasis on our own culture to give us more pride. I think we're all lost, including the Europeans, because we're all just stuck, like, in a bowl of cherries, but we all have to shine in our own identity to give us pride in where we come from and what we're all about. My grandchildren are little blue-eyed blondes but when they come to visit from New South Wales we tell them their ancestry, speak the words, and put on their little yellow, black and red identity colours just so it can't be lost. We're on the brink of it: we get bleached out, we marry Europeans, but our identity and our culture is inside every Australian and we should never lose it no matter who comes to our country. I'm pleased that we share our country with a lot of good people.

MACCA: Exactly, and I think people are starting to realise that now and I think there'll be big changes. People are sick to death of being inundated with American culture all the time. It's fine for Americans but it shouldn't be all-pervasive here and it shouldn't mean the extinction of our own culture. Everybody's facing it, right round the world, not just in Australia. In France they've banned words like le hamburger because they're worried about their language, and we should be just as concerned.

GLORIA: Yes, we should.

Macca: Good on you, Gloria. And thanks to Gary for ringing us, it was nice to talk to you both.

from
DAVID WILLIAMS
ARMIDALE
NEW SOUTH WALES

ABOUT TEN YEARS AGO my wife and I bought a ten-hectare property some twelve kilometres out of Armidale. We were attracted by the rural lifestyle but particularly by the panoramic views. We are located on the crest of a hill with a view extending over hills to a mountain range about thirty kilometres to the east and several kilometres along a north/south valley which runs along the boundary of our property. The landscape is virtually devoid of man-made structures and the view has many moods creating both peacefulness and stimulation.

All that is about to change with the decision of the Electricity Transmission Authority to run the Eastlink transmission line from Armidale to Gatton (in Queensland) right across the foreground of this landscape. We are confronted with having ten transmission towers each forty-five metres high (about a fifteen-storey building) running along our valley. The incredulous response of Eastlink to our concern about this devastation of the environment was that this is the price of development and that as the towers are not actually on our property we have no legal rights in the matter.

Why do we continue to live where we live?!

• • • • • • • • • • • • • • • • • • •

from
KRIS MCLEAN
FREEMANS REACH
NEW SOUTH WALES

MY SIBLING AND I were raised in the little suburb of Canley Heights, smack in the middle of Sydney's fibro belt and just down the road from Cabramatta. I guess we both figured the olds would see their days out there. It was with some surprise when we learned from the old man that they were to sell up and retire to the little hamlet of Stanley, not far from where Mum spent her childhood. Apparently there had been just one 'home invasion' too many in the big smoke for the old man.

My brother and me glanced at each other in stunned silence then both made a dive for the map. Sure enough, there it was, beautiful downtown Stanley, a speck on the map up the road from Beechworth, Victoria, a good nine hours' drive from us. My wife and I made the run a few times, hours on the road down 'truck alley' with the kids in the back '. . . are we nearly there yet?' every five minutes in my ear. There had to be a better way!

There was! I resurrected my old GA pilots' ticket. These days I do it in just two hours in a little Piper Dakota. It's a snap. South from Bankstown I get approval from flight service at the Nowra air station to track through their zone, then down to 500 feet for a coastal sprint to Moruya. On a good day you get to see a dolphin pod. Then up to 8,500 feet over Cooma, in through Corryong and straight over the pines to Stanley. Mate, I just love to come over that hill and see what the old buggers are up to, pottering in their garden or tinkering with the wood heap, whatever. By this time I've really got the warm fuzzies. I've switched off the satellite navigation and I'm fairly cruisin', just following the Dederang high tension lines. I park that plane and wander into another world, 700 km from Sydney and a thousand miles from care. We go for walks in the bush and watch for platypus and echidnas. I always say, '. . . what, no takeaway' when Mum serves up her home cooking—those golden arches haven't made it to Stanley yet! Every day down there with them is a blessing and I'm hoarding them up like treasure.

• • • • • • • • • • • • • • • • • • •

**I** LIVE IN THE GAIRDNER area. It is about 500 kilometres away from our capital city, Perth. From our farm on Meechi Road it is about 162 kilometres to our main town Albany where we do most of our shopping. On our farm we have about 5,700 sheep, counting our lambs. Since it has been dry we have had to feed our sheep oats.

I like living where I live because I can drive the ute around the farm. I can also go and check the sheep with Dad and I love watching him pull the lambs out of the ewes with troubles. I also like living here because it is peaceful.

We live only about twenty-five minutes away from a town where we can go swimming. We can go to the beach if it's hot. It is called Bremer Bay. I like going there a lot because most of my dad's family live there. My dad's family owns a factory there as well. I like going down there and mucking around with my cousins.

My favourite two things on the farm are seeding time and harvest time. I like harvest time mostly because I like playing in the wheat and lupins but I especially like jumping off the super shed roof into them. We live quite close to the Fitzgerald National Park and I like going there, I especially like going to a beach called Point Ann because in winter the female whales go there to give birth to their calves.

I love living on a farm because you can do things that kids in the cities or towns can't do, like driving a ute without a licence. Also on a farm there are no ambulance or police sirens going at night when you're trying to sleep.

from
KELLIE DREW (YEAR 7)
GAIRDNER PRIMARY
SCHOOL
WESTERN AUSTRALIA

• • • • • • • • • • • • • • • • • • •

**M**Y CLASS OF UPPER Primary students at Galiwinku on Elcho Island are a great mob of children—quite proficient at using a computer.

Galiwinku is an Aboriginal community of approximately 1,500 people during the wet season and considerably less during the dry season when many of the people move back to their homelands or outstations. The island is approximately seventy kilometres long and twelve kilometres wide. There are plenty of places to go hunting and fishing, collecting bush tucker and the like.

When I first arrived on Elcho I was adopted by an Aboriginal family and so now I have a much bigger 'family'. The Yolnu refer to me by my relationship to them which immediately makes you feel as if you belong. My Napipi (uncle) and Mukul (auntie) like to take me out hunting and teach me things about their culture. They are proud of their culture and they want to share it. When I was sick recently, one of my Yapas (sisters) went out and got some bush medicine, brought it back home and showed me how to prepare it. After having had to sit on the toilet for three days I was better within a few hours!

Life in any community has its stressful moments but life on Elcho is great (most of the time!).

from
JAN HERRMAN
WINNELLIIE
NORTHERN TERRITORY

• • • • • • • • • • • • • • • • • • •

**I** LIVE SOME OF THE time in a bus and the reason why might become evident as you read on.

Just now I'm cooking bacon and eggs and listening to your program at Warroora Station (pronounced Warra) on the southern end of the Ningaloo Marine Park near North West Cape, Western Australia.

from
PETER MACK
CORAL BAY
WESTERN AUSTRALIA

The scene all about contains the essence of the outback sheep station. I'm parked on a stony ridge with a sparse covering of brown buffalo grass and the occasional stunted mulga bush. Small groups of ewes, heads down, plod along a dusty track to water at the mill in the gully, kicking up red dust as they go. Most are followed by half-grown, long-tailed lambs. The occasional inquisitive emu stalks by, or maybe a feral goat with a floppy eared knobby kneed kid cavorting about. Not far off there is a pigeon bush where the top-knots glide in to rest on their way between the mill and far out in the scrub where they feed. Overhead the inevitable pair of crows completes the scene, flapping in a cloudless sky.

But this is not the reason travellers call at Warroora. Beyond the mill is a white sand drift and past this the Indian Ocean stretches away, smooth and serene, to the horizon. Today there is a land wind and the sea is placid and still—a fisherman's dream. Not far off shore a humpback blows occasionally and lazily waves a fluke into the air. Our nearest neighbours are a country kilometre away up the beach and they are also parked with their own personal view of the sea. The coast here contains a variety of cliffs, beaches, lagoons and bays stretching away along 200 kilometres of coral-filled sea which is our beautiful Ningaloo Marine Park.

Well, that describes the little bit of paradise I'm enjoying at the moment. I was going to leave and head back to civilisation tomorrow but you have just played that song 'In the Suburbs', so I think I might stay here a few days longer!

• • • • • • • • • • • • • • • • • • •

from
PIERRE LOMAY-LYONS
SOOCHOW
CHINA

ONE WOULD LIKE TO be able to hear all four hours of your program but that is not possible when you are linked to Radio Australia and your program goes international. Still, to hear your familiar voice here in Soochow in China (a quaint little place with small houses overhanging centuries' old canals, and many little bridges) a little way up the creek from Shanghai is indeed grand.

Soochow's claim to fame is its place in history of over 1,200 years as a prominent town that grew on the banks of the 'grand canal'. And as a prominent craft (i.e. silk) and art (i.e. small landscaped gardens, calligraphy, painting and books) centre it remains a treasure house of things Chinese.

My wife Cathy is a doctor in the Katale Refugee Camp in Zaire (Rhwandan/Zaire Border region) who has over the last five months assisted in the medical needs of the sick kiddies and displaced people. She had the good fortune to be able to listen to three or four of your programs which I taped and sent her. Your program cannot reach Africa, but the tapes did. Sadly they were confiscated by the gun-toting Zairean military—just as well they made copies.

I am settled in Soochow for a dozen months or so and working on aspects of language, culture, and social issues. I'm told there are something like 200 Aussie families here in Jiangsu (Jang Soo) Province.

from
TERRI A. BREEN
NEGARA BRUNEI
DARUSSALAM

MY HUSBAND WAS AWARDED a contract to teach in Brunei for three years, and off we set with a mountain of luggage and a sense of adventure—sort of mid-life crisis—to what we jokingly described to our friends and relations as 'the wilds of Borneo'.

I am typing this in our temporary accommodation—a cold-water flat three floors up—overlooking the jungles of Borneo—in the heart of Temburong Province, otherwise known as the frontier of Brunei. We monitor the antics of a troop of about twenty monkeys each day as they progress around the accommodation complex; we watch the storms build each afternoon, sending deluges onto the surrounding rainforest; we wake each morning to wonderful mists lifting like a veil from the river valleys—and everywhere we look is tranquil and green.

We are confined to the riverboat system for visits to the capital. Generally this is a simple matter, but a couple of weeks ago we had to go to Bandar, and the river was in flood. We certainly got adventure that day — our little boat skittered through the flood waters dodging floating logs, parts of houses, escaped boats and forty-four gallon drums. I think most of us spent the voyage assessing which floating log or other substantial debris to aim for if the boat went down. It wasn't helped by one of the passengers regaling us with stories of local maritime disasters. The boats are locally known as 'coffin boats'.

As a Muslim society, the family is paramount, and embraces traditional values. We find it a tremendous change from Cairns — there is no alcohol, drug usage is punishable by death, the crime rate is minimal. We can walk the local street at night certain in the knowledge that we will reach our destination unmolested —something we were not able to do in Cairns in recent memory. So, as I sit here above the trees in the wilds of Borneo, listening to our CDs of 'Australia All Over', I can honestly say that I am content — a relaxed lifestyle in a very relaxed society.

• • • • • • • • • • • • • • • • • • • •

IN 1970 MY HUSBAND Lew calmly asked if I would like to live on a tropical island in the Torres Straits. My reaction: 'How long do I have to make up my mind?' His answer: 'I'd like to be there in a couple of weeks.' Easy enough for the two of us, but when you also have three children and various pets, plus I was working, a few things would have to be sorted out. But as I have always been adaptable, what the heck?

Thus began nearly two of the happiest years I have ever known, on Thursday Island, or 'TI' as the locals call her. We were greeted by what seemed half the Island's population, and had a lovely little flat on the waterfront, looking down the Straits.

Lew was responsible for the running of the seafood factory from which prawns and crayfish were exported to the USA and Japan. I am ashamed to admit we used cray tails for bait—I remember when we came back to the mainland we found crays were $26 a pound! We found the Islanders a warm and caring people, and we didn't ever knock back an invitation to share their customs, even a tombstone opening! And you haven't lived until you have heard the Islanders singing on Sunday morning in the Quetta Cathedral without the benefit of an organ, just the drums. I can still hear them.

We did not have TV and for some time not even a radio, and forgot about the newspapers, but somehow it didn't matter. The children thrived at school which had excellent primary and high school facilities. Entertainment? Visiting, parties,

from
DAPHNE HUGHES

KAHIBAH

NEW SOUTH WALES

dances, and after tea our kids would put on a concert. But all things come to an end, and once again we found ourselves on the wharf with the many friends we had made. They sang TI's own song 'Old TI', and I stood there with the tears rolling down my face.

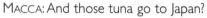

## G'day, this is Macca

YVONNE: Hello, Macca, this is Yvonne here. I'm sitting in a truck in Sydney and you're down in my part of the country so I thought I'd give you a call. We've just unloaded a load of tuna from Port Lincoln at Sydney airport.

MACCA: Is that your livelihood, carrying tuna to Sydney?

YVONNE: Yes, we've got a truck and my husband, Neville, and I do a weekly trip to Sydney. You've probably observed the tuna farms around the area since you've been there, and the company that we cart for harvests two to three times a week and we get one of the loads.

MACCA: And those tuna go to Japan?

YVONNE: Yes, straight from Sydney to Japan.

MACCA: And it fetches hundreds of dollars a kilo, or something, doesn't it?

YVONNE: Well, it varies. It goes from thirty dollars to fifty or sixty dollars; it ranges. It depends on what the market's doing over there and what other tuna are coming in from around the world.

MACCA: And how much tuna do you carry to Sydney from Port Lincoln each week?

YVONNE: That varies, too. This week we have about nine tons and it can be anything from about six tons to sixteen or seventeen.

MACCA: This is not live, is it?

YVONNE: No, it's freshly slaughtered and packed into cartons with ice and sent freshly chilled across to the Japanese, and they obviously like it.

MACCA: You farm the tuna in Port Lincoln in little pens and feed them just like they farm the salmon and trout, I think, on the Huon River in Tasmania.

YVONNE: They harvest them from December through to about March or April and put them into their pens there and fatten them up by feeding them every day. Most time we go down the east coast of Australia, down around Eden and Lakes Entrance, and pick up pilchards and mackerel to take back to Port Lincoln to feed then on.

MACCA: How long have you been doing that, Yvonne?

YVONNE: For about two years. We're actually fishermen turning truckies.

MACCA: Now tell me, when you drive from Port Lincoln to Sydney which way do you go?

YVONNE: Up through Clare and across to Renmark, across to Mildura, Hay, Narrandera, Wagga and up onto the Hume to Sydney. It's about a 4,000 kilometre round trip from Port Lincoln.

MACCA: That's a long way, isn't it?

YVONNE: Yes, you get to know the road after a while. I've been going to ring you because you often talk about the carp in the river systems. Well, hundreds of tons of carp are used in the crayfish or lobster industry as bait.

MACCA: Carp are everywhere in Australia. I heard the other day about a plan to farm carp and use them for fish meal. It would be good if we could use them in some way. It's just a matter of taste, isn't it? In Europe, of course European carp is a delicacy, but here we we just throw them on the bank or blow them up or do anything to get rid of them.

YVONNE: We used to use them sometimes for crab bait but we didn't like the smell of them very much, let alone eat them.

MACCA: No, that's what some people say, but one man's meat is another man's poisson, as they say. Neville's your silent partner, obviously.

YVONNE: Yes, he's in the bunk at the moment.

I'M AN AVA (Australian Volunteer Abroad) teaching at the Provincial High School here in Telefomin, which is one of the most underdeveloped districts of Western Papua New Guinea, even though it is sitting in the middle of the mineral-rich Star Mountains. The rugged terrain has held back almost all development—mountains, thick with jungle, rising to almost four kilometres, and deep gorges, with wild rivers roaring in their depths. The headwaters of the famous Sepik River pass by only a few kilometres away. Another famous landmark, of a completely different nature, is the Ok Tedi copper mine which is about twenty minutes flying time south west of Telefomin, or three days' walk.

Telefomin is the name of the provincial district, and also the name of the government station of which we are part. We are surrounded in our little valley by mountains, some of which reach 3,500 metres, but the average is about 2,800 metres. Also located in our little valley are a number of small villages with names like Drolergam, Ankem, Telefolip, Koprenmin and Framtelin. Many of our students fly in from further out and board with us at the school, and come from places like Oksapmin, Tekin, Eliptamin, Mianmin and Tifalmin. There are eleven teachers here, and about 260 students. Living conditions aren't too bad—we get six hours' electricity every day, have solar hot water services, and mail twice a week, although that depends on flights into the valley. We are very isolated!

It rains usually four or five days a week, sometimes all week, and as a result the ground is almost always muddy. I do miss the sight of a warm, cloudless blue sky like that above Elong Elong in Central Western New South Wales, where I grew up. Even as I write, it is very heavily overcast with a very high chance of rain later on today.

P.S. We only get about two hours of AAO on Radio Australia. Any chance of any more?

from
ANDREW MAY
TELEFOMIN
PAPUA NEW GUINEA

MY NAME IS ANTON KRKAN I am eleven years old and I am in a special class at Morisset Primary School. I live in Rathmines and it is on Lake Macquarie. I like living here because the moon shines on the water at night.

There is a problem because people sometimes throw glass in the lake and we cut our feet.

There is a nice view at the point at Fishingpoint Road and I go abseiling off Fishingpoint Road with my friend Brendan. He takes me everywhere and he is in year 8 at high school.

Thank you for your program, Macca.

We would like you to visit our class please.

from
ANTON KRKAN
RATHMINES
NEW SOUTH WALES

from
MICHAEL BRIMMER

CORINTH

GREECE

'YASSOO' FROM XYLOCASTRO, A small town 30 kilometres west of Corinth in the Peloponnese, Greece. My wife Niki, son Nicholas and I abandoned domestic security in Sydney almost two years ago and have since lived in this beautiful pocket of the Mediterranean. In many ways, our address is like a dream come true. Just off our front verandah is the deep blue Gulf of Corinth. Across this stretch of water sits Mount Parnassus, one of Greece's highest mountains, in whose foothills rests ancient Delphi. The mountain is blanketed in snow at the moment and it is a magnificent sight, literally rising up out of the water. Behind us are hills covered in citrus and olive groves which rise up into the rugged mountains of the Peloponnese. You can swim for about eight months of the year and in the cooler months the hills provide wonderful opportunities for long walks and even longer lunches in village tavernas. Every night in summer the seafront promenade (paralia) is full of families out strolling, savouring the evening and the seafront tavernas and cafes.

We work in a language school, teaching English to Greek schoolkids of various ages. Most English here is heard in American films so my Australian accent can really throw them at times.

Life is very seasonal and the food is usually related to what is being currently harvested or what religious festival is being celebrated. When the olives are being picked, whole families take to the hills to bring in the crop—old grandpas up the trees, the womenfolk in the lower branches and small children picking the strays off the ground and making a nuisance of themselves. I've been fortunate to experience this and will cherish the memory of sitting under an ancient olive tree eating hot lentil soup and crusty bread washed down with home-made wine, surrounded by friends chatting and laughing.

I'd better stop now as it's time to go and teach gerunds and irregular verbs!

• • • • • • • • • • • • • • • • • • • • • • • • • • • • • • • • • • • • • • • • • • • • • • • • • • • • • • • • •

*At the Sydney Cricket Ground outside broadcast there was a bloke there who lived at Long Bay near the famous gaol.*

MACCA: 'What do you live in?'

BLOKE: 'A house with plenty of land around it.'

MACCA: 'Is it a problem living near the gaol?'

BLOKE: 'We think it's the safest place in Sydney. Once they get over the wall they don't hang around — they go whoosh. They're out of here.'

• • • • • • • • • • • • • • • • • • • • • • • • • • • • • • • • • • • • • • • • • • • • • • • • • • • • • • • • •

# 9

# *H*ave a listen to this!

BY COURTESY OF
SUNDAY MAIL
BRISBANE

## THE PAT GRUNDY EPIC

Doctors had just twenty-four hours to find Pat Grundy to give her a new kidney and another chance at life. But the 56-year-old mother of three, who had been waiting four years for a suitable donor, was nowhere to be found. She had left Tasmania for a holiday in Queensland, her pager would not respond to frantic calls from Royal Melbourne, and attempts to locate her through the police, taxi companies and countless phone calls failed.

But there was one final hope—Macca.

Pat Grundy's daughter Kim knew Mrs Grundy listened to 'Australia All Over' every Sunday. When a suitable kidney finally became available late one Saturday night, Launceston Hospital nurse Rose Mace and Kim immediately launched a search. Their deadline was critical—they had to find Mrs Grundy within twenty-four hours of the donor's death. Although the donor kidney could have been kept alive through freezing techniques for forty-eight hours, its function starts to decline after twenty-four hours.

The Grundys had been on the Gold Coast for a family wedding, but decided to do some sight-seeing on the Sunshine Coast. The pager, which Mrs Grundy had been carrying for four years in case a donor was found, had been left in her Gold Coast hotel, so Kim asked police and taxi companies to look out for her parents' car. It became a family operation with Mrs Grundy's son, Chris, arranging to have announcements aired hourly on ABC radio news bulletins. But no-one could find them.

The breakthrough came on Sunday morning when the Grundys, getting an early morning start as they headed to Maleny, near Maroochydore, turned on the car radio. 'It was near the end of Macca's program which I have been listening to every Sunday morning for years,' said Mrs Grundy. 'Then I heard this voice that I knew was Kim's and I told my husband to stop the car. I couldn't hear very well because I was so shocked to hear her voice, but I heard her say "medical emergency" and I thought something must have happened to my eighty-five-year-old father.'

'Then I heard her say there was a kidney available and we should contact her by noon. I just went hot and cold. We were at the base of the Glasshouse Mountains, and raced to a service station to ring Kim but she was on the phone.'

Travelling briskly on the expressway back to the Gold Coast, they were desperately looking for a telephone. At 10.30 am they located a pay phone and called Kim. She told them they were booked on the 2.45 pm plane from Coolangatta to Melbourne. They went back to the expressway and headed for their Gold Coast Voyager Motel, where staff had been mobilised by Kim to pack their suitcases.

'We wondered all the time whether we would make it because the traffic was really heavy as we got closer to the Gold Coast,' she said. 'By 12.15 pm we were at our motel. We dragged the cases into the car, went to Coolangatta airport, left the car with the two front doors open, and made the 2.45 pm plane with two minutes to spare.'

By 6.30 pm Mrs Grundy was in the hospital operating theatre having a kidney transplant. 'It must have had my name on it because it has performed so beautifully . . . I really think it was meant for me.'

# Caps, Hats, Jumpers and a Kilt

16

17

18

19

20

You can be sure of one thing at outside broadcasts (apart from bad weather— see pictures 39-44) or book signings, and that's the wide variety of clothing on display. The Macca jumpers look great, and David (*left*) and Lisle manage 5.35 am smiles while Eddy is a study in concentration.

# *K*ids All Over

Kids' pictures and drawings are always memorable. Here we have a sing-song I had with the entire Coorabie Rural School, South Australia — ten pupils!; Christmas fun at Bidyadanga, south of Broome, for Katherine and friends (see her 'Why I Live' letter); 'fan mail' from Nikki (*right*), Matthew and Lauren (who likes the song 'Bundaberg Rum' because it says 'bum') Lloyd; Pam with smiling faces from Hebel State School, Queensland; and Ben Wheeler from Tinana, Queensland with a gumboot friend.

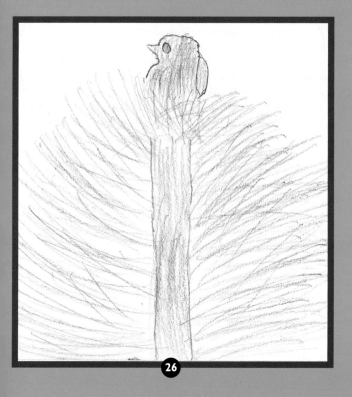

26

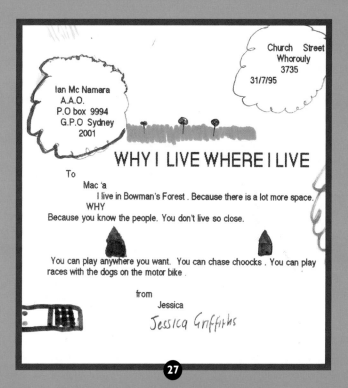

Church Street
Whorouly
3735
31/7/95

Ian Mc Namara
A.A.O.
P.O box 9994
G.P.O Sydney
2001

# WHY I LIVE WHERE I LIVE

To
   Mac 'a
     I live in Bowman's Forest . Because there is a lot more space.
  WHY
Because you know the people. You don't live so close.

You can play anywhere you want.  You can chase choocks . You can play races with the dogs on the motor bike .

from
Jessica
*Jessica Griffiths*

27

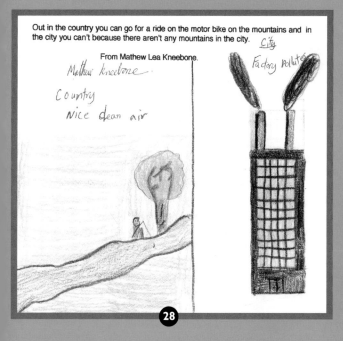

Out in the country you can go for a ride on the motor bike on the mountains and  in the city you can't because there aren't any mountains in the city.  City

From Mathew Lea Kneebone.

*Mathew Kneebone.*

*Country*

*Nice clean air*

Factory Pollutes

28

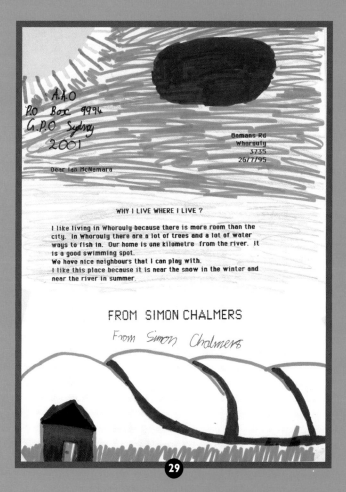

A.A.O
P.O Box 9994
G.P.O Sydney
2001

Bomans Rd
Whorouly
3735
26/7/95

Dear Ian McNamara

WHY I LIVE WHERE I LIVE ?

I like living in Whorouly because there is more room than the city.  In Whorouly there are a lot of trees and a lot of water ways to fish in.  Our home is one kilometre  from the river.  It is a good swimming spot.
We have nice neighbours that I can play with.
I like this place because it is near the snow in the winter and near the river in summer.

FROM  SIMON CHALMERS

*From Simon Chalmers*

29

A selection of drawings (with some nice observations) from Kylie Worthington, Jessica Griffiths, Simon Chalmers and Matthew Lea Kneebone of Whorouly Primary School, Victoria.

# Choirs and Bands

30

32

31

Wherever we broadcast, there's music — groups like this one at Narromine, New South Wales (the little boy seems to be encouraging the reindeer to join in), or the Dalby Christian School, Queensland (choir led by Gwen Langridge); the late Mal Rabe's 'Bush Harmony Band' at Winton, Queensland; and the South Australian Air Training Corps (6th Flight) Squadron Band.

33

Mrs Grundy rang Macca from hospital the Sunday after her operation to thank him for the announcement on his program. 'I wanted him to know that it all had a happy ending.'

••••••••••••••••••••

AN HOUR AFTER YOU broadcast my story on Sunday about the cockatoo that visited me on Friday night, a friend rang to say she would love to take him if no-one claimed him. Her parents had heard my story while driving home from Canberra.

I phoned the vet, explaining who I was and that I had rung 'Australia All Over'. There was a slight pause, then a rather cool voice said, 'Yes, we know.' I answered excitedly, 'Oh, he's been claimed then?' 'Yes, by twenty people!' I felt terrible, realising how much extra work I had given these poor people on a Sunday morning! I hadn't thought to tell them I was ringing you! I know the program is very popular, but I hadn't expected that sort of response!

As a result of the program, our cocky was finally reunited with his owner yesterday afternoon. He has apparently been missing for six months. It's a pity he doesn't talk in our language, judging by the way he charmed me on Friday night, the story of his adventures over that six months would make a bestseller!

from
BUNTY OLDMEADOW
PADSTOW
NEW SOUTH WALES

••••••••••••••••••••

WITH GREAT APPRECIATION I would like to thank you for allowing me to appear on your program to talk about travelling showmen and locating some of my family I had not seen nor heard of for forty-three years. Twenty minutes after the show went to air I received a phone call from Queensland from my younger brother Terry. After forty-three years it was absolutely brilliant. He told me where all the other members of my family were to be located. I also found that the family had multiplied: twenty nieces and nephews, five grand-nieces and nephews. A reunion is planned for the near future.

from
KEN & HEATHER STEVEN
GERALDTON
WESTERN AUSTRALIA

••••••••••••••••••••

I'M HOPING YOU OR your audience can help my dad, Wes Penney. He isn't too well, and is seeing a bit of the country while he can. Unfortunately he left his hat behind on a tea break and consequently left all of his badges and hat pins as well! We're not worried about the hat, but if someone has found it we would appreciate it very much if they could post his badges to him.

He left his hat about twenty-five kilometres south of Tambo at a truck stop around ten o'clock. When he realised he had left it he drove back (250 km round trip) but it was gone.

I hope somebody can help us through your show and give Dad some good news.

from
ATHALIE VAN DE
VEERDONT
PORTLAND, VICTORIA

••••••••••••••••••••

THANK YOU FOR TAKING the time this morning to put over the radio waves an enquiry by my rather distraught family for my whereabouts. I certainly was not a 'missing person' nor had I encountered trouble on the track. But I had failed miserably to keep in touch with home during my month in Perth assuming that the family would know I was safe with friends. And I ought to have rung them

from
RUTH BOULTON
WOODVILLE SOUTH
SOUTH AUSTRALIA

when I left Perth. All this coupled with second-hand news and rumours caused them to push the emergency button.

At 7.30 am today I was safely parked on a side-track beside the Kalgoorlie water pipeline, sixty kilometres from Southern Cross when I heard your request that I contact home. I was aghast, imagining bad news there. With HF radio reception not good due to atmospherics, I quickly packed and headed for the first public phone. Though my daughter Jenny was glad to hear my voice, she was understandably angry that I had treated those at home so badly. She made me promise that I will call in every week in future.

• • • • • • • • • • • • • • • • • • • •

from
CATE ACKLAND
APSLEY
TASMANIA

ON 24 APRIL 1994 you read my letter which told the story behind the Memorial Cross on the Sugarloaf Hill here at Apsley. Part of the letter was a request for families of six of the seven crew members to whom the Cross is dedicated to contact me so I could tell them about the Memorial. The phone started ringing about an hour later, a call from Queensland and the first family was found. It took fifteen months to find all the families, including the one in Scotland, but it was well worth the effort. The families are deeply moved by this memorial in such an unexpected location; only the pilot was a Tasmanian. We have had quite a steady stream of family members to visit, including one from England and another from Scotland. They are lovely people who have greatly enriched my life. It's strange how men who died for their country more than fifty years ago have had such an influence on my life these last few years.

• • • • • • • • • • • • • • • • • • • •

from
DOT CARLTON
MORUYA
NEW SOUTH WALES

LAST JANUARY YOU HAD a lady on your show, Lorraine Welch, who works her way around Australia fruit picking. You asked her where she was off to next and she said she was working her way to Kununurra, Western Australia. My ears pricked up as that was the last place my son had rung me from back in September 1993. It was Grand Final Day in Sydney and he had watched the match and come in for supplies. He rang from the Kununurra Pub and said I will ring you next time I am back in civilisation, which he always did. For years he had been gold digging in the desert on his own and he was having a change and doing some prospecting in the Kimberleys. Well, there was no more word from him, so I thought he had perished. It was a very agonising time for us his parents, his three brothers and two sisters. We had rung the police many times over at Port Hedland which used to be his base, and placed him as a missing person in Perth. All to no avail.

Well, on that day I rang the ABC and asked if I could speak to Lorraine. I explained the circumstances to her and she said she wouldn't get there until the end of April or early May. Well, four weeks ago my phone rang and it was Lorraine! She had found my son alive and well. He is working at Turkey Creek out from Kununurra. She got a message to him that his mum was looking for him and he rang me first thing on Mother's Day, the best present a mother could receive. Thanks to your show and that wonderful woman, Lorraine Welch.

• • • • • • • • • • • • • • • • • • • •

# 10

# Isn't that mighty!

## G'day, this is Macca

BRIAN: (Bungalow, Queensland): I'm up on the Palmer River at the River of Gold slate mines we started about ten years ago. The slate we're mining is absolutely unique for Australia in that it's just full of fossils. In it are fossilised worms and ferns. We had a bloke up in Cooktown and he laid 100 metres and he found a fish fossil in his floor, which was a bonus for him. We give the fossils for free! It's an open-cut mine. Sometimes we blast, and we pull it out just like the pages in a book. We do it in the old way and split it with bolster and hammer and the slate splits like bread, about a finger thickness. Every piece has that much fossil and history to it that it's like reading a book. The pieces come out as big as a man, down to plate size. It's a bugger Sundays. I can't get me slate splitters into the pen until after ten o'clock.
MACCA: Why's that, Brian?
BRIAN: Because they're listening to your program, mate.

GRAHAM: (Townsville, Queensland): I've just come back from Weipa on a prawn trawler. I had a month up there and it's one of the biggest seasons we've had for years. In the first four days we picked up 700 cartons of prawns, and we're one of the smallest boats up there.
MACCA: The price of prawns in the big smoke is still pretty dear.
GRAHAM: Yeah, well these are export prawns. One hundred and thirty-one boats started the season and we're only a fifty-one-footer, *Ali Baba*. The season for banana prawns only lasts three to four days then it's over and done with. Then the boat just changes all its gear and goes chasing tiger prawns. Banana prawns get up and move, where tiger prawns, you gotta get 'em out of the mud on the bottom and catch them at night time.

from
RAY ROBERTS
MOUNT ELIZA
VICTORIA

**I** SHARE WITH YOU A deep admiration of men like Matthew Flinders. My admiration of Flinders was heightened back in 1972, when I was involved in a mining feasibility study which called for a deep water, open-sea, ship loading facility to be located in the Gulf of Carpentaria, about seventy kilometres north of the mining port of Weipa. The only hydrographic chart available for that section of the coastline was one prepared by Matthew Flinders.

Much of the sea floor in that part of the Gulf is gently sloping soil and a jetty would need to be very long in order to reach deep water. It would also be very exposed and costly to construct. Our only hope was to locate a depression in the sea floor extending close in to the shore. There were no physical features along the coastline to suggest any variation of the sea floor. However, a detailed examination of Flinders' chart showed that he had located and taken soundings of a 'gutter' running at right angles to the shore at a point south of the mouth of the Pennefather River.

I was amazed that Flinders should have taken detailed soundings of a minor depression in the sea floor, in such a remote location. There is little doubt that we were the first people to make use of his soundings. We were concerned that the depression may have silted up or moved, so arrangements were made for a hydrographic survey vessel to carry out a check. Sure enough, the depression was exactly as the Flinders chart showed it to be.

The experience made me think long and hard about the character of men like Flinders. Even in 1972, the area was isolated and unforgiving. Yet, 170 years earlier, Flinders had located a minor depression in the sea floor and had delayed his voyage to take detailed soundings. He did this, despite the fact that it would have then been some eighteen months since he left his home in England and possibly six months since he had left the last outpost of civilisation at Sydney. The work must have taken him several days during which time the *Investigator* would have been most uncomfortable pitching in the 'slop'. I can only conclude that men of Flinders' calibre were more hardy, more dedicated and prepared to make more personal sacrifices in the discharge of their profession than most of us know anything about these days. And to cap it off, the French held him prisoner in Mauritius for over six years on the way home!

• • • • • • • • • • • • • • • • • • • •

*About ten years ago The Shopping Trolley Saga began and it still attracts letters, even from overseas. John Bourne from Biloela in Queensland wrote the first letter. Very sadly John, a man with a deep love of rural Australia and a highly developed sense of the ridiculous, died early in 1997. He would have been amused to see the continuation of The Saga.*

## THE FERAL SHOPPING TROLLEY

from
ELVA SCOTT
COOLAH
NEW SOUTH WALES

A feral shopping trolley
thought he'd take a little walk,
to meet up with his neighbours
and to have a little talk.
His wheels were getting rusty
and he thought he'd see the doc
to help him with his problems,
so he went around the block.

The doc was pretty busy
so he had to wait a while,
he didn't mind too much because
the nurse gave him a smile.
She took down his particulars
he came from Coles main store,
and he had worked for many years,
gone all around the floor.

His temperature was taken
doc checked he had no cough,
his pulse and pressure of his blood
were quickly written off.

He stood there to attention
as all his parts were checked
though the doc was rather hasty
and his posture almost wrecked.

'We need a bit of steel wool here'
the doctor said to nurse
'And perhaps a bit of first class oil
will help him check the worst.'
No bandaging was needed
and he didn't need a shot
so trolley really was surprised
the day the bill he got.

It seemed like such a big amount
for just one little chat
but doctors always learn a lot
there is no doubt of that.
But just to pay the money
he would have to go to work,
he had to give up roving
way out there back of Bourke.

So if you get a trolley
that is just a little old,
and if you find it rather wants
to stay out on in the cold
remember he is thinking of
the days out on the hill,
before he had to take a job
to pay the doctor's bill.

• • • • • • • • • • • • • • • • • • •

from
JUDI COX
KENMORE
QUEENSLAND

**I** SEE THAT SHOPPING TROLLEY rage is flaring in Australian supermarkets. So, the next step in the revenge of the shopping trolley is upon us!

Having successfully used tactics of both violence and passive resistance against shoppers and their vehicles to create shopping trolley wars, they are now setting human against human. It was reported that in the latest trolley rage incident one woman pushed another shopper in the rear with her trolley and a brawl erupted, to which the police were summoned. Ha! I bet the so-called pusher had no hand in it whatever! I can just see that trolley smirking to itself, while the other twisted metal minds silently applauded this example of supermarket rage, the next stage of their plan to overcome the world.

Shoppers of Australia, you have been warned!

*A fencer said to Macca:* 'I'm off to my next job — it's about thirteen stubbies away.'

Jᴜsᴛ ᴀ ǫᴜɪᴄᴋ ᴡᴏʀᴅ about Hale-Bopp for those people who would like to find it. You come down from Orion—which is what we often call 'the pot' or 'the saucepan' or 'the frying pan' and . . . well, a couple of months ago we had a woman come in here and call it 'the shopping trolley'.

from
Mᴀʀᴋ Mᴏɴᴋ, Dᴇʀʙʏ Fᴀʟʟs
Oʙsᴇʀᴠᴀᴛᴏʀʏ, Cᴏᴡʀᴀ
Nᴇᴡ Sᴏᴜᴛʜ Wᴀʟᴇs

• • • • • • • • • • • • • • • • • • •

I ɢʀᴇᴡ ᴜᴘ ᴅᴜʀɪɴɢ the Depression and although my father owned his own cattle property he was eventually forced to sell it by the bank. Dad was a great hunter and used to bring home ducks, pigeons and sometimes kangaroo steaks or kangaroo tail. Mum was well known for the lovely pigeon pies she made. She used to boil them whole with some onion and a little salt. When cooked let them cool and then take the flesh from the bones and return to the pot. Bring to the boil and thicken with flour and water. Put in a pie dish and cover with pastry made from plain flour, cream of tartar and soda, with dripping rubbed in and a little water to roll the pasty out. Bake till golden brown. Delicious!

Dad mainly shot squatter pigeons and there's still plenty of them in the area, so he never shot them out!

P.S. Mum once cooked an echidna, a cross between pork and chicken flavour the oldies said, but I don't remember it!

from
Dᴀᴡɴ Rɪᴅᴇᴏᴜᴛ
Mᴏᴜɴᴛ Lᴀʀᴄᴏᴍ
Qᴜᴇᴇɴsʟᴀɴᴅ

• • • • • • • • • • • • • • • • • • •

'KNOT' A PLASTIC BAG

A curse has come upon us
Spread across our wondrous land
From mountain tops, through valleys
And along our surf-washed sand.

Made for our convenience
To help bring our shopping home
So not to be more burden
They were made as light as foam.

When they have served their purpose
And have done this useful chore
They're stuffed up in a cupboard
That they may be used once more.

They have been taken with us
Maybe to a picnic ground
And left there filled with rubbish
For the winds to blow around.

At every tip there's millions
They cling all around the fence
And if some of these escape
It's of little consequence.

from
Eɪʟᴇᴇɴ Kᴇᴀʀɴᴇʏ
Pᴏʀᴛʟᴀɴᴅ
Vɪᴄᴛᴏʀɪᴀ

Then they're carried by the winds
Who could really know how far?
Borne aloft and flying free
They can outpace any car.
But then their journey's halted
By a wall, or fence, or tree
And there to flap and flutter
So that all the world can see.

The sight is not a pretty one—
Reeks of negligence by us.
'Someone else can pick it up
For I must not miss my bus.'

We have no want to touch them
We don't know where they've been
They're dirty or they're smelly
Have all sorts of germs; unclean!

There's a way to cure their progress
Try to stop these dreadful things
Just squeeze the air out of them
And then tie them up in rings.

When time comes to discard them
With these knots that you have tied
By winds they'll not be carried
All about our countryside.

There is not any turning back
Plastic bags are here! No doubt!
So it's up to us—tie 'em up
So they cannot fly about.

• • • • • • • • • • • • • • • • • •

from
ANGELA PERRY

ADDINGTON

VICTORIA

## THE LAUNDRY LAMENT

Everyone who's done the washing,
Either by machine or by hand,
Should listen to this verse, because
I know you'll understand.

You gather all the clothes,
And you turn them inside out,
You poke them, and you search them,
And you shake them all about.

You go through all the pockets,
You peer up every sleeve,
There's nothing that should not be there—
Or so you would believe.
And you wash them, and you spin them,
And you hang them out to dry,
You stand back, well satisfied
Then something takes your eye.

A fine white mist is covering
Every sheet and shirt and sock—
A tissue has escaped your search,
And is powdering the lot!

No matter how you look for them,
One always tends to miss you.
The bane of every washday—
The one elusive tissue.

IN THE MID-1950s a cricket match was being played in Carnarvon, Western Australia, on matting on a concrete pitch, which in turn was on ankle-deep, loose sand spread on the then recently levelled town rubbish tip. It was a pretty hot day, too. The game had been underway for several hours when a motorbike and sidecar rattled past, ridden by the officer of the local Salvos. (I say rattled because of the corrugations on the road.) He was also a bugler. Perhaps half an hour later we heard the sound of The Last Post coming from the cemetery which was just a few hundred yards away. Our senior umpire—himself an old soldier—called, 'Hold the ball, fellers. That has to be an old soldier being buried!' Whereupon he removed his hat, and we our caps, to stand and listen and reflect on things. Then, after The Reveille, it was on with the game.

*from*
RON MITCHELL
DARLINGTON
WESTERN AUSTRALIA

. . . . . . . . . . . . . . . . . . . .

## THE DAY THE REPLAY WENT DOWN

*from*
GEOFF MILLER
DEVONPORT
TASMANIA

'Good one,' the old fellow muttered,
'As good a catch as I've seen.'
A hint of smile cracked his stony old face,
and the players danced all round the screen.

They'd just won the game and the series
by less than a layer of skin.
Just one ball remained to be taken,
and them needing four runs to win.

A moment eternally treasured,
the nation stood proud to the core.

This brilliant catch deep in the outfield,
had steered them to victory for sure.

The fieldsman unwound like a cheetah,
exceeding the limits of Man.
Diving full length, an inch from the fence,
he juggled the ball in one hand.

Delirious commentary babble
clogged up the airwaves with praise.
Never they said had they seen such a catch,
in all of their cricketing days.

When the ball left the bat it was smoking,
barely a yard from the ground.
The wind it pushed out in its passing,
spun several fieldsmen around.

Courageous and fearless he took it
a warrior confirming his worth.
The ball split the tips of his fingers,
his nose dug a trench in the turf.

Stretched straight as an arrow he held it,
ignoring his personal pain.
The blood trickled out of his fingers,
but the ball in his fingers remained.

The roar fairly rattled the grandstand,
the nation as one gave a cheer.
Sculptured in stone, the old man sat alone.
It was the replays he feared.

'That's not a catch for repeating,'
the thoughtful old man quietly said.
If they think he can do that for replays,
they have to be out of their heads.

Each time they replayed the replay,
the old fellow questioned their sense.
Until at the eighth or ninth replay,
the ball rattled hard on the fence.

From running so hard for each replay,
the fieldsman was feeling the pinch.
He still covered the ground like a rocket,
but his fingers fell short by an inch.

Shattered the fieldsman lay weeping,
his nose buried deep in the earth.
Though fearless and tough, they expected too much,
and the outcome could not have been worse.

The umpires conferred at mid wicket,
not eager to break the new ground.
For not in the history of cricket,
had there been a replay put down.

Compressed by this weight so enormous,
they pondered the problem at hand.
Then lifting their heads like melons of lead,
they signalled the four runs would stand.

'I knew it,' the old man exploded,
what could the damn fools expect.
If you run a man round till he's ragged,
he'll finish up totally wrecked.

Not happy he's done it just one time,
they expect it again and again.
Thinking by some crazy logic,
the outcome will still be the same.

He'd suffered some pain in his lifetime,
he'd marched off to war in his prime.
When fighting in jungles with mud to his waist,
he'd suffered, but not like this time.

To win it then foolishly lose it,
brought suffering right into his home.
So he put a big sign on his telly,
'This house is a replay free zone.'

*A lady rang up with a personal memory:*
'When my second daughter was born I was listening to you—and when my third
was born it was Sunday morning. Guess who I was listening to?'
MACCA: 'Tell us all about it.'
LADY: 'Oh, Macca, the whole of Australia is listening!'
MACCA: 'Doesn't matter—tell us.'
LADY: 'Well, when you're giving birth it's good to have the radio on to distract you .'
MACCA: 'They have radios going in the bails while milking the cows, don't they?'
LADY: 'It's the same thing—we're all women.'

from
TONY PETERSON
JANNALI
NEW SOUTH WALES

SORRY I MISSED YOU on Sunday at the Sydney Cricket Ground. I was coming over to speak to you, but the opportunity to play cricket was too tempting.

Using a garbage bin as a wicket, Denis (an old bloke whose bat you'd signed), in his Drizabone and Akubra took guard on the perimeter of the SCG. I bowled a couple of looseners with a very bald tennis ball before we were joined by four or five kids who took up positions around the bat.

In the field I found it difficult to concentrate. Here I was on the turf where I'd seen so many of my heroes while selling newspapers at the ground. I looked up at the dressing rooms and imagined the drinks being prepared; looked up at the Members' Stand and imagined the stands starting to fill in anticipation of a great afternoon's cricket. I got a bit emotional.

Denis handled himself well before giving a difficult chance to the bowler, who accepted it. But then disaster. A security guard came over and proclaimed, 'You can't play cricket here,' to which everyone replied in unison, 'This is the Cricket Ground.' But there was no arguing with the umpire. We were sent packing, but not before everyone shook hands and congratulated each other.

......................

from
WALLY HAYS
ULVERSTONE
TASMANIA

THIS IS A FACTUAL story of a time when eight runs were taken off one ball in a Bill O'Reilly over. In 1949 a team of Test cricketers toured the RAAF bases. The team consisted of Bill Brown, Sid Barnes, Stan McCabe, Don Tallon, Colin McCool, Bill O'Reilly, Clarrie Grimmett and others I have forgotten. Our base was at Iron Range on Cape York Peninsula and comprised about twenty personnel. Understandably, as far as talent is concerned, we were a bit thin on the ground against the internationals.

The field was a patch of level ground with scattered clumps of thick coarse grass and a concrete pitch. Clarrie Grimmett had a phobia about snakes and he was regaled with stories about big snakes, little snakes, death adders, taipans and pythons. During the course of the match, our batsman deflected a ball down the leg side in the vicinity of Clarrie Grimmett. The ball came to rest in a clump of grass and the spectators called on Grimmett to look out for snakes. By the time he had run to get a stick to rake the ball out of the tussock our batsmen had added eight runs to the score!

The game finished in a draw, with a little help from the umpires. (I know because I was an umpire.)

......................

from
BERNICE FISCHER
DYSART
QUEENSLAND

I'D LIKE TO TELL YOU about Alice who came to Dysart to be an artist-in-residence for the state school. I volunteered to have her at my home, and being Aboriginal myself (from Stradbroke) we had lots of things to talk about. Alice showed me a book on New South Wales Aboriginal culture and as I flipped through the pages, mainly viewing the photographs, I came across one showing the La Perouse Gum Leaf Band.

I asked Alice if she knew your program and told her that on Sunday you got a call from a lady at Kempsey who wanted to tell you about the Burnt Bridge Gum Leaf Band. Alice sat and listened and then said, 'I'm from Burnt Bridge.' I nearly died! Alice told me that all the Aborigines from the Armidale area were rounded up and put on Burnt Bridge Mission. She spoke of mission life and how she remembered the Gum Leaf Band. One thing she described that will always stay with me is the day they opened the mission gates and told the people they were free. Alice said the people just didn't know what to do. I just couldn't imagine that feeling. Could you?

. . . . . . . . . . . . . . . . . . . .

IN REFERENCE TO MEG'S request for information on playing the gum leaf (her bush band had 'tried and tried but couldn't get a note from a gum leaf') may I offer some help. My family used to gather around the piano in the 1940s for a musical bash: violin, mouth organ, mandolin and piano. Anyone who dropped by without an instrument would grab a gum leaf and join in. To play a gum leaf, break a fresh, young gum leaf in half, pull apart gently to leave a transparent film of about two centimetres in the centre. With the film between slightly relaxed lips, blow gently. Select the notes by opening lips a fraction and varying the wind power on the moist film.

from
LESLEY FERNANCE
NEWRYBAR
NEW SOUTH WALES

. . . . . . . . . . . . . . . . . . . .

MY SISTER, NIECE AND I recently travelled on the Cairns to Forsayth train called the 'Last Great Train Ride', and it was like a breath of fresh air.

The train is the weekly mixed goods service (with a few passenger carriages tacked on) to a dozen small bush communities in the Gulf country. The old wooden train carriages pulled out of Cairns on the Wednesday evening and we ambled into Forsayth twenty-three hours later. Our average speed was forty kilometres per hour, dropping down to twenty kilometres per hour going up the ranges. We travelled through rainforest, the Atherton Tableland, and then the vast openness of outback Queensland. We were treated to wonderful bush hospitality all along the way. Every tiny stop seemed to have a pub nearby, with hot pies, cold beers and a cheery hello. At Einasleigh, the station mistress served up freshly cooked scones, cakes and tea for the train crew and passengers. Later on the return leg we were treated to home cooked chocolate cakes by the train driver!

from
SUZIE DAVIES
TOWNSVILLE
QUEENSLAND

As we were travelling at such low speeds and there was plenty of time we had many opportunities to see lots of wildlife and countryside. My sister and I felt we had stepped back in time to a slower, calmer, saner age. The train crew obviously love their old train and its slow, cumbersome journey. They went out of their way to make our trip enjoyable. In this age of glitz and forced 'customer service' it was wonderful to see genuine hospitality and friendliness.

Sadly, the Queensland government has decided to close down this service. The stated reason is that it is no longer economical. Apart from the obvious tourist potential of the line, with its old wooden carriages and spectacular scenery, it seems almost criminal to take away such a vital communication and social link to bush communities. Those people have suffered through a severe recession and are still battling drought. The last thing they need is to be further isolated. This train provides employment for people all along the line and brings in money each time a tourist buys a beer. Maybe we Australians and our governments need to rethink our priorities. There always seems to be money for new parliament houses, for high-speed, high-profile car races. Why not put some emphasis on service to the average Australian. Why not give something back to the bush? God know the bush has given its fair share.

*George from Bairnsdale, Victoria rang in about water diviners.*
'The council were trying to find a water main and this water diviner called Barney said he'd find one. He got a couple of wire coathangers, twisted them together, walked along and put a pick mark in the bitumen and said, "She's there." It was too. Barney said later, "I didn't tell them, but I put the bloody thing down myself thirty-two years ago." '

> from
> DOUG TWELL
> SANDY BAY
> TASMANIA

WITH THE APPROACH OF VJ Day, there has been a lot of interest shown in troop trains. Perhaps you may be interested in my experience—on a hospital train travelling from Cairns to Melbourne in 1944.

It was quite uneventful from Cairns to Townsville, but because the track was cut by floods at Tully we were diverted out to Charters Towers and then down through Hughenden, Longreach and Emerald and back to the main line at Rockhampton. Travel on the inland line was quite slow, so on the second day we were pleased when the train suddenly speeded up. However, the brakes were applied, we went backwards for a short distance, and finally ground to a halt. Being flat on my back, with one leg encased in plaster, I couldn't see anything. But we could hear people running about outside and much shouting. Apparently the driver got bored and decided to climb out and do some oiling, and in so doing, he fell off! The fireman panicked and pulled the wrong lever, causing us to speed up. The driver was not badly injured, but we had to sit there for some hours before his replacement was brought out.

The following day we once again ground to a halt in the middle of nowhere and slowly backed up for quite a long distance, but not to pick up the driver. On this occasion we had to re-connect the last few carriages which had dropped off!

• • • • • • • • • • • • • • • • • •

> from
> R. L. IRVINE
> NARACOORTE
> SOUTH AUSTRALIA

FIFTY YEARS AGO I used to travel the Ghan with other drovers and stockmen who came down to Adelaide during the Northern Territory's wet season. There were first- and second-class carriages, the second-class carriage for Aborigines only. However, the special carriage was not necessary as the stockmen worked with the Aborigines for eight months of the year and there was a bond between them. The carriage for Aborigines was usually empty by the time we reached Port Augusta.

The train stopped at all towns on the way down, although 'towns' would be an exaggeration as there were no railway platforms, just a pub on the edge of nothing. When the train driver wanted the passengers back on the train he would blow the whistle but no-one would leave the bar until the train started to move. The driver would stop the train further down the track to make sure everyone was aboard.

Some women and card sharps from Adelaide worked the Ghan when they knew the stockmen were coming down, hoping to relieve them of their hard-earned cash. But the majority of stockmen travelling were too wise to become involved. Their interests were a nice room, soft bed, beautiful meals at the Adelaide railway canteen, mixing with girls at dances, a swim at Glenelg and to renew their wardrobe.

Advertisements list the Australian features
Resorts, Casinos and Sunlit beaches
Hotels, Motels, Tours with meals,
Attractively priced with discount deals.

As the package tours speed far and wide
(Note — it's always air-conditioned inside)
The patrons recline, see the rolling scenes,
Windows like substitute TV screens.

But the number of features is rather small
A couple of months will cover them all:
Uluru, The Olgas, Kakadu and back
The Flinders Ranges, The Birdsville Track
Fraser Island and the Barrier Reef,
The Duty Free Shop a quiet relief.
With souvenirs packed and a book to read
Look out of the plane, see Australia recede.

But the real Australia was somehow missed,
The people for instance were not on the list,
The towns, the countryside, the sight and sound
Of the normal Australians moving around.

At Apsley, Bargo, Calca and Dargan
Elmore, Forbes, Girgan, Huddleston
Innisfail, Jugiong, Kapunda, Laverton
Marla, Normanton, Oldin, Pemberton
Quilpie, Robinvale, Stirling, Toolibin
Ulladulla, Veresdale, Walpeup, Yelarbon
And all the rest from Ayr to Zeehan.

from
KEN WILLIAMS
PARK ORCHARDS
VICTORIA

I MAY BE ONE OF THE few persons to have flown in the old Southern Cross. My mother, brother and myself flew from Sydney to Brisbane in the 'old bus' as it was known. On board with us were an English lady, an engineer, Judge Macrossen and his wife. I recall the flight very well. Minties to chew, cotton wool for the ears, a paper bag for bad fliers. I believe the pilot was Captain Taylor. Apart from being sick we enjoyed the flight. Three days later we learnt that the Southern Cloud was missing over the Australian Alps.

from
IAN MACLEAN
CUNNAMULLA
QUEENSLAND

from
BILL GLASSON
CLIFTON
QUEENSLAND

## SMITHY

Now, heroes are a dying breed, not many left, I fear.
Most young folk worship film stars, or their favourite brand of beer.
Shane Warne and Alfie Langer both receive their share of cheers;
But dinkum Aussie heroes haven't been around for years.

But there were heroes, long ago, for Aussies to admire,
Maybe 'Smithy' was the greatest, our world record breaking flier.
He flew when planes were bits of tin and canvas, tied with cord.
With Ulm, he flew around old Oz, in ten days, a record.

His trip to London took twelve days; he then flew the Atlantic.
Then home again, we waited by the radio, quite frantic.
The Tasman Sea quite often passed beneath the Southern Cross.
They nearly crashed when one old 'donk' stopped from an oil loss.

Engineer Gordon Taylor, a real hero on the boil,
Climbed out beneath the port wing and took a quart of oil
From the good 'donk', then he climbed back and went out the starboard side
To pour it in the sump of the old engine that had died.

'Smithy' got the engine going and they flew along till when,
Poor old Taylor had to risk his life again, and then again.
The King presented Gordon with a shiny EGM*
For Taylor, just like 'Smithy', was a hero among men.

'Smithy' broke near every record, he was our most famous Knight,
But in 1935 he made his final gallant flight.
From India he headed east, this paragon of men,
And sadly neither 'Smithy' nor his plane were seen again.

His fame and memory linger on, though younger folk may scoff.
He flew when airmen risked their lives each time that they took off.
He was part of a gallant band; great heroes, every one.
Today we fly because our 'Smithy' showed it could be done.

* Empire Gallantry Medal

• • • • • • • • • • • • • • • • • • •

from
DR KEN HUTTON
PORT VILA
VANUATU

**I** HAVE A TALE TO tell about Banjo Paterson. He was a patient of my uncle's dental practice at Double Bay, New South Wales, where I used to work after school in about 1938. One afternoon a rather poor looking upper denture was passed to me for immediate repair. I was rewarded by being introduced to the great Banjo. As I remember he was a very tall, rangy-looking bloke, and smoked a pipe. And that was my brush with fame and a treasured memory.

34

35

36

37

Since AAO2 was released we've travelled widely and done more than twenty outside broadcasts. The next four pages feature pictures from just a few of them. At Guyra, New South Wales, I talked to Gordon Youman, winner of a tree-planting award (note, I'm holding the Jam Drop Hole Putter-Inner which 'disappeared' at a concert); the community hall was suitably decked out; Anne Finlayson and the St Mary's of the Angels School beautifully sang 'I am Australian'; 'Macca Crackers' — the new all-Aussie biscuit— was launched; and 'Haggis' was ordered from the hall for indiscriminate fighting!

38

# *Christmas Day at Narromine*

As I've said before — and we've had several letters and poems confirming it — outside broadcasts usually bring rain, and Christmas Day at Narromine, New South Wales, was no exception. Just look at these pictures — cold, wet and miserable. But, as always, the large crowd was full of fun. Santa turned up and I loved it!

45

46

47

48

We were at Junee, New South Wales, in mid-winter and at 5.15 am it was very cold! We broadcast from the magnificent railway refreshments room, with its huge mirrors and ornate columns, and later saw the Junee Roundhouse, one of several in Australia being used by railway heritage groups.

49

# Woomera

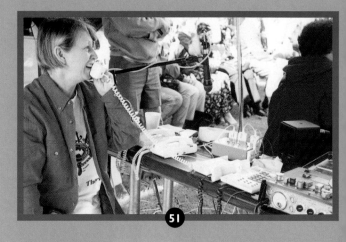

LEN BEADELL
O.A.M. B.E.M. F.I.E.M.S (AUST)

1923 - 1995

SURVEYOR  EXPLORER  ROADMAKER

A UNIQUE CHARACTER

WHOSE SURVEYING SKILLS AND ENDURANCE

ENABLED HIM TO OPEN UP THE OUTBACK

FOR ALL PEOPLE

NEVER 'TOO LONG IN THE BUSH'

Woomera in South Australia was wonderful, the landscape magical. Kel was kept as busy as ever; the large crowd enjoyed the early morning sun; I had a chat with Anne Beadell, widow of Len Beadell (the roadside plaque sums up his amazing life); and along the way the AAO team — Perce (*left*), Kel, myself and Lisle took in the sights at Clare.

WHAT A MEMORY JOGGER—Bob's call from Well 26 on the Canning stock route in search of thorny devils. I was born and raised in Neutral Bay, Sydney and in the mid-1950s Len Beadell, a family friend, came to visit from Woomera. This created great excitement as even then, at the beginning of his surveying career, Len Beadell was a larger-than-life character. He came to Sydney yearly and this time he had a car full of kids from the rocket range. Some of them had never seen the sea—something we coastal dwellers found hard to believe.

Once the introductions had been made, Len noticed a line of ants moving along the garden path and said to one of his group, 'There's a feed for our little friend. You'd better get him out of the car.' And from out of a shoe box came a thorny devil. I couldn't believe my eyes. The little creature was tethered with a string tied around its leg close to the ant line. Len then explained that being a desert dweller the reptile had evolved to carry its own water supply in the form of a barrel at the back of its neck. I was fascinated—its prehistoric appearance, its deadly darting pink tongue making a meal of the passing column of hapless ants.

For me this childhood incident remains a magical experience, as do a number of other Len Beadell stories that have become part of my family folk memory. It was good to hear your tribute to him. He was and remains a memorable Australian.

from
MORLEY GRAINER
TOOWOOMBA
QUEENSLAND

• • • • • • • • • • • • • • • • • • •

WHEN I WAS FIVE and a half years old my parents decided that I was going to be a 'world famous' violinist! So after years of threats and frustrations and telling fibs about doing my practice, when I was really out in the lane playing ball, I eventually at age of twelve or thirteen became lead fiddler in a jazz band. Well, my dad and I went to a recital at the Sydney Town Hall sixty-nine years or so ago and heard Fritz Kreisler play. I've never forgotten that evening. When Kreisler came on stage a gasp went through the audience. His hair was very bushy and looked as if it had never been combed. He held his violin by the scroll, hanging down, dragging the bow almost along the floor, and did a bit of a stagger. Somebody near us said, 'This man is drunk!' He just stood there and let the audience settle down. Then he played and the wonderful music flowed through the great hall. Everybody was spellbound. That night made a big difference to me, though not the way my dad hoped. I realised that I'd never be able to play so wonderfully and when I left school I stored my fiddle and went bush. I still have the fiddle and get it out now and then to make a tune for my grandchildren— the whole ten of them!

from
BOB LUGTON
SCOTTS HEAD
NEW SOUTH WALES

• • • • • • • • • • • • • • • • • • •

REGARDING BILL FORDYCE,* the RAAF veteran you had on your program, there's another side to Bill which listeners may not know but which I discovered when researching for my film script *Still Waters Run Deep.*

Bill is a maternal descendant of Horatio Wills, the son of a convict and the sole survivor of the massacre of a trading schooner crew by Pacific Islanders early last century. Horatio Wills took up land in western Victoria, became a friend and supporter of the Aborigines and watched with interest the game of

from
FRANK VAINS
BEACHMERE
QUEENSLAND

'kick, catch and chase' they often played on his property, using a large ball of hair, fur and feathers.

Later he and his friend and relative by marriage, Dr Harrison, felt there was a need for a game which would help occupy the time of unemployed gold miners who were crowding into Melbourne after their unsuccessful hunt for gold during the early rushes. There was no competitive football at that time, in the early 1850s, so Wills and Harrison toured Britain, Ireland and America, taking note of what they thought to be the best points from soccer, rugby, Irish football and American gridiron to formulate a new more free-flowing game of football—Australian Rules. The first game of the new code was played in Melbourne in 1855 and it flourished immediately.

But Wills became dissatisfied, probably over taxes applied by the Victorian government, and he overlanded to Queensland with his family, station staff and ten thousand head of sheep at the beginning of 1861. Nine months later, after an epic journey, they settled on land south-west of today's city of Emerald, about 200 kilometres or so inland from Rockhampton, on the Nagoa River.

Immediately, they set about building a new station, which Wills called Cullen-La-Ringo, on land which had formerly been the preserve of the Kairi people. The Kairis had made every effort to live peacefully with the wave of white settlers who had moved in before the Wills party. However, their efforts were in vain, for they were treated brutally and, only three weeks before Wills and his group arrived, a party of whites from neighbouring Rainworth Station had swept through a Kairi camp, killing men, women and children.

The Kairis had had enough. They decided on revenge. It is believed that they may have mistaken Horatio Wills for the leader of the raiding party, an English-born overseer from Rainworth, who was not only the same build as Wills, but rode a similar horse and dressed in similar clothes. In any case, two weeks after the Wills party had arrived at Cullen-La-Ringo, the Kairis swept down on its camp while Wills and his staff and their families took their usual early afternoon siesta to escape the worst of the heat. Wills and eighteen others were killed within minutes, but four men survived—two shepherds who had been out with the flocks and Horatio Wills' son Thomas and another man, who had been away at Rainworth Station getting supplies.

This remains the worst massacre of whites by blacks in the history of modern Australia, although it pales into insignificance when compared to the murder and dispossession of the Aboriginal people.

Thomas Wills remained at Cullen-La-Ringo until 1864, then returned to western Victoria, becoming Victoria's best-known cricketer in the mid-1860s. On Boxing Day 1866 he led an Aboriginal team on to the Melbourne Cricket Ground before a big holiday crowd in what must rank as one of the greatest acts of white-black reconciliation in our history. While his team of Aboriginal players did not win, it delighted the crowd with its lively brand of cricket against an experienced white team from the cricketing establishment.

After an unsuccessful attempt to take this team of Aboriginal cricketers to England during the next few weeks, essentially the same team did leave for England a year later, in February 1868. Wills did not go on the tour, which was a great success. The first Australian cricket team to tour abroad, the Aboriginal side played forty-seven matches, including games at The Oval and Lords. They won or drew about half of that total and drew big crowds at every game. Not only did they play exciting 'Calypso' cricket, but they were well managed, well disciplined and were honoured as a skilled sporting side wherever they went. During breaks in the game they would give demonstrations of spear and boomerang throwing and these were eagerly looked forward to by the cricket fans.

The team returned to Australia one year later in February 1869. The Aboriginal tour preceded the first official Australian cricket tour by ten years. Significantly, no Aboriginal cricketer has played for Australia since that first and last tour.

So, with his maternal lineage connection to Horatio and Thomas Wills, Bill Fordyce is deeply embedded in Australian history.

*Ian's interview with Bill was published in *AA02*.

⦁ ⦁ ⦁ ⦁ ⦁ ⦁ ⦁ ⦁ ⦁ ⦁ ⦁ ⦁ ⦁ ⦁

**I** WANT TO TELL YOU something about Qantas pilots saying 'Dangle the Dunlops'. I can't be sure where it came from but the pilot may have not been first to coin the phrase.

In my motor racing days of yesteryear (1937–88) drivers who had an accident would say 'The car fell over when I came around the bend and dangled the Dunlops' (or whatever tyres they had—Goodyear, Bridgestones, etc.). It would mean that the car rolled over and ended up with four wheels pointing skyward. I can remember first hearing this at Bathurst in 1937.

Thank goodness none of my racing cars ever 'Dangled the Dunlops—Goodyears, etc'.

| from |
|------|
| BILL WARREN |
| SNAKE GULLY |
| NEW SOUTH WALES |

⦁ ⦁ ⦁ ⦁ ⦁ ⦁ ⦁ ⦁ ⦁ ⦁ ⦁ ⦁ ⦁ ⦁

**A**BOUT TO LAND, so in the new descriptive language the cabin crew announce that the pilot is about to:

| | | | | | |
|--------|-----|--------------|---------|-----|--------------|
| Dangle | the | Dunlops | Oggle | the | Olympics |
| Bangle | the | Beaurepaires | Flop | the | Flaps |
| Tickle | the | Tarmac | Scrape | the | Strip |
| Mangle | the | Michelins | Burnish | the | Bridgestones |
| Grope | the | Gravel | Rub | the | Runway |

I could go on and on, but Ample the Sample.

| from |
|------|
| BOB NICOL |
| ARMIDALE |
| NEW SOUTH WALES |

*Anthony was at the Wodonga, Victoria, outside broadcast.*

MACCA: 'What do you do?'

ANTHONY: 'I run a motel just down the road.'

MACCA: 'What's that like?'

ANTHONY: 'It's interesting.'

MACCA: 'Do many things get broken?'

ANTHONY: 'We're always getting broken beds. I've had a bed in my house for twenty years, and it's still good, but in the motel they only last about two months. I just don't know what they do to them, but they wreck them.'

from
JOCELYN KING
ROSEBUD
VICTORIA

## ODE TO A TEABAG

I'm a little teabag
Dangling from a 'mug'
I always get a nasty squeeze
That's different to a hug.
I'm always in hot water
So please remember that
When tossing me so rudely out
And no time at all to chat.
I'm not wanted at a party
When someone 'reads' the cups
Yet sip my brew in dreaming
Will make all your 'downs' come 'ups'
I often get a headache
From jiggling on the edge
Or stopped on Sunday's country drive
To be tossed on someone's hedge.
I'd be a happy teabag
If all folk saved the grains
And served them to the compost heap
Instead of clogging up the drains.
So, all you tired teabags
Who've littered all these years;
Rise up and jiggle back to 'mugs'
Who started all my tears.

• • • • • • • • • • • • • • • • • •

from
DAVID L. GREEN
NEERIM SOUTH
VICTORIA

**I** HAVE JUST LISTENED to a little verse about the teabag and it reminded me of a story concerning my workmate Ken Kercheval.

Ken was with a contractor upgrading a forest road. He and another three men were seated on the side of the road having lunch one day, when he noticed an unusual butterfly in a bush. He was intrigued by its blue colour and other markings, so after watching it for a while he went to have a closer look only to find it was the blue and white tag on a teabag hanging in the bush!

• • • • • • • • • • • • • • • • • •

from
NOLA LLOYD
BUCASIA
QUEENSLAND

I'm in a bit of a quandary,
So Macca please help me—
When we have visitors at night for a meal,
Is it for dinner, supper or tea?

Dinner to us was a midday meal,
With breakfast in the morning,
And tea was the meal we had at night,
It gets more confusing, I'm warning.

Where I was brought up (near Mackay),
And we kids were all around,
Mum used to call out 'Your tea's ready now'
And that was when the sun was down.
And then sometimes on a winter's morn,
As we headed off for school—
'Come home for dinner today' she'd say
'We'll have soup 'cos the weather's cool.'

Then some days Mum would inform us,
That she wouldn't be home until two.
'So what would you like on your lunch today?'
We'd reply—'Vegemite will be fine thank you!'

Then someone else would ask us—
'You're all invited over tonight,
Come around about six or seven
—the supper will be a delight.'

Etiquette says—breakfast, lunch and dinner,
But it's become quite difficult for me,
You see where I was brought up in the country,
It was always breakfast, dinner and tea.

• • • • • • • • • • • • • • • • • • •

I CAME ACROSS 'Rules for Women Teachers, 1915' when visiting central Queensland earlier in the year. How times have changed!

from
CORAL WHITING
HENTY
NEW SOUTH WALES

1.   You will not marry during the term of contract
2.   You are not to keep company of men
3.   You must be home between the hours of 8 pm and 6 am unless attending a school function
4.   You may not loiter down town in ice-cream parlours
5.   You may not travel beyond the city limits without the permission of the chairman of the board
6.   You may not ride in a carriage or automobile with any man unless he is your father or brother
7.   You may not smoke cigarettes
8.   You may not dress in bright colours
9.   You may not in any circumstances dye your hair
10.  You must wear at least two petticoats and your dresses must not be any shorter than two inches above the ankle.

• • • • • • • • • • • • • • • • • • •

ACCORDING TO THE DICTIONARY, bowyangs helped stop snakes from crawling up your legs. They were straps tied over trousers just below the kneecap and were worn in particular by swaggies, navvies, miners and labourers.

from
MAUREEN DOUGHTY
RHODES, NSW

• • • • • • • • • • • • • • • • • • •

from
BARBARA RANDELL
SOUTH BRIGHTON
SOUTH AUSTRALIA

**I** AM NOT GOING TO contribute to the argument about where the word bowyangs came from, but I can give you a couple of stories about men who wished they had been wearing them.

The first was a young man teaching at our one-teacher school. Fresh from the city, he was filled with amazement at things we country kids took for granted. One of those was a mouse plague. At the time he was boarding with my family. I vividly remember being at the tea table one night when he let out a blood-curdling scream and fled. My brother followed him onto the dark veran- dah and then returned almost helpless with laughter. A mouse had mistaken his hairy leg for a ladder to the larder and scaled the heights accordingly. As an inno- cent female student, I was never told whether or not it sampled the only food available!

The second concerns my father, and again involved a mouse plague. We had an old Ford utility with a wooden frame on the back for transporting pigs and calves. The bench seat had wire springs stuffed with straw which provided ideal nesting material for the marauding mice. Father was driving to the weekly pig sale when he, too, felt the patter of little feet in a place where they shouldn't be. Unable, because of traffic and road conditions to scream and run, he grabbed his thigh and squeezed—hard. When he reached the sale yards and climbed down from the utility his friends were somewhat startled to see a dead mouse drop from his trousers.

So you see bowyangs would have been useful in both cases. Even if the mice were not as dangerous as snakes!

• • • • • • • • • • • • • • • • • • • • •

from
RAY ROBERTS
MOUNT ELIZA
VICTORIA

**Y**OUR TALK WITH FRED MCKAY brought back many memories for me when place names such as Tibooburra, Innamincka and Wilcannia rolled from his tongue. You see, when Fred was a twenty-seven-year-old parson making his first visit to these places, I was a thirteen-year-old boy 'packing ice' for delivery by mail truck to the same locations. Many will no doubt ask, 'what is packed ice?' Further it is unlikely that many of today's travellers pause to consider how, in the past, peo- ple living in these remote areas kept their food fresh and drinks cold without modern refrigeration. The answer is that prior to World War Two, a few stations and bush hotels had refrigeration driven from lighting plants, but most relied on Coolgardie safes and cool cellars, plus 'packed ice' delivered by mail truck or railway during the very hot weather.

I grew up and worked in my family's iceworks at Broken Hill. The standard size block of ice in western New South Wales at that time was fifty-six pounds and measured about 32 x 14 x 5 inches. When ice was ordered by bush hotels, stores and stations, two blocks were placed side by side to fit neatly into a bran bag. The bag was sewn at the top and a second bag slid over the bag of ice to provide a space for packing sawdust insulation. After packing the sawdust, the outer bag was sewn tightly. Packed in this manner, 112 pounds of ice would sur- vive reasonably well under a tarpaulin on the back of a mail truck, or in the guards van of a train, for about eight hours on a summer day.

I cannot remember having talked to people who received 'packed ice'. At this distance in time, the mind boggles at the thought of a bag of 'packed ice' deliv- ered by a mail truck which had been broken down or bogged for two days!

I HAVE NEVER HEARD MENTION of the invisible army of tradesmen, labourers and apprentices who, behind the scenes, were responsible for the overhaul, maintenance and manufacture of Australia's vast fleet of steam locomotives. The craftsmanship that was applied to those steam work-horses was superb, providing a system with an outstanding safety record and a reliability that allowed people to set their clocks when a train passed by. I had the good fortune to secure an apprenticeship at the Eveleigh Railway Workshops during the Depression, and people will remember that when the Sydney suburban trains left MacDonaldtown or Erskineville towards the city it would look like Dante's Inferno outside the huge workshops, where smoke and steam would erupt from the dozens of locomotives.

Between 7 and 7.30 am trains would spew out a torrent of workers at Redfern Station giving the appearance of a flowing mass of humanity as they climbed the steps to the overhead walkway and down into the grounds of the workshops. The workshops trained thousands of apprentices over the years and was one of the few establishments to do so during the Great Depression. Because of this, not only did they have a continuous supply of skilled tradesmen for their own requirements but they also filled a gap in private industry both during and after the war.

A number of these apprentices went on to become engineering graduates and filled managerial jobs throughout industry. They were sought-after, having had one of the finest practical training experiences. This behind-the-scenes workforce deserves some recognition among the stories of the great steam era that played such an important role in Australia's development.

from
BOB JOHNSTONE
CRONULLA
NEW SOUTH WALES

• • • • • • • • • • • • • • • • • • •

THANK YOU FOR WHAT you said last Sunday about the problem there seems to be with regard to so many men being violent. The reason it was so good to hear from you and that other lovely man talking about it was because whenever I have raised the subject with men to see if they can come up with any clues as to why such violence exists among men—their chief targets being women and children—even the nicest of them have gone immediately into 'defensive mode'. They have felt that I was just another man-hater, which couldn't be further from the truth. However, I choose male company rather selectively, and there are lovely men. But you are the first I have ever heard admit that there is a huge problem of violence among the male population, and that is I feel an all-important start. Thank you.

from
CAS
NORTH IPSWICH
QUEENSLAND

• • • • • • • • • • • • • • • • • • •

I AM WRITING IN REGARD to plastic notes. I know several people in shops who hate them because they are so difficult to put in the till. I have a different reason for hating them.

In February 1995 I became legally blind. It took little time to learn which notes were which because they were different sizes. Now the notes are all so similar it is hard to tell them apart.

There is a radio advertisement which offers blind people a gadget to measure the length of the notes. I need another gadget like I need a hole in the head! It is already difficult enough managing a long white cane plus shopping articles.

from
TONI
CAIRNS
QUEENSLAND

Please don't let your listeners be persuaded that the device suddenly and wonderfully overcomes a vision-impaired person's problems. It does not. It actually slows us down and makes us more awkward.

. . . . . . . . . . . . . . . . . . .

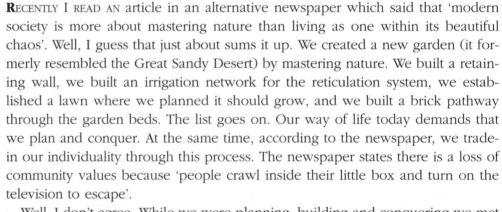

from
'THE DREAMERS'
BATHURST
NEW SOUTH WALES

WHILE I HAVE ALWAYS been prompted to write for one reason or another I have never actually made the final effort. Time now is not a worry as I am serving a sentence at a correctional centre near Bathurst, New South Wales. I listen in on Sunday mornings and the nostalgia is easily evoked through your wonderful program. As this is a minimum security institution we have some very special privileges. One of them is to have a singing group that visits old people's homes in Bathurst, under supervision of course. The joy that we inject into those communities is most welcomed by those at the hospices. We sprinkle our repertoire with many old favourites and in particular many Australian songs. We are at present preparing some Christmas songs along with the traditional carols. We have a few guys on guitar and one keyboard player. I hope next time I correspond I will be part of the normal community again.

. . . . . . . . . . . . . . . . . . .

from
ELIZABETH BURRELL
FORRESTFIELD
WESTERN AUSTRALIA

RECENTLY I READ AN article in an alternative newspaper which said that 'modern society is more about mastering nature than living as one within its beautiful chaos'. Well, I guess that just about sums it up. We created a new garden (it formerly resembled the Great Sandy Desert) by mastering nature. We built a retaining wall, we built an irrigation network for the reticulation system, we established a lawn where we planned it should grow, and we built a brick pathway through the garden beds. The list goes on. Our way of life today demands that we plan and conquer. At the same time, according to the newspaper, we trade-in our individuality through this process. The newspaper states there is a loss of community values because 'people crawl inside their little box and turn on the television to escape'.

Well, I don't agree. While we were planning, building and conquering we met many people who were interested in what we were doing. During our breaks we sat in the shade of the pergola and shared many conversations with curious passers-by. Each morning and in the late afternoon the park across the road resembled a busy thoroughfare as pet owners walked their dogs. And they often stopped for a chat. We found a new sense of community. It was nice.

We think our garden is pretty good too. We planted a host of Australian native shrubs and we think that's kind of special, don't you?

. . . . . . . . . . . . . . . . . . .

*This is another one of those believe-it-or-nots. Something gets mentioned, in this case the name Ronald Biggs, and Aussies all over ring, write and fax their brushes with him. Just amazing. And then there was the call from the man himself.*

*Most of the calls and letters came in 1995. Then in 1996 we were in Wagga doing the program, because I wanted to go back to nearby Junee to shoot some more footage for my long-awaited (by who?) TV series. Anyway, as is per usual, anything goes. Ross, an interstate Greyhound-Pioneer driver, pulled up outside the*

*Radio Riverina Studios and rang us. At the end of the conversation he said, 'Can't talk any longer Macca, I've got a schedule to keep, but I'll write you about my mate who took the last photo of Ronald Biggs!' Then, while the news was on, we got a call from a 'Deep Throat' Aussie who said, 'Ronald Biggs would like to talk to you.' Next thing Lee comes in and says, 'I've got Ronald Biggs on hold!' I said, 'Call the police!'*

*After the interview we got fourteen letters of complaint, the most I've ever received about a particular subject. As to the call, most — including me at the time — couldn't believe it. It's an interesting chapter in Australia's recent history. Now read on:*

BERNIE: G'day Macca, you're lookin' well. It's Bernie here from Harlin, Queensland. You were just talkin' about Ronnie Biggs. Well, I'm the last authenticated person in Australia to have spoken with him — in fact, I gave him a lift in my car.

MACCA: Did you?

BERNIE: That's for sure. Down in Gippsland. I had a caryard in Morwell and I was taking a lad up to Rosedale and this fellow was thumbing a lift. In those days we often used to pick up fellows going out to the RAAF base at East Sale. This fellow was on the side of the road just out of Traralgon and looked like an air-force boy. I picked him up and he was very much the gentleman sitting in the back seat.

Mac, I don't know why, but I had a funny feeling. Couldn't put my finger on what was wrong and I offered him a cigarette. He kept his face slightly turned away, but accepted the cigarette. I tried to draw him into conversation but it was 'yes sir, thank you sir', and I finally let him out at Rosedale, just out of town, making the excuse that I had to take the other lad to his people. I then shot back into town and went to the police station. You wouldn't believe it, 'Back at 6 pm' on the door!

MACCA: That was on the door of the police station, 'Back at six'?

BERNIE: They were the good old days, mate! I went home and told the wife how uneasy I was and she said, 'Go down to the local boys.' I knew them well, being in the car game, and the sarge took me out the back and showed me three great mugshot books. In the second one I saw a familiar face and said, 'That's him,' and he said, 'Are you sure?' He showed me another book and I picked the same bloke out and he dialled a hotline number in Melbourne. The next morning when I went to the police station to register a car I said, 'Hey, what was all that about last night?' The sarge said, 'Mate, you're the last B one . . . that was Ronnie Biggs!' That's God's honour, mate, and you heard it first on the Macca show. A real gentleman, very nattily attired. And they say you can't disappear in Australia!

* * * * * * * * * * * * * * * * * * * *

RAYMOND: This is Raymond Rhodes from Ulverstone, Tasmania. When I heard you talking about Ronald Biggs it brought back a lot of memories. My wife and I were on a ten-month tour around Australia and we got to a little place in New South Wales called Gloucester. I thought, 'What a place to spend a few days.' But it didn't turn out like that!

I went to the hotel and had a few beers and because I was an agent for Ruston

Bucyrus, 'RB' was on a lot of things that I had. Well, three policemen suddenly surrounded me. They insisted that I was Ronald Biggs! They roped me into the police station and said, 'How about coming clean now.' I said, 'I'm Raymond Rhodes.' I showed them my licence, my pilot's licence and things with my name on. But they wouldn't wear it; they insisted that I was Ronald Biggs. So I said, 'Ronald Biggs is two inches taller than me. I've got a finger missing. He speaks with a real cockney accent. And I haven't got that amount of money!' They said, 'Well, where's Charmian?' I said, 'Charmian who? My wife's name is Moya!' But they still wouldn't wear it. I told them I went around oil wells and rigs checking on RB equipment, that's where the RB comes from.

MACCA: And they said, 'Don't give us that line of bull, mate — we didn't come down in the last shower!'

RAYMOND: At the time I didn't know who the hell I was because the grilling they gave me just didn't make sense. I thought when is it going to stop? What happens if they don't believe me and they lock me up and I serve Ronald Biggs' time? They sent for a squad from Taree who gave me a going over. Then they waited for some cops from Sydney. Eventually, Ronald surfaced in Perth and they finally had to believe me and let me go. I tell you what, when old Biggsy gets back, I've done three days for him!

• • • • • • • • • • • • • • • • • • •

RONALD BIGGS: This is Ronald Biggs in Rio de Janeiro.

MACCA: It's Ian McNamara here. Hello Ronald, how are you over there?

RONALD: Good morning to all you Aussies.

MACCA: We've had a lot of phone calls about Ronald Biggs and people who met you along the way. So what have you got to say for yourself?

RONALD: I can only imagine what they are saying about me, some 'Good old Ron' and others 'The bugger should be hung!'

MACCA: I don't know about that, Ron, but we've had amazing calls from people who gave you lifts and stuff like that. You must be pretty fond of Australia?

RONALD: I got to like Australia very, very much indeed. I'm often asked if I'd like to go back to England, and I say no. But I'd certainly like to get back to Aussie one day.

MACCA: Do you reckon that's a possibility?

RONALD: Who knows what this wonderful life has in store for me?

MACCA: One of our listeners said you were very quiet. Another that you worked in his furniture factory. One bloke said he was the last to see you before you left Australia. How long were you in Australia?

RONALD: Four very happy years. I made some very fine friends. I kicked off in Botany Bay — where else? I went from there to Adelaide where I lived in The Grange. It was difficult not being able to tell people I considered friends my real identity. That was very difficult. But certain people I did confide in, tell who I was, and I'm glad to say we remain fine friends until this day.

MACCA: What years were those?

RONALD: I arrived in Kings Cross, Sydney, on New Year's Eve 1965. And I was having a happy old time with a bunch of girls singing 'Waltzing Matilda'.

MACCA: I'm a bit non-plussed. You must have had a pretty scary life on the run? Looking over your shoulder for four years.

RONALD: Yes, that was part and parcel of being on the run. We had to change names quickly, which was difficult for the wife and kids too. For me to tell my children, 'From here on it's not going to be Nicki Biggs, it's going to be Nicki something else.' And there was always that feeling that you might get caught one day and that your happy life in Aussie might just come to an end. Which in fact it did.

MACCA: Did you get out by the skin of your teeth?

RONALD: I guess I did really. I was amazed to think that I got on a ship in Melbourne and out of twelve hundred people only one person recognised me. I thought because my picture had been in the papers, and all the coverage on TV, I would be recognised. But I disguised myself and was travelling on a friend's passport, of course. These were all very, very hairy moments. A lot of heart-in-the-mouth stuff.

MACCA: The fact that you could survive here for four years shows Australia was a sleepy little hollow?

RONALD: The person who escaped from prison with me went to Australia about two weeks before I did. I was in Paris recovering from plastic surgery when he phoned and said, 'Ron, you've got to come to Australia, it's a wonderful place. It was made for people like us!'

MACCA: Well, that's how it started, really. It was wonderful to talk to you — I think! Give us a quick weather report for Rio.

RONALD: Cold and getting colder.

· · · · · · · · · · · · · · · · · · · ·

*And finally, just a couple of the many other calls we received.*

MACCA: Father Brian from Fremantle?

FR BRIAN: I just wanted to say that in 1969 Ronnie Biggs made it to Sydney and came into my church. I was in the confessional.

MACCA: He must have wanted some counselling.

FR BRIAN: Yes, and he had a gun under his coat. It's amazing the advice you give people when they've got a gun under their coat. More Catholics should do it, they'd probably get better advice!

*Another caller:* I was in a bar in Melbourne about 1979 or 1980 and thirty or forty police and detectives were celebrating a farewell to one of their mates. There was a fair bit of noise when over the loudspeaker came a message: 'Would Mr Ronald Biggs please come to the foyer.' All noise ceased as the cops looked at each other. Then a bloke put his head around the corner and said, 'It's not for real!'

## G'day, this is Macca

ZIG: This is Zig from Korlobidahda in the top end of the Northern Territory, roughly Central Arnhem Land. You won't even see it on a topographical map so it's fairly minute.

MACCA: And what are you doing there, Zig?

ZIG: I'm here working with the Aboriginal people. I wanted to talk to you about a rather

unfortunate occurrence on Friday: the Old Man here passed away. In some ways it wasn't unexpected but it's always a shock and a bit of a trauma for the whole community. This man was very old: he grew up in the days before white people were around, but he seemed to settle into their coming. He did a lot of droving and stock work and I'll always remember him yelling out to his wives—he had three wives, which is not unusual for traditional Aboriginal people—he'd always call them 'boy', which probably came from a habit that he picked up from his droving time. I just thought I'd tell you about it because it's a little bit of history and a real loss for Australia for someone like that to have passed on.

MACCA: What was his name?

ZIG: I can't say his name; maybe in time, but at this particular stage it's just not done. We just refer to him as the 'Old Man' or 'the one who passed away'.

MACCA: I understand. How long have you been at Korlobidahda?

ZIG: I've been here full time for eighteen months but I've spent a month of each year here for the past five years or so. I've had a long-term relationship with this group and with the Old Man.

MACCA: I was talking the other day to a Presbyterian minister who was with the Pitjantjatjara people in the Musgrove Ranges during the sixties, and he was saying what a privilege it was to be there and work with the Aboriginal people. I suppose you must feel the same.

ZIG: Very definitely. I try to show the people things that they haven't had experience with or have limited knowledge of, but I think the return to me is far greater. I'm learning a lot more about the people, about the culture and the language. I can even speak a little bit of the language myself.

MACCA: And you've got a duty now and in the future to let other people know about that and to spread the word. It's a bit like the Aborigines in the old days, isn't it, when the older people had a duty to let younger people know. To be there among those people—just wonderful.

ZIG: Yes, it's a tremendous privilege, and one day the way of the people and their lifestyle and beliefs will be in the past. They're fading a little bit. When they do their traditional dancing here the young people sometimes dance with baseball caps on back to front; they've obviously picked this up from videos when they've gone into the towns.

MACCA: I don't know what to say about that!

ZIG: It gets back to the fact that young people are impressionable, whether they're black or white, and they see these images and begin to mimic them.

MACCA: The American culture is certainly very attractive to youngsters but it's a threat to all sorts of cultures, isn't it? You'd think that in the middle of Arnhem Land you'd be removed from all that.

ZIG: Yes, and this is what makes the passing of the Old Man even more tragic. So much has gone with him that can never be recovered.

MACCA: A friend of mine says that when an old man dies a library burns. Thanks for calling, Zig.

# 11

# **K**eep taking the tablets!

from
M. LLOYD
TOOWOOMBA
QUEENSLAND

MACCA, I NOTICE THAT YOU have been fighting a raspy throat and cough. I know you have been sent cough mixtures, but here is another. Mix thoroughly equal parts of honey, glycerine, lemon juice, vinegar and sherry. Bottle in a clean, scalded bottle and cork well. Fill a medicine glass and take in sips. I find it A1.

•••••••••••••••••••

from
RUTH EVERS
COONDOO
QUEENSLAND

YOUR VOICE WAS NOT up to its usual quality on Sunday last, and when all the remedies started coming in, realised you were in the clutches of the dreaded flu. Let me add my remedy to those you already have. It does work but you may have to repeat it a couple of times if you are game.

Into a small glass put about three mouthfuls of brown vinegar, add to this about enough bicarbonate of soda to cover a two dollar coin, heaped. Let it fizz, then gargle and spit out until it's all gone! It tastes bloody awful, but guaranteed to take the soreness away.

•••••••••••••••••••

from
REG
GORDON
NEW SOUTH WALES

COLD AND SORE THROAT CURE

1/2 cup honey
1 lemon, grated rind and juice
2 cloves garlic (crushed and mixed in)
1 tablespoon cider vinegar
1/2 cup boiling water
Take one tablespoon every half hour.
* Another idea—add one teaspoon of ginger
* Another—add sage and thyme.

•••••••••••••••••••

from
MARGARET THOMPSON
ROCHESTER
VICTORIA

LISTENING TO YOUR PROGRAM about oranges given to a family to cure the flu reminded me of a story my mother told me about her uncle and aunt's family who lived in Bendigo when the epidemic hit in 1915. Whole families died, and in my grandmother's brother's family seven passed away, only two remained.

Bendigo's large Chinese population at that time offered to go into the local hospital free of charge and cure the patients. Their services were refused and hundreds of people died, but not one Chinese person was lost. So you can see the Chinese have a lot of cures for all different illnesses.

•••••••••••••••••••

from
CHEZ BUCKBERRY

JUST TO LET YOU HAVE some feedback on the boiled oranges to remedy the symptoms of the flu. Last Sunday after your show we boiled up a couple of oranges. My hubby Buck and I both had the flu which we have not had for years. Anyway, we both ate the oranges. Buck ate all the skin of his orange while I ate only a little of the skin. Eating that boiled orange was the greatest challenge of my week and not one I cherished. There is something very peculiar about munching into a hot orange. I think it worked because I was back on the ball by Tuesday morning and if anyone had told me on Saturday or Sunday that I'd be okay as soon as that I would not have believed them.

I HAVE HAD A NAGGING problem with my jaw which I tried to solve by having (at great expense) every tooth on that side removed at one sitting. At the suggestion of the lovely lady on your show I tried the capsicum. It works. I rang my daughter Kris who is a trained nurse (better than most doctors) to tell her about it. I recalled that her girls (now three and fifteen years) used to walk around chewing red capsicum when they were little. She tells me they still do and they never had any trouble cutting teeth.

from
ARTHUR COLLESS
CURRUMBIN
QUEENSLAND

· · · · · · · · · · · · · · · · · · · ·

I HEARD YOU MENTION THE therapeutic values of capsicum and it brought to mind my experiences with an old traditional remedy made from capsicum. That was 'Eichorn's Remedy'. I'm sure many of your older listeners will have rather vivid memories of it if it was ever used to disinfect their cuts and scratches as it really 'packed a punch'! It certainly seemed to work. It was a clear, rose-coloured liquid made from capsicum, ginger and nutmeg in an alcohol base that could be used straight on 'cuts, scratches, festering sores, abrasions, boils, carbuncles and insect bites' or diluted for gargling for 'ulcerated throat and tonsillitis'. The label was red, black and yellow.

It certainly was a tradition in our family from the early 1920s. My father and both his parents were doctors in the homoeopathic, herbalist, naturopathic and chiropractic area. We were born and bred on this 'smarting remedy'. It never let us down and I suppose it was like applying pure vitamin C. Unfortunately this wonderful product came to its demise in the 1980s and all I have left is an ancient bottle with a few precious drops in it!

from
CORAL BRODERSEN
ORANGE
NEW SOUTH WALES

· · · · · · · · · · · · · · · · · · · ·

AFTER LISTENING TO ALL the cures for your sore throat I thought I would just add a little to the subject.

Firstly, the use of kerosene on sugar. Many years ago a neighbour's child had diphtheria. The doctor was called and he said there was no hope for the child (this is pre-immunisation days). The mother decided to use the old remedy of kerosene on sugar and the child lived. My sister always used this method at the first sign of a sore throat or cold. Three drops of kerosene on a teaspoon of sugar placed on the back of the tongue and let melt slowly. Take about twice a day and it usually only needs one or two doses.

The other remedy kerosene is good for is for burns—unbroken blisters. My son ran through hot ashes and while I was running round trying to find someone to take him to the hospital a neighbour took him, applied kerosene to the blisters, bandaged his feet and continued to do that for a few days. His feet healed and there were no scars or hospital bills either!

from
JESSIE COVERALL
VILLAWOOD
NEW SOUTH WALES

· · · · · · · · · · · · · · · · · · · ·

I KNOW YOU ARE TIRED of hearing cures for this and that but can't resist telling you this. Kerosene is useful for rubbing on where arthritis is causing pain. However, I don't think this should be told to the general public because someone might rub it on and then get close to a fire or some such thing!

from
JESSIE
OR
'YAKKA'

· · · · · · · · · · · · · · · · · · · ·

from
BERYL VERTIGAN
AKOLELE
NEW SOUTH WALES

I WAS INTERESTED TO hear a chap (sorry, I've forgotten his name) talking about the prickly pear. When I was fifteen (I'm now seventy-six) my stepfather gave me the following recipe from his mother, so it is very old. Our family didn't try it as it wasn't prescribed by a doctor, also none of us developed diabetes, thankfully! I presume it was used in the early days.

PRICKLY PEAR PRESCRIPTION FOR DIABETES

1 lb prickly pear (leaf)
1 dessertspoon of bicarbonate of soda
1 pint of water

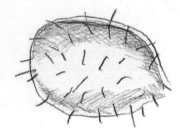

Cut prickly pear into pieces as for potato chips, place portion in bottom of basin, sprinkle portion of bicarbonate of soda over it, place another layer of prickly pear over that, then some more bicarbonate of soda and so on until all is used. Pour the pint of water over the lot (cold water can be used but hot is preferable), let stand for twenty-four to thirty-six hours (thirty-six hours preferable) and drink two cups a day (do not strain off but pour as required through strainer).

Dieting has also to be done—most emphatically!
Nine to twelve months is the usual time required.
I'm only sending you this recipe out of interest, not for anyone to try it unless they get advice from a doctor first!

• • • • • • • • • • • • • • • • • • • •

from
MARGARET STAFFORD
SOUTH HOBART
TASMANIA

IF YOU CAN GET A taste for the much-maligned gargle, it can nip flu in the bud. I have a 'gargle-and-swallow' when I first come into the kitchen every morning, and can't remember when I last had flu. I enclose the recipe—just in case I can convert you!

GARGLE

1/3 cup honey
1/3 cup cider vinegar

Mix together over hot water. Then add 2/3 cup boiled water. Mix and bottle. Gargle and swallow as often as it takes your fancy. (Helps clear catarrh too). Remember the old adage: An apple a day keeps the doctor away? Well, cider vinegar is made from . . .

• • • • • • • • • • • • • • • • • • • •

from
KRIS MCLEAN
FREEMANS REACH
NEW SOUTH WALES

I'M THE PRODUCT OF a mixed marriage. Mum was a country girl and Dad a city kid. Mum's views on medicine were always a bit 'back woods' (note the spelling please if you read this on air, she listens!). Never mind the few drops of kerosene on sugar, Mum's notion was always to gargle the kero neat! Dad once said to me from his sick bed, 'If you ever see that woman walking me down behind the garage I want you to check for the rifle. If it's missing come running!'

• • • • • • • • • • • • • • • • • • • •

I THOUGHT I HAD BETTER write to you quickly in case many men try to grow hair using black sulphur and lard. It won't work on bald-headed men! I know because I tried it years ago. I spent two weekends with my head in a cloth bag to stop the black, gooey mess running down my face and back. It is as hot as hell also.

However, it works wonders on horses and cattle when applied to areas where hide has been knocked off. I have even grown hair on fairly new fire brands on horses. The brand is not obliterated as the new hair grows through in a darker, richer colour than the rest of the coat and remains that way.

from
GEORGE BLACK
INGLEBURN
NEW SOUTH WALES

• • • • • • • • • • • • • • • • • •

I WAS INTERESTED TO HEAR on your program that you got a 'sore bum' from sitting on a wooden bench. I would like to suggest a remedy you might not be aware of. Buy yourself a nice five-litre cask of red and empty the contents with a couple of mates. When the cask is empty blow it up and sit on it. They are strong enough to support your weight and when deflated easy to carry in your pocket.

from
JOHN WINWOOD
CLEARVIEW
SOUTH AUSTRALIA

## G'day, this is Macca

CAPT. SLIM: Good morning, Macca, this is Captain Slim on the *Iron Whyalla*. We're down in the middle of the Great Australian Bight on our way east, returning from Japan where we took another export cargo. We came back to Port Hedland and loaded our twenty-millionth ton which we're taking over to the Port Kembla steelworks.

MACCA: How far offshore are you?

CAPT. SLIM: I'm using a mobile phone and we're 170 miles from the nearest station, so we've got exceptional radio conditions. We're picking up ships at seventy miles on radar and land at 120 miles.

MACCA: What's the sea like?

CAPT. SLIM: It's like Lake Macquarie! I think this is a bit of a payback by nature. When we were up in the North Pacific, as soon as we got across the Equator we had four typhoons lined up in a string. We had Theresa, Verne, Wilda and Zelda, just like a picket fence, and the one we had to go near was Wilda, with winds near the centre of 190 miles an hour. We had twenty-two metre waves and we were riding the biggest surfboard in the world, I think—we're 930 feet and we were surfing down the sides.

MACCA: That must have been frightening.

CAPT. SLIM: No, it wasn't, because this is a very well-found ship and we were sealed up tight. We had everything dogged up, all the watertight doors closed. We were using our skills and using the typhoons to sling us along our way like a woomera, but I wouldn't like to have been coming the other way. Anyway, I'd say this is the payback now: beautiful sunshine, flat seas and generally nice conditions.

MACCA: I was scared when I was out in a little dinghy with three other blokes. I don't know how I'd cope with surfing down the side of huge waves but I suppose you get used to anything, don't you?

CAPT. SLIM: Well, I wouldn't like that dinghy of yours very much either; this is certainly quite a bit bigger. As I say, we've lifted our twenty millionth ton this time and this year altogether we've lifted one-and-a-half million tons.

MACCA: Flying to Sydney I've seen those big coal trains in Queensland and New South

Wales. They're huge, aren't they? Huge amounts of coal coming out of the ground.

CAPT. SLIM: They say that by the turn of the century Newcastle will be exporting one hundred million tons a year. I think there's something like fifty million a year going out of there now. Sixty per cent of our work this year has been on export cargo, earning a bit of export income. We've taken 850,000 tons of coal up to Japan. We're shifting things and trying to get a few bucks in for the country. Incidentally, we got excellent reception of the show in Japan on Radio Australia.

MACCA: Good morning to the listeners via Radio Australia. Thanks for calling us, Captain Slim, nice to talk to you.

*Macca met a bloke at Winton during the centenary of 'Waltzing Matilda' who said amid much laughter:*

'My Mum had eleven children and my Dad was a drover—just as well he never had a town job!'

# 12

## *I*t's lovely to talk to you

## GRAHAM VANZELLA

*About the time the Letona Canneries fell over, a bloke rang us up and said, 'Macca, I've got an orchard here full of pear trees and thirty or forty tons of pears which are all going to fall on the ground and be wasted and ruined.' We had a yak about it on the air and Graham said, 'Look, I don't mind if people come down to my joint and pick them,' and this is what happened after we talked:*

GRAHAM: Well, in a matter of about five days thirty tons of pears just vanished off my property. People just came from everywhere: you wouldn't believe what happened. The longer the time went on the further away they came from. There were some classic runs: a lady from Tahmoor loaded her little car absolutely to the roof and I said to her, 'Look, you be careful with this car. It's not going to stop and it's not going to go like it should.' But she said, 'Oh, it'll be right,' and she wrote me this letter afterwards addressed to 'The Pear Giveaway Man in Batlow'. It found me, and she listed who she gave the pears to: to the Meals on Wheels lady, to this and to that, it was quite incredible where they went.

MACCA: You're still growing pears?

GRAHAM: Yes, well, I had to push the bulk of them out because there wasn't any market for them, but I still grow a few.

MACCA: What do you grow now?

GRAHAM: Mainly apples; that was always the big thing. The pears were just a sideline, but I still grow pears. There's still a market for them, but I couldn't grow the thirty or forty tons like I was for the cannery because consumer attitudes have changed. People want apples—pears have just, shall we say, fallen out of favour.

MACCA: Isn't that amazing? When I go to the markets in Sydney I talk to the bloke who supervises the unloading of all the trucks, and he said Australians aren't eating nearly as much fruit and vegetables as before; it's all processed stuff, things in packets and bits and pieces.

*Very sadly, just over a year after this chat with Graham at Junee came the news that he had died—a great loss to the Batlow, New South Wales, community.*

## RICA ERICSON

*I count myself very lucky to have met a lady called Rica Ericson at the Royal Perth Show. She's not famous but she's a great Australian, like a lot of people I meet. Rica loves her home state of Western Australia; she loves the flowers, the bush and she loves people. She's been compiling and writing books for most of her eighty-seven years; books about plants and families in Western Australia, including Aboriginal families. Rica Ericson says she loves helping people find information. She's the sort of person you could talk to for hours.*

RICA: I was born in Boulder in 1908. I've got a fair life behind me and I've used it well, I think. I went as a teacher in country schools because I wanted to go bush, and I was lucky enough to marry a farmer. We were utterly compatible and I had every support from him. My father was a farmer before he came over to the goldfields in the gold rush, about 1905. The gold rush started at Kalgoorlie in the mid-1890s and at that time the Victorians were suffering from the bank failure so we were really an island up there at Kalgoorlie/Boulder of eastern states. We helped Federation along. We were very isolated, more so in those days because we had no railway link, and I think we still are very isolated: it takes so much money for people from the eastern states to get here. We often complain that the eastern states know nothing about Western Australia, but I think also Western Australians don't know much about the east.

MACCA: We're here at the Stockman's Hall of Fame exhibit and you've got a couple of little books in front of you, simply called *Wheat* and *Wool*. Tell me about them.

RICA: They're magnificent books, beautifully produced, and they should be in every school. They're aimed at children inasmuch as they've got funny little skits in them and things to make the children look again. They have wonderful photographs and they take children and adults right through the process of the wool industry from the lamb to what comes on your back. A lot of people who live in towns should read these. When I was a child on the goldfields I got cream out of a tin; I didn't know that butter came from a cow, and the same thing applies these days: I've seen children at the Royal Show see a cow milked and they wouldn't drink milk after because they just didn't realise where it came from. But these books tell you about the whole industry from a child's point of view and they also instruct adults.

MACCA: You've always lived here, and you wouldn't leave Western Australia?

RICA: I've only been away on holidays. I went to Europe for a long holiday when I had to wean my husband off the farm as he had a bad back. We spent about nine months away and that really was an education. I spent a lot of my time at Kew Gardens because I had produced and illustrated three books on wildflowers, and it was an eye-opener just to get into the original records.

MACCA: What's special to you about the west?

RICA: It's my birthplace. I feel so utterly at home, especially in the outback. I don't mind seeing red sand and yellow, dry grass; they're beautiful colours. I think it started off with my grandmother, who had a green thumb; she could grow anything but her garden needed watering every day, and then when the rains came all the little flowers came up in the bush, and that was what inspired me, I suppose, to be interested in the bush, and I could always draw. It's a fascinating country, but there's something about the people who are always helping each other and sharing. I suppose it's my long love.

· · · · · · · · · · · · · · · · · · · · · · · · · · · · · · · · · · · · · · · · · · · · · · · · · · · · · · ·

## JIM SIBRE

*I got a note from Jim Sibre about two Australians who swam the Dardanelles this year. Jim, you'd better tell us the whole story.*

JIM: The swim was secondary, really. I'd always had a yen to visit Gallipoli and find out what it is to be an Australian, and I've found that a lot of people feel the same way. I got a call from an old mate I used to swim with thirty-six years ago who'd heard I was going to stop off in Turkey on my way home from England, and he said, 'Jim, I've always wanted to swim the Dardanelles,' and I said, 'If you want to do it, Andrew, I'll do it with you.' I made enquiries and found it was swimmable and unpolluted but you had to watch out for shipping. There's a current of up to twelve kilometres an hour from the Black Sea end, and although the swim from side to side is only about 1.3 kilometres, because of the current you end up swimming at least three times that distance. So I trained hard and we met up and did the swim.

MACCA: What did the Turkish authorities say?

JIM: Andrew insisted upon doing things the right way, and it took us months to get permission from about eight different authorities. They told him they'd knocked back every application for the last two years and they only gave us permission because we're Australians.

MACCA: Isn't that amazing, but it's really nice too, isn't it? I remember one of the old diggers who went on the pilgrimage to Anzac for the fiftieth anniversary saying 'It's good to be back in Turkey as a cobber.' There's a bond there.

JIM: Yes, and once they gave us permission they just couldn't do enough for us. They provided a harbour authority boat and doctor and told us to swim at 3.30 pm because that's when shipping is at its slowest, and then they radioed all the ships and slowed them up to give us the break through.

MACCA: That's wonderful! How long did it take you?

JIM: Forty-one minutes forty seconds. Andrew and I have been swimming against each other for all those years and it's the first time in my life I've beaten him! When we stepped ashore the local press and TV were there; it was unbelievable.

MACCA: Can you explain why you've had this thing about Turkey and the Dardanelles all your life?

JIM: There's always been something special about it, and when I stood on this little point between Anzac Cove, where the Australians landed, and North Beach, where the Kiwis landed, I looked up and saw this eroded cliff and you wonder how they did it. The other thing is that it's not just young Australian tourists who are there but busloads of Turkish schoolkids, because it's important to them: the successful defence there by the Turks catapulted this unknown military officer, Kemal Ataturk, into international prominence and he went on to become the founder of modern Turkey.

MACCA: As you say, lots of Australians go over there as part of their pilgrimage overseas.

JIM: And the Turks are so impressed by this because they're young people. The Turks would like to set up an annual marathon on the Dardanelles. They've had a go at it but only a few people turn up, and I think Australians could help promote it to become one of the big international swim events of the year.

MACCA: Well, it's certainly a different swim; I think it's great.

*Keith of Katherine offered a tribute:*

'I've got a mate in the RAAF up here and they call him "Lander". That's a good name for an RAAF bloke—there's lots of good fliers in the RAAF, but it's more important to be a good lander.'

## TOM BIGGS

*One of the most unusual growth industries in Australia is rescuing thousands of people who go bush in their four-wheel drives, sometimes a bit unprepared. More and more breakdowns are occurring and Dr Tom Biggs of Brisbane has made a business of rescuing Australians in distress. Tell us about it, Tom.*

TOM: We started a business in 1983 assessing and rescuing people with personal and medical problems all round the world. People today are so mobile that they get sick a long way from home, and when you're in that situation you want to talk to a mate, someone who can help you get home. I think the thing that fired me was the great hospitality and mateship of the Australian bush; that's what kept people going, and these days with sophisticated vehicles there are Aussies all over northern and central Australia, and a lot of overseas people are coming to look at what's probably the last place on earth where you can get solitude and the kind of natural environment we've got here.

MACCA: They do things I wouldn't do. I've seen people in the most amazing places towing caravans with a Falcon stationwagon on the Birdsville Track and all sorts of half-unmade roads.

TOM: I remember one woman who rang us. The vehicle was working but she said oil was flowing over the rear hubcap, and after some difficulty our guy got there to find that the problem was actually a dead chook in the boot which had started to disintegrate. I guess that's one end of the spectrum, but in some cases we've had people with catastrophic problems with accidents, right through to the trivial things. When you're stuck a long way from home you definitely don't want to talk to a database that says 'Press A if you've got a wheel problem, press B if you've got a heart problem, press C if you're on fire'. When you're anxious and in a remote area you want to talk to a person who can solve the problem.

MACCA: Exactly. How do you get to these people?

TOM: Nationally there are about 14,000 people we call 'providers' who work for us. In remote areas it might be a park ranger. We use the appropriate local people to provide the response.

MACCA: If the vehicles can't be fixed do you tow them out?

TOM: You can. But there are a few places where it's very hard to tow them from, particularly twenty feet under in a river in the Northern Territory—that's hard!

MACCA: And you rescue people with medical problems, too.

TOM: Last week we picked up a woman in the highlands of New Guinea who'd come into labour at twenty-six weeks and the child is doing well for a premature infant. Our mission is to make sure that people in the remoter parts of this country have got a lifeline. The ability to respond to one another's needs in times of crisis is very characteristically Australian.

## DAWN SCHMIDT, MYRNA NEVILLE

MACCA: There are two ladies I want you to meet: Dawn Schmidt and Myrna Neville. Now, why did you two come to Winton?

DAWN: Because of our ancestors and our connection to 'Waltzing Matilda'. Our great-grand-aunt was Sarah Riley who was engaged to Banjo Paterson on and off for nine years. Our version of it is that he was a bit of a romantic man and had his eyes elsewhere and that's why the engagement was on and off. Sarah came up here to our grandfather, Frederick Whistler Riley, to get away from him, and he followed her up here to get her back. And after all this she never married. That's our family story.

MACCA: What's this you've got here, a letter?

DAWN: Yes, I found a cousin to my father in 1981 and I wrote and asked her if she could tell me the reason why the engagement was broken.

MACCA: She didn't like his poetry!

DAWN: No, it says here: 'The reason why Aunt Sarah did not marry Paterson was that he flirted with the sewing mistress on Dagworth Station on McPherson's property. It was when Banjo, Miss Chris McPherson and Aunt Sarah set off in a dray to visit Aunt Marie at Winton. When they arrived they took possession of the piano and said they would not leave until they were satisfied with the story and music of 'Waltzing Matilda'.

MACCA: Myrna, where are you from?

MYRNA: I'm from Townsville now. I was born in Winton.

MACCA: And what have you done since you came here, since the celebrations started?

MYRNA: We haven't stopped. We've been to two concerts and we've been out to Vindex Station. The owners were very good to let us have a tour over the station. We had a particular interest to be out there: our great-uncle, James Brookes Riley, is buried there. It was really great to go and see the old grave and look over the homestead.

MACCA: There's nothing more to tell us about the romance?

DAWN: No, it's only what we know.

MACCA: Nice to talk to you both. Thank you.

• • • • • • • • • • • • • • • • • • • • • • • • • • • • • • • • • • • • • • • • • • • • •

# KIWI WHITE

KIWI: I'm a commercial fisherman. I've been involved in the fishing here for about twenty-five years and I've spent about twelve years in the aeroplanes, spotting tuna for Port Lincoln Tuna Processors. We spent a lot of time out of Nullarbor Station and we'd fly out in the Great Australian Bight and patrol the area from the Western Australian border right down to Kangaroo Island on the Continental Shelf. We had some really good years there: one year we caught 21,000 tons of bluefin tuna and at that time there were about forty-eight boats and seventeen aeroplanes flying. But the government could see the writing on the wall: we were just wiping out the tuna, so they brought in quotas and only the big guys survived. It finished up with about five or six boats and two or three aeroplanes, and everybody was crying gloom and doom, but really it's been a benefit to the community. Things have changed and the tuna are coming back.

MACCA: They found them in the river at Adelaide the other day. Is that right?

KIWI: I don't know, but that's possible, because I've seen them up here in the Gulf, and the other day I went looking for a school of salmon here in Port

Lincoln Bay with a guy in a little aeroplane and I actually saw some wild tuna feeding on pilchards out here in the Bay, which is quite good to see. But what I wanted to tell everyone about is that since they closed down the whaling station we've noticed a great increase in the whales, especially sperm whales, and in the last couple of years we've had a lot of hump-backed whales in the Bight, and we saw a fantastic sight on the last day of tuna spotting. I was with a guy called Derek and we were just finishing an aerial survey when we saw this commotion about ten or fifteen miles away, so we flew over and circled and there were fifteen sperm whales head-to-head in a daisy pattern and seven killer whales were attacking them. They were putting their heads together and splashing their tails to try to protect themselves. There was a big stream of blood coming out and as we circled we could watch these killers coming and hitting individual whales and then they would slide up on top of their air hole and try to block the air off so they'd drown one. They would kill one and then eat the tongue and then let it go, so it's quite phenomenal. An expert from the museum in Adelaide said only two or three people in Australia have seen that phenomenon.

MACCA: What a story! That must have been great to see.

KIWI: And just a little bit about great white sharks. I was out squidding at Boston Island in my little tinny one morning and there was a big swirl, and I thought oh, no, not another seal, because they give me a lot of trouble. But it was a white pointer, about fourteen foot, and I was only in a twelve-foot tinny. It came right up alongside me; we were actually eyeballing each other! It would go ahead, turn around and come back, and I thought this was not too good, so I started my motor and went off, and he actually turned around and chased my boat. He was like a Polaris submarine: he came out of the water with his tail and fin out and the water was coming off his nose, coming for me. That was about three weeks before a woman was killed up here by a great white shark.

## ARCHBISHOP HICKEY AND FATHER HARDIMAN

MACCA: I'd like to welcome the Archbishop of Perth and Father Hardiman here to Leonora.

ARCHBISHOP HICKEY: I was born here in Leonora and so was my friend here, Father Hardiman. Our fathers were both mining registrars at different times.

MACCA: So mining's in the family for you.

ARCHBISHOP HICKEY: It really is. We've got gold in the blood but that's the only place we've got it.

MACCA: I'll have a transfusion!

ARCHBISHOP HICKEY: It's great to be here. People have been so friendly. Some of the sisters who taught in the local school have also come back, and although they're getting on in years now they've found plenty of students who've swapped memories of the old days. These events are marvellous.

MACCA: Yes, I love them. Do you travel a lot?

ARCHBISHOP HICKEY: I do. I go overseas a fair bit, to Rome and other places, but not so much in the country now because I'm based in Perth.

MACCA: Are places like mining towns more unchristian than the cities? Do they need people like you more?

ARCHBISHOP HICKEY: No, I think it's the other way around. People in the bush have good, strong family traditions and they hang on to them. The trouble is back in the cities.

MACCA: Thanks, Archbishop. Father Hardiman, tell me your story.

FATHER HARDIMAN: Well, I was born here in 1943 when the wartime economy production standards were strictly enforced, and that's why I'm so short!

MACCA: You're sitting down; I couldn't tell!

FATHER HARDIMAN: Actually, I'm lucky to be here at all. When I was an infant here I was very sick and the doctor gave me up for dead, but I finished up in the hospital for a long time, undergoing all sorts of tests to find out what I could eat. They couldn't understand why I was putting on weight when they were giving me so little and they finally discovered that another patient, an Italian miner, thought it was cruel to be starving a baby so when no-one was looking he was feeding me cheese and salami!

MACCA: It must be a true story—you're a priest!

FATHER HARDIMAN: When I was a kid my father told a story about a visiting Redemptorist priest who was preaching a blood and thunder sermon in the church here. The fire brigade is opposite the church, and when he cried, 'And if you don't repent you'll go to hell, where you'll burn in everlasting fire—fire— fire!' they came running in from over the road thinking the church was on fire!

MACCA: I'm going to come to your services.

FATHER HARDIMAN: Well, we try to work on the theory of mixing the useful with the agreeable. We hope people won't get so distracted by your program that they don't come to listen to ours!

## MIKE McDERMOTT AND COLIN AKLAND

MIKE: It's Mike McDermott, from Mosman in Sydney and I've just returned from a visit to Vietnam after twenty-five years. I served there in 1969 with the Australian 5th Battalion and went on to the Australian Army Training Team to act as an adviser to the South Vietnamese. My wife and I went back and we hired bikes and cycled about sixty kilometres out into the jungle west of the coast to a spot where I was in 1971. We climbed up on the hill where there had been a five-day battle and I put my hand in the rock where I'd left my prismatic Australian Army compass and the compass was still in the rock.

MACCA: Really! I don't believe that story!

MIKE: It's a good story, isn't it? The only signs of the battle were a lot of holes in the ground. Two Australians I've never met supported me on that day; they had the call signs of Helix Zero One and Helix Zero Three. One's name was Col Akland and the other was Bruce Woods and they were forward air controllers bringing in the air strikes that came to help us. They only spoke to me that day then flew away and we never got together. I think there were also about twenty-five American airmen who came in over the five days and supported us to stop us being over-run and I think a few of them were killed; a couple were shot down. But after twenty-five years I went up the hill and there was the compass—a great rush of adrenalin!

MACCA: And you brought it home with you.

MIKE: It was an interesting time. The most interesting thing for Australians is that when I looked down in September 1971 across the battlefield it was covered in low green scrub and open paddies. Now I looked down and there must be two million Australian grey gums, so the whole of the landscape has been changed from a green Asian landscape to the blue-green of Australian gums, which are now about thirty-five feet high.

MACCA: Do you know why they planted gums?

MIKE: Australians are quick to forgive and forget. We don't hold grudges, and about eight years after the war we went over there and gave them the trees to re-forest the area that had been devastated by the war.

MACCA: Isn't that mighty! Tell me why you left the compass.

MIKE: I was in rather a hurry! After five days we were pushed off the position and we were being followed down the hill by a lot of very angry people, so I grabbed the radio and left the compass under the rock where I'd kept it. I thought about it for years because my father was a quartermaster in the army and he never let me forget that I'd lost my compass.

*A week later Mike McDermott came into the AAO studio.*

MACCA: Last week you mentioned a couple of pilots, Col Akland and Bruce Woods, who supported you in Vietnam. You'd better say hello to Colin Akland, because he's on the line.

MIKE: Oh! G'day Col. I've never met you but we spoke on the radio many times when you were bringing in the air strikes. For the two hundred or so people on the ground I think you were the turning force that got us out of trouble. Thanks very much, mate.

COL: Well, it's nice to talk to you. Until this moment I've never known who I was supporting down there, only that it was Australians. We usually supported an American division and when your Australian voice came up it was unique. I didn't know how many of you guys and how many bad guys were down there, but from the sound of your voice I could tell you were in a spot of bother!

MIKE: Yes, the sound of my voice went into a high pitch because there were a lot of bad guys. Prior to that Bruce Woods had supported us when a chopper went in and thirty of my fellows were burned to death. I looked up your name in a book called *The History of the RAAF in Vietnam* and saw that you'd received a decoration. Was it for that same action, Col?

COL: I think it probably was. A fairly big North Vietnamese force came through and I put in a lot of air strikes. It was a bit tricky because they kept on moving closer to you.

MACCA: It's Ian McNamara here Colin. Can I ask if you heard the story that Mike told last week about finding his compass all that time ago?

COL: I did, but I missed the first part of his call so I didn't hear my name, but as I listened I thought that maybe it was the mission I was involved with. Then a couple of friends rang me later and said my name was mentioned earlier on.

MACCA: Well, it's lovely to get you both together, and the next thing you'll have to do is meet some time.

## PETER OLDE

MACCA: We've been talking about grevilleas and Peter Olde is a grevillea expert.
PETER: G'day, Ian. All this about Australia's flowers not being scented, particularly grevilleas, isn't true. There are some beautifully scented grevilleas and when you go out in the bush you can smell Australia, you really can. Some grevilleas have a beautiful honey scent, although a few are fairly horrific because they've designed themselves to attract blowflies for pollination, but most of the scented ones have a very delightful sweet scent which is attractive to bees and butterflies and other pollinaters.
MACCA: I'm a big fan of growing Australian plants, because they attract little insects and Australian birds.
PETER: I think that plants give us a definition of what we are. Australians say they are searching for what they are, but plants actually define your environment. And a native garden defines what you think about your country. And if you love your country, you love the plants in it and you love the birds and the animals. If you push all that out and plant exotics you are really saying, 'I'd rather be somewhere else.'
MACCA: You've got a couple of grevillea books. How did you get interested in grevilleas and flowers generally?
PETER: Well, through my garden, and then we decided we'd do a work on grevillea. We didn't realise what we'd got ourselves into, because we decided to photograph every species and give a comprehensive description and treatment to each one. This necessitated us travelling right round Australia many times to get that elusive photograph. Looking for the plants took us into some very inhospitable and remote places, particularly in Western Australia, which is just the most sensational place for a botanist or anybody interested in native plants. One of the most interesting things that came to light in this quest was the rediscovery of a plant that had been lost to science for 150 years.
MACCA: Your life with plants obviously gives you a lot of pleasure and fulfilment.
PETER: It gives me immense fulfilment because I feel we're still in an age of discovery and we have to be careful not to lose our heritage.
MACCA: And everybody can help by having one Australian plant in their garden.

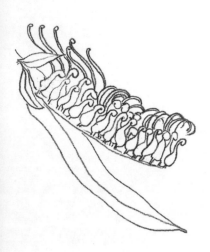

## BETTY LOITERTON

MACCA: Here's Betty Loiterton who knows a little bit about what happened in wartime. You've got a story to tell about the war and troop trains and something that happened to you. Tell me about it.
BETTY: I was unfortunate enough to lose a leg. American servicemen were coming through Junee and the loading on one of the trains worked loose, and one of the servicemen came down the street carrying his sawn-off shotgun. He came into the shop where I was working and wanted to know my name. I was quite a young prude at that stage and I told him I didn't tell strangers my name but he heard some of the boys calling me Betty so he called me and whistled at me, and I told him I was not a dog. He pointed the gun at my feet and said 'Which

foot would you like it in.' I naturally thought he was joking, but the gun went off. He said he didn't realise the gun was loaded but just before that he had loaded it while showing the children how to do it.

MACCA: He shot you in the leg and you lost it and now you have a wooden leg.

BETTY: No, I've got a fibreglass and nylon leg now!

MACCA: That's an amazing story. Did he want to go out with you or something?

BETTY: No, he'd only been there about ten minutes.

MACCA: At that time all the troop trains stopped at Junee. Did lots of Americans stop here?

BETTY: No, I'd never seen one before in my life. We didn't seem to get Yanks here at all.

MACCA: That's just one legacy of the war. You hear about Changi, or people getting shot or wounded or bombed, and here's Betty who's minding her own business in a little town called Junee and a soldier comes along with a shotgun and boom! no leg. Somebody told me that you're full-bottle on most things around this place.

BETTY: I keep busy.

MACCA: Did it make you bitter about Americans?

BETTY: I didn't have much time to think about that part of it, really. I was going to toss the sponge in completely until I saw my father cry for the first time, and I think it was Dad's tears that made me think, well, you've got to get up and get going, old girl. And it hasn't stopped me doing anything.

MACCA: We're glad you're still here to talk to us, Betty.

## CLARRIE AND DR MICHAEL GIBLIN

CLARRIE: It's Clarrie, from Dubbo. I was prompted by the talk of Smithy's celebrations to tell you that from 1965 to 1970 I worked at Sydney Hospital, and one of their treasured possessions was the flag that came with Smithy on that epic flight. I wondered if it was still there and if it could be brought out for the occasion. It's a national treasure, I think, and it would be a pity if it's still just hidden away in a safe.

*The following week Dr Michael Giblin, who's an ophthalmologist at Sydney Hospital, came into the studio.*

MACCA: So you followed up Clarrie's phone call about the flag?

MICHAEL: Yes, I did. I'd never heard of it and neither had the superintendent or anyone else until we spoke to Barbara McAndrew, a secretary at the hospital, who said she believed the flag was in a vault at the Westpac Bank. So Dr John Graham, chairman of the medical staff, Ian Rule, the superintendent, and I went down to the bank and conned them into giving us the box. We opened it up and what do you think we saw—seven flags! Our eyes were out on sticks. There were two Union Jacks, two New Zealand flags, two Australian flags and one RAF flag. They were on drums and we thought we shouldn't disturb them, but temptation overcame us and we unrolled one of the Australian flags. It was silk, in reasonable condition, a bit faded, probably coloured with vegetable dyes, hand-sewn, possibly home made because of the Depression at the time. On the fly of the flag were signatures of Charles Kingsford Smith and CTP Ulm, co-commanders, Southern Cross flight on the Australia–New Zealand flight across the Tasman, 1928. The signatures were authenticated by the then secretary of Sydney Hospital.

MACCA: Isn't that a lovely story, and all because of a phone call from Clarrie. What do you intend to do with them?

MICHAEL: They're back in the bank now, but we think they're national treasures and obviously we'll have to restore them. It seems the flags had been in the hospital chapel for many years and the box was especially made to store them. I understand there should have been eight, but one had decayed. Why did Sydney Hospital have them? It turns out that the flags were put on the Southern Cross to be auctioned later to raise money for hospitals in Australia and New Zealand and St Bartholomew's Hospital in London. Sydney Hospital is Australia's oldest hospital and St Bartholomew's is the oldest in England, so there may have been a connection there. Speaking of that flight, there's a beautiful quote at the airfield at Wigram near Christchurch where Smithy landed after his overnight flight—'They came on the wings of the morning'.

* * *

## GRAHAM MIDDLETON

*In the second AAO book we included an interview with Graham Middleton who had just completed an epic swim of the Murray. He raised $200,000 for kids with cancer. Very sadly Graham died of a heart attack in 1995, so as a tribute to this true son of Corryong, Victoria, here's a short extract from that interview:*

MACCA: G'day Graham, how are you? How's it going?

GRAHAM: We've finished.

MACCA: Was it every bit as hard as you thought it would be?

GRAHAM: It was harder, and I guess the biggest part was that at the end it was the mind that had to be activated more than the body. The cold water and the cold winds were really getting at me, but it's been done now so I thought I'd let you know.

MACCA: It's probably the hardest thing you've ever done. What did you think about?

GRAHAM: It's certainly the hardest thing I've ever done! We were hoping that we'd get a great result for our kids. It was very much on my mind to make certain that the challenge was a charitable event, but I guess when it really got hard I had to exclude everything from my mind except what I was doing. In the middle part of the river I had plenty of time to contemplate and philosophise, but at the end it was absolutely a battle to keep my mind on the job and keep going. It took 138 consecutive days, more than four and a half months, and it meant being in the water just on six hours every day.

MACCA: That's a long time. You probably never want to see the Murray again.

GRAHAM: I loved it, actually. There are so many beautiful things on the river and the people are just fantastic. I think the river was kind to me in the end and let me hang in there. It fought me all the way and at the end it let me through. I feel a bit humble about it, really.

# 13

# *Australia remembers*

from
HEDY TRIFFET (SCHAFLI)
SURFERS PARADISE
QUEENSLAND

**I** WAS LISTENING TO YOUR wonderful program on Sunday (for me it is a must) and heard a Canadian war bride telling you her story. I came to Julia Creek, Queensland, in October 1946 as a war bride, having met my Aussie husband in Switzerland following his escape over the Alps from an Italian prison camp. We married in Switzerland in September 1945 and I arrived in Sydney on board the *Stirling Castle*. With me was my baby daughter Susan, just a couple of months old. For me, a young woman from Switzerland, Julia Creek was somewhat of a culture shock, but the country folk were most welcoming and there I stayed for some years. I had to learn to drive a 5-ton truck, to make camp each night, cook for the men over an open fire and in the camp oven, make damper, boil the billy and sleep under the stars. In those days there were no such luxuries as caravans. Our chairs were kerosene tins. The water bags hung from bars on the side of the truck, food was kept in a large wooden tucker box on the back of the truck and the meat, salted with coarse salt, was in hessian bags also on the back of the truck. My two daughters used to love to ride with their father and the stockmen. They were schooled in Toowoomba but joined their father and myself from boarding school during the holidays, and in their early years did correspondence with me as their tutor.

At the age of seventy-seven I decided to retire and now live on the Gold Coast near my two daughters and family. My grandson, who is now fifteen, bought me some of your tapes for Christmas. Every time I listen to 'The Man with the Big Hat' tears come to my eyes. Ian, I did love people in the bush. They are a special breed—kind with big hearts. I have no regrets joining my husband in the bush. It was the obvious decision for him to make after six years in the war—being in a prison camp, chained to the wall (four hours on, four hours off), fed on rotten food. My husband was a Rat of Tobruk and decorated at Buckingham Palace with a DCM.

## AUSTRALIA REMEMBERS

from
CHILDREN OF
GREGORY PUBLIC
SCHOOL
NEW SOUTH WALES

Come and I'll tell you a story of war
About farmers and husbands and wives;
Butchers and bakers and drovers and shearers
The soldiers who gave up their lives.

And now Australia remembers
The sorrow, the anger, the joys.
Memories heroic and special
So many were only just boys.
And now Australia remembers;
Remembers because we are free.
Our mothers, our sons, and our daughters;
Australians just like you and me.

I think of my uncle in his uniform,
I've a photo of him and his friend
On a ship to New Guinea with other young soldiers
Kokoda was where it would end.

56

57

58

60

59

61

There are so many interesting people in Australia, and here are just a few of them. Bill Scott, a welcome program veteran and contributor to all of the books; I asked Lily Ah-Toy what she thought of Darwin — 'God's Own Country!'; taking a break from signing books; chatting to some great bush kids at Charters Towers, Queensland; Australian sprint champion Melinda Gainsford-Taylor stops for a natter at Narromine, New South Wales; accompanying Robert Keane in 'The Old North Queensland Accent'.

# *A Little Bit of Everything*

62

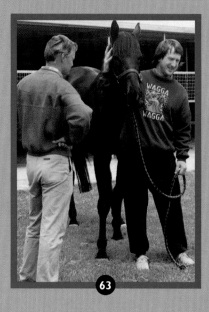

63

64

65

66

One of the many amazing things about the program is that I never know what the next call or letter will bring. And that's reflected in these pictures, a wide variety of unusual and everyday life in Australia. At Parramatta Park in Sydney the excellent Andra and me sang a few songs; the look on my face says it all, 'Sunday with Macca' has seen more tails than Hoffmann, as a taxi driver once said; with my mum, Lorna, opening an art show at Oatley West Public School, Sydney; the pound note signed by Ronnie Biggs and used as a fundraiser for kids with cancer; even dogs like Freddy from Narromine, New South Wales, wear shades these days; Betty King, supposedly the first white woman to come ashore in Australia, is buried at Magra, Tasmania; every year millions of Christmas Island crabs migrate from the rainforest to the ocean to spawn.

67

68

# A Little Bit of Everything

MAGPIE CAKE.

eat together 1 cup of sugar and 6ozs. butter u
my, add 3 eggs well beaten, and then 1 cup milk
in 2 cups SIMPSON'S SELF-RAISING FLOU
de the mixture and add to one half 1 cup sultan
lla, and enough chocola to make it dark. Flav

69

70

71

72

73

74

76

75

The magpie cake — many called for the recipe; taking in the floods at Wodonga, Victoria; the hazards of outside broadcasts!; magnificent tulips at a farm on the Table Cape, Tasmania; here's Henry who reported the storm and flood at Olary, South Australia; AAO goes to air via satellite dish from Leonora, Western Australia.

77

78

A great way to relax after the outside broadcast from Dalby, Queensland — swinging on some huge vines in the Bunya Mountains; during the outside broadcast from Broken Hill, New South Wales, John Dynon painted this very amusing image and presented it to us after the program.

*For Alec*
*Killed in the battle of Pozieres 10 August 1916*

Today I opened once again
The small blue box so lovingly treasured
By my grandmother through many years.
It holds the few, poor, sad reminders
Of her son, whose life was worth a medal and a cross
Somewhere among a thousand others far away.

Beneath the lid were laid with tender care
Some postcards,
Stiff tourist scenes of Egypt
With a few lines penned of flies and sand;
Some gaudy greeting cards from Paris,
Intimations to those at home of strange, unknown lands.

What dreams of patriotism
Took him on that voyage?
Or was it just a job which must be done?
Just another number in the ranks of that vast army
And yet, unique,
As every man.

No works of art, no symphonies
Carry forward in time his fame.
No wife or child to give posterity his name.
A simple, unlettered man
He died by violence
Far from family and home.

I read those letters to his mother
Sadly. The homesickness shows through
Those ill-spelled, pencilled notes on scraps of paper.
'I miss you all, you seem so far away.
How's old Blue? Give him a pat for me.
I haven't heard from you as yet, I guess the mails are slow.'

And then I read the latest one of all.
'We're going up the line tomorrow.
I wish the mail would come,
I haven't heard. But there's no need to worry,
We've been trained real well.
Maybe I'll see you soon.'

The telegram arrived before the letter.
His disk, together with a lock of baby hair
Are folded with most loving care

from
HELEN FLOWER
KYOGLE
NEW SOUTH WALES

Into a paper serviette made gay with flowers
Placed beside the official letters
And a small scroll from the King ('for service to your country').

And now on Anzac Days some say
This celebration of our wars should cease.
But surely men like him have earned
A celebration of their brief existence,
Some compensation for their unlived lives
Destroyed by this world's violent search for peace.

THE VICKERS VIMY RE-ENACTMENT FLIGHT

THE FLIGHT OF A replica Vickers Vimy from England to Australia has been hailed as the aviation event for 1994. On arrival in Darwin this replica World War One bomber, created and piloted by my son Lang and his partner Peter McMillan, will receive a tumultuous welcome.

> from
> RICHARD L. KIDBY
> SUNRISE BEACH
> QUEENSLAND

> from
> ROBERT LESLIE
> BURWOOD
> VICTORIA

I AWOKE THIS MORNING IN time to hear Lang Kidby call from Singapore to advise on the leg from Singers to Jakarta. I heard Lang confirm that Vimy is pronounced Vim-me. Vimy is close to Arras in France where appalling battles occurred during World War One. There is a great monument near Arras to the Canadian Army who successfully took Vimy Ridge. The trenches are in places a mere twenty metres apart.

A friend of mine's father, Doug Joycey, was a medical orderly with the Canadians who took the Ridge. Joycey is now in his nineties, lives in Brisbane and when last was heard of is upright. The Canadian Veteran Affairs send him a new glass eye every second year!

*Eleanor (Balgo, Western Australia):*
'We've got a plane, but it's only got one propeller — I like two propellers and grey-haired men driving them.'

> from
> KEITH MAYNARD
> KATHERINE
> NORTHERN TERRITORY

## WHY WEAR A POPPY?

'Please wear a poppy,' the lady said,
And held one forth, but I shook my head.
Then I stopped and watched as she offered them there,
And her face was old and lined with care;

But beneath the scars the years had made
There remained a smile that refused to fade.
A boy came whistling down the street,
Bouncing along on carefree feet.

His smile was full of joy and fun,
'Lady,' said he, 'may I have one?'
When she'd pinned it on, he turned to say:
'Why do we wear a poppy today?'

The lady smiled in her wistful way
And answered: 'This is Remembrance Day,
And the poppy there is a symbol for
The gallant men who died in war.

'And because they did, you and I are free—
That's why we wear a poppy, you see.
I had a boy about your size,
With golden hair and big blue eyes.

'He loved to play and jump and shout,
Free as a bird, he would race about.
As the years went by, he learned and grew,
And became a man—as you will, too.

'He was fine and strong, with a boyish smile,
But he'd seemed with us such a little while
When war broke out and he went away.
I still remember his face that day.

'When he smiled at me and said "Goodbye.
I'll be back soon, Mum, so please don't cry"
But the war went on and he had to stay,
And all I could do was wait and pray.

'His letters told of the awful fight
(I can see it still in my dreams at night),
With the tanks and guns and cruel barbed wire,
And the mines and bullets, the bombs and fire.

'Till at last, at last, the war was won—
And that's why we wear a poppy, son.'
The small boy turned as if to go,
Then said: 'Thanks, lady, I'm glad to know.

'That sure did sound like an awful fight,
But your son—did he come back all right?'

A tear rolled down each faded cheek
She shook her head, but didn't speak.

I slunk away in a sort of shame,
And if you were me, you'd have done the same;
For our thanks, in giving, is oft delayed,
Though our freedom was bought—and thousands paid!

And so, when we see a poppy worn,
Let us reflect on the burden borne
By those who gave their very all
When asked to answer their country's call
That we at home in peace might live,
Then wear a poppy! Remember—and Give!

• • • • • • • • • • • • • • • • • • •

<table>
<tr><td>from<br>VIVIENNE ACKERMAN<br>BALLINA<br>NEW SOUTH WALES</td></tr>
</table>

**W**HEN YOU WERE READING incidents in Australia during World War Two I remembered a tale my father told me. He was a fisherman; he and my Uncle Fred used to go down to Cape Northumberland in a boat called the *Nelippar* for three to five days. One day at dawn, at the height of the Japanese submarine scare, they were hauling in their shark (gummy) lines when a submarine started to surface. Both immediately thought it was Japanese and stood on the rails, scared stiff, ready to dive overboard. However, it turned out to be a 'T' class British sub and a very 'pukka' voice inquired politely if they would care to swap some fish for fresh bread. This they duly did with great alacrity and pleasure and never spoke of the incident until after the war. The sub *Tapir* visited Portland after the war and I often wondered if it was the same one.

• • • • • • • • • • • • • • • • • • •

<table>
<tr><td>from<br>DAVE BAKER<br>TEA GARDENS<br>NEW SOUTH WALES</td></tr>
</table>

**I** SPENT A LOT OF TIME at Humpty Doo, Northern Territory, in the 1950s with an Aboriginal from Melville Island. His name was Holder Adam. He was much older than me and had worked with the Australian Intelligence Bureau during the war. In 1942 he had accompanied Australian Intelligence teams to Timor in US submarines where he acted as a forward scout. Great sense of humour and delightful company and I learned a lot from him. He died a couple of years ago, but I hope to visit his family next year. Lovely people.

Our work for the Department of Works gauging streams for water flow was in hindsight bloody dangerous. Mostly we stood in water on logs or concrete paths built across streams in the dry. With a meter in one hand you walked along so many yards at a time, immersing the meter to varying depths each time. Holder and I had been camped for some time on a big bend in the Adelaide River beneath the only tree. We went to bed one night in fine good conditions. About one I heard Holder splashing around. It had rained upstream, the river cut the bend and we had to go up the tree. At dawn as far as the eye could see there was only water and as it kept on rising we kept on going up the tree.

About four in the arvo it started to subside. I swam, following Holder, and by dark we gained higher ground. After a couple of days and nights we got into drier country and for the first and last time in my life I was treated to the sight of Holder making fire from two dissimilar sticks.

• • • • • • • • • • • • • • • • • •

THIS BEING THE 50TH anniversary of the end of the Second World War, I thought you may be interested in this little poem. I think it sums up the tragedy and futility of war.

The author, although being in the same battalion as my husband, is unknown. My husband Syd found it when looking through his war mementos. Syd was in the Islands, 12th Advanced Australian Workshop, Bougainville.

from
J. BIGGS
ASCOT VALE
VICTORIA

## BOUGAINVILLE

We've nineteen dead on the Buin Road,
Ten more on the jungle track.
And all day long there's a broken tide
Of our wounded coming back.
We've fought all night by the Hongoria
With never a bite or sup,
And tomorrow's back page will quote
Our forces are 'mopping up'.

*Anon*

• • • • • • • • • • • • • • • • • •

I MET AN OLD DIGGER the other day. Yarning with him he brought up the matter of the current trend to call it the Kokoda 'Track' instead of 'Trail'. He'd fought on it, as had his mates, and they are (certainly he is) very distressed about this. From what I can gather the politicians have checked with the Australian War Memorial boffins who assure them that the Yanks called it 'Trail' but the Aussies called it 'Track'. I have original Aussie wartime publications and all of them refer to it as the Kokoda 'Trail'. I also have the Australian War Memorial's official pictorial history of the war and it refers to the Kokoda 'Trail'.

I guess it's a few young historians who've found some obscure papers that call it the 'Track,' or perhaps it's just another insensitive politician getting something else wrong! Anyhow, it's a matter of great importance to these old blokes (and ladies). Can you and your tribe put your weight behind getting it referred to as the Kokoda 'Trail'.

from
ED CAMERON
CABOOLTURE
QUEENSLAND

• • • • • • • • • • • • • • • • • •

THE SCENE IS WARTIME London in July 1944. An RAAF Lancaster crew is on leave, doing over the regular haunts in Piccadilly, Leicester Square, Fleet Street and finally the Boomerang Club (home away from home for Aussies). The crew is halfway through a tour of operations and looking for a relaxed week off ops. On this particular day Alan, our rear gunner, had received a parcel from home. He opened it and held up a small brown paper bag with a note attached which read, 'Just a reminder of the smell of the Australian bush. Love, Grand-dad'. In

from
ROSS DENT
GROVELY
QUEENSLAND

the bag was a bunch of dried gum and wattle leaves which we took turns at sniffing, relishing the long-forgotten fragrance. Frank, our bomb-aimer, put some in a saucer and put a match to them. Soon the room was swirling with fragrant bushfire smoke and we revelled in the aroma.

Suddenly there was a hubbub in the upstairs lounge area. A rush of feet down the steps and we were surrounded by dozens of fellow Aussies. For some minutes nostalgia reigned supreme.

• • • • • • • • • • • • • • • • • • •

from
A. L. 'DARBY' MONROE
OURIMBAH
NEW SOUTH WALES

**I** SERVED ON THE CORVETTE HMAS *Shepparton*, which was named in honour of the township of Shepparton in Victoria. Shepparton townspeople adopted us and sent comfort parcels. We were so pleased with their kindness we decided to do something in return.

While we were surveying in the Admiralty Islands area a party of sailors went ashore in our motor launch. After scrounging around they came across a wonderful souvenir, a Japanese mountain gun, dismantled it and man-handled it onboard. A suitable box was made, the gun packed in it, and after arriving back in an Australian port in 1944 it was entrained to the town of Shepparton. There it was mounted in the park where it remained before being refurbished and placed in their museum.

Another story about comfort parcels. While in Townsville doing a boiler clean, half the ship's company were given two days' leave, while those remaining had to carry out various jobs such as storing the ship. We did this by lining up and passing the stores hand-over-hand until they were safely stowed below. On the truck this day was a large tea chest marked 'Comfort Fund' so the truck was unloaded in smart time. The chest was bundled down below to the mess decks and we were just like a lot of kids on Christmas morning.

'Stand clear,' called our supply PO armed with a pinch bar. Off popped the lid. 'Strewth,' he said, 'It's full of sanitary pads!' A three-badged AB from the back of the crowd called out, 'Don't send them all back Herb, keep some for my bleedin' piles.' On a closer look at the address we discovered 'WRANS', C/- Naval Depot, Townsville.

• • • • • • • • • • • • • • • • • • •

from
ROSA MILLS
GOSNELLS
WESTERN AUSTRALIA

**I** WAS A LITTLE GIRL in England at primary school during World War Two. My father was a soldier in Europe and of course there was very little money about. We were called into a class one day and told to select one toy each. I was wishing I could have a wooden 'horse', a horse's head on a stick with wheels on the bottom, but missed out on that. Instead I got a koala knitted in grey wool stuffed with cotton wool. He wore a jacket of green and a pair of fawn shorts and in his pocket was a tiny white handkerchief and an Australian sixpence.

This bear became my great friend and was loved for years until my mother— who at the time wasn't forgiven for this—gave it to my younger brother. Then my dear little brother decided to rub koala bear in the muck and so it had to go. I have often wondered about the people who made those toys, and where they came from. I came to Australia twenty-five years ago and we are now a family of Aussies. I have wondered if I have been to where my koala bear came from.

Anzac Day is here and once again I set to wondering about a brass plate I saw in London. It was on the fence of The Horse Guards quarters near Buckingham Palace and it read:

from
Bob Nicol
Armidale
New South Wales

> In Memory of Gunner Arthur Sullivan VC
> 9th April 1937
> Killed whilst serving as a representative
> of his country at the Coronation of George VI
> By his comrades of Australian coronation contingent

I wonder how he was killed. I have heard an extraordinary explanation about how he was on his way to distribute the ashes of a fellow VC on the Thames river and was run over by a bicycle!

All of the coronation contingent were VC holders, and the mate whose ashes he was to spread was to have been there, but he had died before the trip, expressing beforehand a wish that his ashes be spread on the Thames.

· · · · · · · · · · · · · · · · · · ·

Over the past couple of weeks you have had many people talking with you about this being fifty years of peace. I will be fifty years of age on 8 June. My father, Corporal Joe Martin, was killed in action on Bougainville Island on 12 February 1945 so I never ever got to meet him. He was in the 31/51 Battalion. My mum tells me about the time when my dad, who had spent eighteen months on Thursday Island, got wind that they were to be deployed and could not get leave to come home before they left, so he went AWOL. If he had not done that, I would not be writing to you today! Apparently he was quite a good carpenter, and when he went back his CO asked him to build a very strong, inescapable pen. When he'd finished it they put him in it! I often wonder about him and do console myself that I am not alone. I know my mum had a very hard time but she eventually married again, a great fellow, who has been wonderful to me.

from
Merle Moss
Newman
Western Australia

*Percy Tresize, Aerial Ambulance Pilot from Cairns, describing some of his flights:*
'One trip I was flying a DH-86 under low cloud at tree-top level. I was so scared I couldn't spit.'

In your second book there is an article marking the fiftieth anniversary of the Japanese invasion of Sydney Harbour by way of torpedoes and small submarines. Most stories tell about boats and naval activities, but may I add my story with a human flavour.

from
Beryl Wicks
Armidale
New South Wales

On 24 May 1942 my baby daughter was born in the George 5th Hospital which is right in the heart of Sydney. Very early on 31 May lights suddenly lit up our ward and a female person clad in dressing gown and slippers said to us, 'Ladies, I am your matron, I am very sorry to disturb you so early, but during the night we had a red alert and the Japanese have invaded our harbour. So I want you all to put on your gowns and slippers and sit on the edge of your beds in readiness. When you hear the siren each one is to go down to the nursery, collect your baby and wait there.' Prince Alfred Hospital was on the opposite side of the street to King George Fifth and apparently a tunnel was built connecting both hospitals. The matron said that we and our babies were to be shunted down this tunnel until the all clear was sounded. We sat in awe all that day just waiting, but fortunately nothing further happened. When we saw matron next in her crisp, snow-white uniform and long white veil it was hard to imagine it had been the same person.

• • • • • • • • • • • • • • • • • • •

from
TED MCPHEE
BELL
QUEENSLAND

IN ALL THE CELEBRATIONS of the ending of World War Two, I wonder how much thought has been given to those fourteen to fifteen year old telegram messengers, boys and girls, who delivered urgent telegrams from the War Ministry. The telegrams with something like 'It is with deep regret'.

I left in early March 1945, my parents' secluded dairy farm near Bell in Queensland to start work in Kingaroy as a Junior Postal Officer. (They had glorified names even in those days!) I was fourteen-and-a-half years old. One day an urgent telegram arrived advising that a certain person's fiance had been killed in action. I had to deliver this and on the way hoped that her mother would answer the door. Unfortunately mother didn't answer but the girl herself. I can still see today the state of shock and disbelief on that girl's face. So during these times of celebrations, remember those very young people who just had to deliver those sad telegrams.

• • • • • • • • • • • • • • • • • • •

from
KERRY A. SMITH
BARGARA
QUEENSLAND

A COUPLE OF WEEKS AGO, on the Sunday prior to Anzac Day, a caller spoke to you briefly about the Korean War and its veterans, and you said that perhaps other veterans would phone in. I tried desperately to phone as there were a number of facts which I wished to be made known, but alas I could not make contact. The Korean War, like the Malaysia/Borneo confrontations, is indeed, the forgotten war. Most people seem to think that the Vietnam War followed World War Two. Here are some facts about that war which I was a part of as a nineteen-year-old.

1    Those who served in Korea were all regular, full-time service-people who had volunteered to do the job.

2    Over 16,000 Australian service-people served, including the 1st, 2nd and 3rd Battalions of the Royal Australian Regiment, the RAAF with 77 Squadron and supporting elements, and the RAN with eleven ships in Korean waters, eight of which served two tours.

3    The War lasted just short of three years with 339 Australians killed, 1,216 wounded and 29 POWs.

4    On our return from Korea in April 1954 we marched through Brisbane feeling proud of our efforts for our country, yet some of us were spat on and called 'killers' by minority groups. So Vietnam Vets are not the only ones to have suffered indignities.

5. Some forty-two years after the cessation of hostilities the Korean Veterans have still not been honoured with an official War Memorial.

So many of the Korean Vets. have felt for so long that they are the forgotten ones. Hopefully they may be recognised and remembered for the job they did under extremely difficult conditions.

•••••••••••••••••••

A REFERENCE TO KOREA MADE me prick up my ears, for my Salvation Army leaders posted us there in the early seventies. I thought I would tell you of an experience there. To mark Anzac Day the Trade Commissioner invited us to visit Kapyong for a remembrance service. There were about forty of us present and a fine service was shared at a beautiful Anzac memorial which had been built in the very centre of the Korean village.

In 1951 an Australian force shared in the defence of this village which was wiped out. Many Australians died and were wounded. The villagers never forgot and themselves erected the memorial and built their little grass-roofed cottages all around. At the service they quietly and respectfully stood by.

from
ALISTAIR &
MARGERY CAIRNS
REDCLIFFE
QUEENSLAND

•••••••••••••••••••

IT WAS A PLEASURE TO hear Col Joye and also to hear of his efforts to help kids with cancer. Not many people would know that Col, along with Little Pattie, was the backbone of Australian entertainment for the troops in Vietnam during the years of this country's involvement there. In 1966, when I was stationed at Vung Tau with 9 Squadron, RAAF, we were tasked to take the Col Joye concert party to Nui Dat to entertain the troops and then fly them back for a concert in Vung Tau. The month was August and the date was the 16th. The concert at Vung Tau didn't happen that night. The reason was that at a village called Long Tan all hell broke loose. Our choppers became committed elsewhere as a result. We managed to fly the concert party back to Vung Tau, except Col Joye who stayed behind. He helped in practical terms by dispensing coffee and cheer at the Nui Dat army base, keeping spirits up and providing that so-necessary sanity link.

The stories that don't make the history books are those like the Col Joye story. He stayed behind to help.

from
DAVE COLLINS
DARWIN
NORTHERN TERRITORY

•••••••••••••••••••

## A CHILD'S VIEW

My Daddy's helping win the war
In some land far away
And Mummy says I must be good
for he'll come home one day.
I wonder who my Daddy is
He left when I was one
Now I am big for I've turned six
And still he hasn't come.

from
LES BARTLETT
(B. M. LUNT'S FATHER)
WANNEROO
WESTERN AUSTRALIA

We had to hide at school today
Sit in a nearby ditch
Then if the air raid warning sounds
We'll hide without a hitch.
The boys are making nets to send
To hide the men at war
The girls have made survival bags
If bombs land at our door.

From pages of *The Broadcaster*
We cut out funny jokes
To send to all our fighting men
And make them happier blokes!
My Gran and Mum and all my Aunts
Have knitted socks galore
They have written many letters
Sent parcels by the score.

When playing on the porch today
A man came to our house
He called my name—I turned away
Then Mummy heard his voice.
They were surprised, they kissed and cried
And looked at one another.
I ran inside, it scared me so
'Twas Daddy with my Mother.

*B. M. Lunt*

from
DOROTHY B. WATT
BRIAGOLONG
VICTORIA

## ANZAC DAY

When men come marching down the street
With shoulders squared and heads held high,
They march, their fallen mates to greet
On Anzac Day, they're marching by.

They may be old with hair turned grey,
Their shoulders stooped with years of toil,
Once they were boys who marched away
To fight for peace on foreign soil.

The watchers waiting in the park
Don't notice how those lads have changed,
They hear the Duty Sergeant's bark,
As round the Cenotaph they're ranged.

With each command the men comply,
A little stiff, a little slow,
But still they are alert and spry
As once they were so long ago.

The bugle sounds and time stands still,
For just two minutes silence reigns
In honour of each Tom and Bill
Who sacrificed their worldly claims.

But in our hearts they live again,
Not old and grey but young and free,
The memory of them will remain
Enshrined in Freedom's history.

## G'day, this is Macca

CARMEL: Macca, I rang to tell you that I've just been on the trip of a lifetime. I was born in Quilpie and I went all the way back there by train. It was absolutely wonderful. I had a day in Brisbane and caught the train again that night. It only goes as far as Charleville now and the railways run a bus from there to Quilpie. Oh, it was beautiful out there: they'd had some rain and the place was just alive with flowers of every colour you could imagine. It was about 210 kilometres from Charleville to Quilpie so I had a good view out the window. When I got there I went on to the properties, but I didn't get to the one where I was born because there just wasn't time, even though I had ten days out there.
MACCA: It must have been great. Carmel, where do you live?
CARMEL: I live at Westmead in Sydney now. I came to the program you did in the Parramatta Park.
MACCA: Oh, right, and you had that lovely little Aboriginal painting for me. How long since you left Quilpie?
CARMEL: Oh, don't ask me on the air! It'd be about sixty years ago.
MACCA: And was it a good return?
CARMEL: Oh, it was wonderful. The hospitality, and talking to everybody.
MACCA: And they've had lots of rain out there.
CARMEL: Yes, they have, and they asked me to come again when there's another drought!
MACCA: Isn't that nice. It's a long way from Brisbane.
CARMEL: Yes, it is. I came back in the day train from Brisbane to Sydney and I'd never imagined that there was so much beauty out there; I didn't read, I just gazed out the window.
MACCA: You should have told me you were going; I'd have gone with you! There's something nice about sitting in a train and watching the world go by.
CARMEL: Oh, yes, and meeting those wonderful people out in the bush.
MACCA: Are you still painting? Did you get any inspiration out there?
CARMEL: I did. I've started on one I'm calling 'The Road Goes on Forever', because that's just what it seems like, and on either side there's the red soil and the flowers and the trees, and the air's so fresh . . .

MACCA: Carmel, stop, because in a minute I'll walk out of here and go!

CARMEL: The second night I was there I saw a bright light outside the bedroom window and I pulled the curtain back and I never saw so many millions of stars in all my life; you could almost put out your hand and touch them.

MACCA: The best things in life are free. Thanks for calling us, Carmel.

* * *

*Arthur Morris, an outstanding Australian batsman, was asked on being inducted into Melbourne's Sports Hall of Fame:*

'How does it feel to be inducted?'

Morris replied, 'I steer clear of any word with "duck" in it.'

* * *

# 14

# **W**omen and men of the cloth

from
REV. GARY SHEARSTON
HAY
NEW SOUTH WALES

YOU WILL, I HOPE, be pleased to know that the Anglican priest in the Parish of Hay says 'strewth' perhaps more times than he ought, abhors the insistent use of 'guys' by sportscasters describing whatever's going on 'out there', estimates measurement in feet and inches and distance in miles (though with the amount of travel I do, I'm forced to think of so many kilometres to such-and-such). All of which, I guess, makes me a paid-up member of the Australian Dinosaurs' Club. Ah, well . . . Amen. (Which means, 'so be it'.)

•••••••••••••••••••

from
SR URSULA GILBERT
DUBLIN
IRELAND

GREETINGS FROM DUBLIN! What prompts me to write is something very dear to my heart. On the second weekend in February, the little bush place where we lived—Tolmie near Mansfield, in the beautiful mountains of Victoria — will be celebrating its 100th Sports.

I claim that Tolmie was 'founded' by Ned Kelly because after he was hanged the government decided that the area must be opened up for close settlement so that no more bushrangers could hide there. The early settlers came from other parts of the state and from overseas—Italy, Scotland, Ireland. Our family went to live there in 1945. We have all moved away but kept our love for the place.

Dublin reminded me of Mansfield a few weeks back with the snow on the nearby hills. The lead-up to Christmas here is fun. In Henry Street there is a great entertainer who sells 'gold' chains. He squats (ready to run) and places them carefully on a piece of red velvet. A crowd always gathers and he says something like this: 'Now look here. What you see is what you get. This one is worth £14.00; this one—this is my favourite—is worth £12.00—this one which the young ones like is worth £16.00. £42.00! I'll sell them all to you for £4.99. Don't ask me where I got them and I won't ask you where you got your money. Actually, they fell off a low-flying aircraft. See! I put them into this bag—with these earrings and this bracelet. There are more carats in that little bag than all of the vegie shops. If you love your wife you'll buy her one; if you love someone else's wife like I do, you'll buy two.'

P.S. There's an old Sister in Mildura in Victoria who must go to Mass on Saturday night so that she can be in bed with Macca on Sunday morning!

••••••••••••••••••••

THE LOCAL ONE-STOP SHOP

from
SR VERONICA
MCSWEENEY
NUNDAH
QUEENSLAND

Often on 'Australia All Over' you advocate supporting the corner shop. Enthused by this, I did call at our 'One Stop Shop' on Buckland Road, Nundah. The gentleman behind the counter and I had a laugh together as I spoke of you and your support of such convenience stores. He said he always enjoys Sunday mornings with you, then said, 'Try me!' as I wondered if he would be able to supply my needs. To each of the following, he chuckled a 'Yes'. Who can get a chuckle from a supermarket shelf? The list was white cotton, a pencil sharpener, blue shoe laces, correction fluid, Colgate toothpaste, and there was another that I can't think of right now. So I got everything I needed, plus a most enjoyable encounter with a person behind a counter.

•••••••••••••••••••

BUSH TURKEY CHEEK

from
TINA GREENWOOD
LANDSBOROUGH
QUEENSLAND

One big trouble for me up here at Landsborough is the bush turkey. I had been hoping secretly that some neighbours would have had it for Christmas dinner, but there it was on my return to my country retreat—from the rat-race of suburbia—waddling by, apparently impervious to the nearness of people or dogs. It had a red head, a yellow band around the neck and a black body. The yellow band around the neck is loose and could be described as a collar. I have seen it flapping about with the turkey's movements. And what has stirred up my anger and annoyance with the darned pest?

When I found pumpkins growing through the wire on top of my mulch heap (the wire was to stop the turkeys eating the lot) I decided to plant them. I started a new bed with a good supply of mulch, cow manure and dead leaves and, after planting them covered it with more dead grass and leaves. On my return from suburbia I found that the little garden bed was gone—the ground bare. What's worse the turkey had moved in next door! A firefighter had cleared quite a bit of land next to mine and had made a nice big pile of all the cuttings. So the turkey had moved in from the state forest across the road.

After I planted cabbage tree palms, I went to get some of the cuttings from the big pile to put around them. And that was when I discovered the area had become the bush turkey's territory. As I started taking cuttings and putting them into my bucket, a turkey rushed to the top of the pile, turned its back and began scratching feverishly at the cuttings so that they were flying all over me. Was I angry with such cheek! I found a long stick to chase it away but it kept coming back until I found a stick long enough to give it a good wallop. Ho!

Hum! It's rather pathetic to realise that scratching is its only defence!

*Sent in by Sr Veronica McSweeney of* Over the Top with Jim *fame. Tina has been deaf since age eleven and following an accident a few years ago is partially blind.*

*A priest describing the Force 7 gale he got caught in up north:*
*'I got out the rosary beads and the vodka and tried them both.'*

## LOST

from
MARY MARTIN
BAUPLE
QUEENSLAND

One local Church,
Last seen Sunday night,
Sitting looking cute and bright.

I waited patiently to hear back from those supposed to care,
To let me know if I might put that Church on another site.
It had to go from its place where it was at,
Ninety-five years is how long it's sat.

I waited for the phone to ring and checked for a note in the post,
To let me know if I might bring the old building home to rest,
Filled in time checking up if banks would help me to shift and fix
Another old grand building full of memories,
Finally I could wait no more. I picked up the phone to find out clear
What would happen to that old building so dear?
'Sorry didn't you know that the men are up there pulling it down,'
Goodbye to history of this town,
My stomach feels all tied in knots
I can't seem to make any sense,
I feel like I've just put to rest an old friend, one of the very best.

It's a sad futility to think about what might have been
Years of people from around the world enjoying
A glimpse of Bauple's past,
Reaching out and touching people in some future years,
Speaking to them of how it is that love and caring in our town abounds.

So now I wonder to myself if those boards that made up that little church
Are somehow crying in the night,
For the chance they nearly had for their glory to go on
Instead there's only silence from old songs.

• • • • • • • • • • • • • • • • • • •

from
REV. CANON
FRANK WATTS
SOUTH YUNDERUP
WESTERN AUSTRALIA

*Text: Acts 2:14*
*Peter stood up with the eleven*
*and was bold.*

O great and mystic game of Cricket;
There's no other sport can lick it.
Straight from God's Eternal Halls
Came those red and seam stitched balls.
Behold the stumps—note three there be
Clear symbol of the Trinity.
Of bails it's plain there are but two
As Testaments both Old and New

Who are these Angels dressed in white
Whose powers immense decide your plight.
They never sleep nor harbour doubt,
But give you guard and point you *out.*

Much prayer to Heaven is swiftly sent;
Tho' oft with slightly selfish bent.
The batsman seeks his Paradise—
'A wicket flat and slow—no flies.'
The bowler carves a different heaven;
Where cracks and bumps his skills will leaven.

The game must last beyond our years
Perfected midst celestial spheres.
Verily! Eternity's its milieu—
So with joy may it ever fill yer.
For over and over, Amen

*Canon de Batton-Ball*

• • • • • • • • • • • • • • • • • •

THIS MORNING I HEARD you read a letter from a lady who had seen a 'moonbow'. I was very happy to hear that someone else had a similar experience that I had out in the middle of the Pacific. We were travelling by canoe from North Tabiteuea to South Tab on the lagoon. We had set out at about 5 pm at high tide, but about 11 pm the tide was going out and it started to rain lightly. As we were about to get out of the canoe to make our way onto land I saw it. The moonbow was high in the sky opposite the moon. It was a marvellous sight. Any time I mentioned this experience to fishermen none of them had ever seen it. So I was delighted this morning to hear someone here in Australia had seen it.

from
SR MERRILYN LEE
OLSH CONVENT
MASCOT
NEW SOUTH WALES

• • • • • • • • • • • • • • • • • •

THANK YOU SO MUCH for the wall poster and the signed greeting. I immediately moved my portrait of the Pope to a lesser location and my original of the 'Mona Lisa' ended up behind the fridge in the kitchen. Now as each person walks through my reception area the first thing they see is 'Macca'. Some swoon, some faint with excitement, others just stand and stare. The burning question on all lips, 'Is he really like that?' My reply, 'Ah well, you must remember that was taken a long time ago.' Various amounts of money have been suggested by adoring fans, and such is our worry that a security company keeps a careful eye on this old relic, I beg your pardon, this wonderful photo poster!

from
FATHER BRIAN
WEST PERTH
WESTERN AUSTRALIA

*Geoff of Tumbarumba, New South Wales, Uniting Church minister rang in about mobile phones:*
'This bloke in the front seat of the church got a call on his mobile in the middle of my sermon and carried on a five-minute conversation. I think I'll put up a sign: The only connection you need in this place is with God — no mobile phones allowed.'

## G'day, this is Macca

CAROLINE: It's Caroline Paul ringing from Argentina.

MACCA: Isn't it strange, we just had a call this morning from the Amazon. Where are you from, Caroline?

CAROLINE: I'm from Bahia Blanca in the province of Buenos Aires. I'm an exchange student this year from Phillip Island in Victoria.

MACCA: I can tell from your pronunciation of Buenos Aires that you've picked it up and got right into the spirit of things.

CAROLINE: Oh, yes. It's a beautiful country. I went on two tours, one to Northern Argentina to one of the world's largest waterfalls—very spectacular—and then to Southern Argentina to see the world's largest moving glacier.

MACCA: That would be really interesting. I've got too many things to do here in Australia, but I suppose if I went anywhere I'd like to go to South America. It must be a marvellous place.

CAROLINE: It's spectacular. I've only got a few weeks left so I thought I'd take the opportunity to ring you and say g'day.

MACCA: Tell us your greatest impressions of living in Argentina.

CAROLINE: I've learned a lot and it's been the best year of my life. Obviously there are times when I miss home; how can you not miss Australia? But my impressions are of the people, my friends, the spectacular places to see—it's a beautiful country to travel. This year was fantastic. I just can't even begin to describe some things. I hope to study tourism next year, which means that I'll be able to come back to Argentina a little faster than usual.

MACCA: And then what—travel the world?

CAROLINE: Oh, in my dreams, but it is possible. That's what I've learned this year—the world is possible. I've lived with three families and so I've learned new customs with each family, which has been brilliant.

MACCA: It's good for everyone, I think, to see another culture. I often think it'd be good for country kids to come to the city and vice versa.

CAROLINE: That's right. It opens your eyes. You see a lot more and you learn a lot, too.

MACCA: Well that's good. Hope to see you sometime. It was lovely to talk to you.

CAROLINE: It's fantastic to hear an Australian voice.

# 15

# *T*hings are crook in Tallarook!

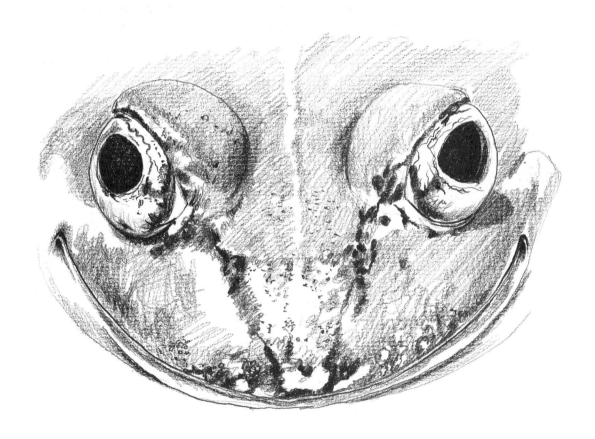

from
DAVID BEARUP
GUYRA
NEW SOUTH WALES

## GET WITH THE STRENGTH

Bugger the bush! said the boss of the bank, I've decided we're closing the door
It's profit we want, not fleeces or crop—past histories don't count any more
The top end of town, not the cockies who are down, the bank is wishing to nurture
To drive forty K to pick up your pay, that most certainly won't hurt ya
From the 49th floor, on a million or more, I've important decisions to take
About dining at Doyles, on some of the spoils, from various cronies who make
Their principal caper, the shuffling of paper, the floating of stocks and shares
From the room of the board, raking in a nice hoard, if it sinks or swims who cares
I've 'Down Sized' the staff, to just over half, most blokes over forty redunded
By trying to collar, the very last dollar, that's how a balance sheet's funded
It's the numbers I need, for the 'bottom line' greed, the almighty dollar my God
How the bush can depend, so much on a friend, is something that I find quite odd
You came as the strength, now deserted at length, as adieu I give a white feather
A stab in the back, seems par for your track, a companion for only fair weather
At my grand final muster, should my friends choose to cluster, to hear whom I'm
    wishing to thank
Of those who chipped in, for life's ways thick and thin, I'll write:
    Bugger the Boss of the Bank.

. . . . . . . . . . . . . . . . . . .

from
DAVE BURTON
PETRIE
QUEENSLAND

Once, when you had some spare money
You lent it to one of the Banks,
They gave a little interest
As just a small token of thanks.

They then advanced chunks of money
To people who needed more dough,
Who in turn paid more interest
That Banks used for running the show.

Now when you make cash deposits
They charge you account fees, what's more
They make you pay for transactions
When any you try to withdraw.

They tell you they're very caring
With what they do on your behalf,
But just how caring can they be
When they're sacking most of their staff.

They're closing most of the branches
It's cheaper, we're told, if you phone.
Instead of meeting a person,
You press buttons, at home, alone.

You're welcomed into the service,
Instructed what buttons to press,
But with account and card numbers,
You find you can't cope with the stress.

Sternly, the voice reprimands you,
Making you feel a complete fool,
Taking too long means a failure,
It's just like exams back at school.

So you hang up in frustration,
Sit down with a nice cup of tea,
Wishing for re-regulation
And the way it all used to be.

## DAYLIGHT ROBBERY

from
R. A. 'RUBE' CHAPPELL
TWEED HEADS
NEW SOUTH WALES

Two blokes withdrew some money from the Westpac Bank today
They used two guns instead of forms and made their getaway
It created mixed reactions with some folks being quite upset
While even more are elated and think it's the best thing happened yet
There's others disappointed too that the National wasn't done
It seems unfair that they missed out while Westpac had all the fun
The police allege they got away in a stolen Brumby ute
They probably thought they'd need a truck to carry all the loot
It's just as well Fig wasn't there, he'd have given those bandits hell
The National would have got touched up and Deans Superstore as well
No doubt the police will catch those blokes somewhere down the track
And they'll probably be disgruntled clients getting some interest back
The Banks think it's a shocking crime when someone steals their poke
But they rob people every day and think that it's a joke
Everything's within the law no guns or masks or stockings
They use pens and paper but the result is just as shocking
People who have worked real hard being sold up every day
While banks announcing record profits carry on their merry way
Until they change their attitude and treat people fair and square
Someone can rob them every day and precious few would care
One thing I can safely bet unless good fortune shines
It won't matter to me which bank they hit 'cause they won't get none of mine.

*R. J. Lewis*

from
JOHN WEIR
BUNDABERG
QUEENSLAND

**O**NCE UPON A TIME, the Australians and the Japanese decided to have a competitive boat race on the Brisbane River. Both teams practised long and hard to reach their peak performance. On the big day, they were as ready as they could be. The Japanese won by a mile.

Afterwards, the Australian team became very discouraged by the loss and morale sagged. Senior management decided that the reason for the crushing defeat had to be found and a project team was set up to investigate the problem and recommend appropriate action. Their conclusion: the problem was that the Japanese team had eight people rowing and one person steering. The Australian team had one person rowing and eight people steering.

Senior management immediately hired a consultancy company to do a study of the team's structure. Millions of dollars and several months later they concluded too many people were steering and not enough rowing. To prevent losing to the Japanese next year, the team structure was changed to four 'steering managers', three 'senior steering managers' and one 'executive steering manager'. A performance appraisal system was set up to give the person rowing the boat more incentive to work harder and become a key performer. 'We must give him empowerment and enrichment. This ought to do it.' The next year the Japanese won by two miles. The Australians laid off the rower for poor performance, sold off the two oars, cancelled all capital investment for new equipment and halted the development of a new craft. They then awarded high performance awards to the consultants and distributed the money raised to senior management.

• • • • • • • • • • • • • • • • • • • •

from
HELEN FULDING
KINGSCLIFF
NEW SOUTH WALES

## O'CONNOR'S REACH

I once strolled through O'Connor's Reach
From Fingal to the Break
And discovered rare Durobi trees
Beside a forest lake

They've built a highway through the land
I called O'Connor's Reach
That glorious stroke of nature's pen
Which reached down to the beach

They've ripped and wrecked O'Connor's Reach
These mindless, ruthless folk
And plundered through our heritage
As though it was some joke

Our Valley is a special gift
That rests within the grace
Of a very mystic mountain
It's a magic, magic, place

But what will happen next, dear friends
When Our Valley's torn apart
As farmers lands and sacred sites
Get a highway through their heart

Will we weep to see God's pastures
Piled dead by the dreaded snake
That will stretch from the Bridge to Brunswick
Destroying all in its wake

They'll hail it as 'real progress'
And when the deed is done
They'll cheer and say 'how great we art'
We won! We won! We won!

Well, I am but a single voice
And yet, for what it's worth
I'll fight to save this special place
Help the meek to inherit the earth

I still walk by O'Connor's Reach
With its soul laid bare and blind
To catch a glimpse of days since past
If only in my mind

## IT'S OUR ABC

from
'ME'
INVERLOCH
VICTORIA

How's things with you Macca old mate
And how's your dear old Mum,
Listen each Sunday—Enjoy every one
Am sad when your program is done.
Heard you say just a week ago,
That they've cut your staff by a third,
They've gotta be jokin' makin' three into two,
I'm sure a third's what I heard.

Who's the mug who's out of touch,
For any old fool can see,
That your Sunday Morn's the best in the land,
It's 'Australia all Over' for me.
There must be a fool with power to play,
Someone who's never tuned in,
Hope it's not Little Johnny himself,
Or the QC who needs fillin' in.

175

So Macca, I s'pose in times like this
We'll just have to find a way
To keep your show goin' at its best,
And please all in the land on a Sunday.
Infrastructure, a new word they've found,
Everyone knows what it means (!!!)
In your case it's just doin' what you do now,
So it's now I'll be spillin' the beans.

Because they tell us it's our ABC,
We'll change the rules a bit.
You have an audience—three million or more,
And to all you're a bloody great hit
Because they all like you they'll pay you a fee
A dollar a week from the lot,
You can hire your time from our ABC
And from Johnny you won't have to bot.

So from now on Macca just send us the bill,
We'll be waiting to pay.
You can please yourself what you do with the purse,
So long as we hear you each Sunday.
And if Johnny 'blues' about what you take
Tell him the owners agreed,
It's our ABC at work at its best,
Of his thoughts we have no need.

All the pollies who listen should pay more,
Their expense account is extensive,
They can pay a fiver out of the rort,
For them that's not very expensive.
You can pull down the unemployment list,
Put on a dozen or so,
To help you give us the best in the world,
Go on Macca—give it a go.

• • • • • • • • • • • • • • • • • •

## AN AILING AUNT

from
DAVID BEARUP

GUYRA

NEW SOUTH WALES

Dear old Aunty's quite unwell, she's almost Rookwood crook,
You'd be white around the gills, if you'd taken what she's took,
Lacerations and abrasions, plus cuts to ten per cent,
With a razor gang to her family, their mission seems hell bent,
On dissecting her vital organs, trying to subdue her will,
Attempting to pin her arms down, hoping her tongue will still,
Her young son little 'Triple J', a voice of youthful vision,

Seek a hollow log m'boy, you're in for circumcision,
Delicate 'National FM', no Sir Galahad to save her,
A ruthless swipe of the reaper's hook, she'll be a semi quaver,
Wilko, Sunday arvo, that's football for the bush,
Stay away from cliff tops mate, you'll cop a gentle push,
There's TV and regional radio, news, a seven-thirty report,
Hack and slash the lot of 'em, send them back real short,
…'though Aunty's on the canvas, she's far from down and out,
She'll rise to fight another day, those with political clout,
She was born to lead the infight, the stoushes and the biffin',
Which puts the noses out of joint, around Lake Burley Griffin.

## RURAL RAMBLINGS

The rural recession has been explained in simple terms by an old time farmer who said, 'It all started back in '66 when they changed from pounds to dollars—that doubled me overdraft. Then they brought in kilograms instead of pounds—me wool clip dropped by half. After that they changed rain to millimetres and we haven't had an inch of rain since. If that wasn't enough, they brought in Celsius and we never got over forty degrees. No wonder me wheat wouldn't grow. They then changed acres to hectares and I ended up with only half the land I had. By this time I'd had enough and decided to sell out. I put the property in the agents' hands and then they changed miles to kilometres. Now I'm too far out for anyone to buy the bloody place . . .'

from
SHIRLEY O'BREE
ECHUCA
VICTORIA

## OPTUS OF THE OVERFLOW

*(With apologies to Clancy and to Banjo Paterson)*

I had written them a letter
In which I said, 'You should know better,'
Than to roll your rotten cables out
Across the wide brown land.

And an answer came, expected,
To the householder, it was directed,
'We're the men from Optus Vision
and we bring you pay TV.

'You know things you used to get for nought,
Now from us they can be bought,
It's this wonderful idea we brought
From the USA.'

And what's a bit of cable,
Strung across the kitchen table?
God, that's a small price to pay
For the best of Hollywood.

I started dreaming then of Clancy,
In my wild erratic fancy,
Gone a droving down the Canning,
In the west, where real men go.

And he's dreaming of his Mabel,
When he rides into a cable,
Strung across the Canning Stock Route
And he cries 'Well spare me days.'

And in place of his dear Mabel,
He sees miles and miles of cable,
Criss-crossin' in the Never Never
From every rock and tree.

And then a little bloke named Bert,
With Optus Vision on his shirt,
Rudely addresses Clancy,
And this is what he says:

'Clancy, we're the men from Optus Vision
And we bring you television,
Re-runs, movies, game shows,
All the news that's fit to print.

'And there's trotting and there's cricket,
Provided you have bought your ticket.
Right out there in Donga
Where the breezes come and go.

'And in place of lowing cattle
You'll see the Broncos battle
The Auckland Warriors
And the Eagles v. the Pies

'And as your stock are slowly stringing,
You can ride behind 'em singin'
The theme from
Beverly Hills 90210.

'And then you'll see our Vision Splendid,
Of our cables all suspended
And at night (oh at night Clancy)
The wondrous glory of all them movie *stars*.'

'Jeez, Bert,' says Clancy,
'But I don't think I fancy
Any of that I love Nancy, or is it Lucy?
And all them TV shows.

'I don't wanna see the Broncos battle
I'd just as sooner 'ave me cattle,
You can keep your TV programs
If it's all the same to you.'

I am sitting in my cosy little cottage,
Where an endless line of cable,
Hangs down
Between the houses tall.

From Tasmania to Broome
And soon up to the Moon,
We can hang our washing out to dry,
On the Optus washing line.

And if you see some cables hanging from
The goal post at Moorabbin
Or at Lang Park or the Wacca,
Then you'll know who put 'em there.

And I somehow rather fancy
We all feel the same as Clancy,
Say *no* to Optus Vision
And who owns those telegraph poles?

And the language uninviting on those programs,
Just *keep* writing.
Yeah I doubt he'd watch much TV,
Clancy of the Overflow.

*Macca*

. . . . . . . . . . . . . . . . . . . . . . . . . . . . . . . . . . . . . . . . . . . . . . . . . . . . . . . . . . . . . . . . . . . . . .

*Cliff Hardy, a stock and station agent, in an interview with Macca:*
'The last two things to leave in a drought are the emus and the stock and station agents—
in that order.'

. . . . . . . . . . . . . . . . . . . . . . . . . . . . . . . . . . . . . . . . . . . . . . . . . . . . . . . . . . . . . . . . . . . . . .

IT'S THE EARLY HOURS of the morning and I'm up writing to you because the train song is going round and round my head and I thought, 'It's that McNamara's fault! I'll get up and make him read one of my letters.' And it's that Penny Davies' fault too, because the particular part of the song that's keeping me awake is the

from
JIM BUTLER
PARKES
NEW SOUTH WALES

chorus where her voice goes up a bit to harmonise with Roger Illot's on '...going back to Erskineville' and all I can say is, 'Gees, I wish *I'd* written those words.' My real motive, Macca, is to thank you for the great pleasure of hearing my song 'At Bogan Gate' on your new CD. So many of these lyrics are pulling me up and making me listen to them, especially 'Beside the Railway Line', 'Travelling Showman' and 'Menindee'. Then 'At Bogan Gate' comes on and I feel like I'm in rare company.

Doesn't Jim Low's voice sound great. It's just like him. I taught next to him and he was a man and a teacher of great strength of principle and yet possessed a gentleness that drew children to him . . . the kind of man I admire most. The original poem 'At Bogan Gate' that I sent him was a fairly strong piece. When Jim put it to music, I thought, 'Well, isn't that just like the bloke. He's taken the venom out and left the story intact.'

The world and Australia in general, Macca? It's a paradigm shift. Used to be that farmers were important . . . like mothers and policemen. Now our nation turns its back on them as economic rationalists kick them off their land with the claim that the banks' shareholders really do have a right to a profit. What a load of garbage. It's about time the banks acknowledged they were risking venture capital and took responsibility for half of the risk.

• • • • • • • • • • • • • • • • • • •

from
JEAN GOADBY
MANNING
WESTERN AUSTRALIA

**T**HE REASON FOR THIS letter is to warn you! One of your songs is in danger. An endangered species. Which one? 'I Made 100 in the Backyard at Mum's'. You see, like Australia's railways, backyards are disappearing fast and soon will be no more. No-one will be able to play cricket in the backyard at Mum's or anyone else's place because there soon won't be any more backyards. Or front yards. Why?

What used to be the Town Planning code and compulsory set-back distance from fences is no more—people are dividing up their blocks, knocking down all the fences and building two, even three units on each block. No trees—no birds. Local governing authorities are loving it of course because they reap in extra rates. Making millions.

Can you imagine—two or three times as many cars—more pollution—less fresh air and gardens all cluttered up in congestion of buildings. 'Infill' it's called!

*In 1993 the drought was bad. A Victorian farmer rang in.*
MACCA: 'How're you going with this drought?'
FARMER: 'I put a sign up at the gate, "Fifty dollars or best offer" and no-one came in. Today the sign reads "Six-to-four the bushfire, or two-to-one the drought."'

from
MALCOLM REED
SYDNEY
NEW SOUTH WALES

**I**S 'AUSTRALIA ALL OVER' going to publish the ABC Guide to Regional Botanic Gardens? I have this vision that a family driving interstate will chuck the guide into the car.

The first picnic that this family has at their destination will be at the regional botanic garden, because there are samples of the local fruit trees, crops and worst weeds; there is a bed of local endangered plant species, and an explanation of why the town's streets are lined with pepper trees. As well, some beds are regrown examples of the region's pre-agriculture vegetation.

The next day, our family can drive around the tourist route signposted by the shire council and actually know what they are looking at.

I am president of the Australian Flora Foundation (a small voluntary organisation backed by various societies for growing Australian plants). Directors of the foundation are trying to orchestrate a network of regional botanic gardens to provide skilled centres for propagating endangered species around Australia.

Australia's botanic gardens are in our usual muddle of federal, state or local jurisdiction with enormous jealousies between and within levels of government. Who owns Australia's native plants? As a lecturer about plants at Macquarie University, I am constantly staggered by the number of students who are unaware of the wheat industry, the growth of vegetables, where pasta comes from, what a seed is, etc. Sometimes I think I should be teaching potato peeling.

• • • • • • • • • • • • • • • • • •

IT'S GREAT TO HEAR you giving weeds the up-front profile they need! Like many communities we have dedicated people removing weeds from open farmland and also the bush, on both private and public land. Stirling, the weed capital of the world, invites you to its special Weeds 2000 celebration from 1 December 1996 to 30 December 1999. Special events include: Blackberry Challenge Marathon—through weed-infested paddocks; Weed Dash—how many weeds can you collect in thirty seconds?; Best Weeds Display; Gorse Jumping; Most Weedy Property Competition; Count the Broom Seeds; Best Roadside Watsonia.

from
DEB CANTRILL
HEATHFIELD
SOUTH AUSTRALIA

• • • • • • • • • • • • • • • • • •

THE MAJOR WEED PROBLEM on coastal areas of eastern Australia is a plant known as Boneseed or Bitou Bush. The plant is from South Africa and is capable of completely out-competing our native flora. It was planted out deliberately by the Soil Conservation Service of New South Wales from 1946 to 1968 and by sand mining companies from 1950 to 1970 to stabilise/revegetate sand dunes.

It is worth noting that a number of Australian native plants have become weeds in other countries. There are species of wattle (acacia) which have become weeds in South Africa and *Melaleuca quinquinervia* (paperbark) is a problem in the Everglades in the USA.

from
TODD DUDLEY
ST HELENS
TASMANIA

• • • • • • • • • • • • • • • • • •

I FEEL I NEED TO REPLY to one of your listeners who expressed their sense of disempowerment and lack of influence in matters that affect them. Becoming apathetic is precisely why people become disempowered. People vote, people buy products, people accept and reject decisions. We the people as a collective body are the majority; those in positions of power and decision making are a minority relying on us to maintain those positions. It is up to us to reject detrimental decisions. We are the controllers of our destiny and until we understand this the rich and powerful will prevail.

from
GRAHAME SPEED
THE ROCK
NEW SOUTH WALES

• • • • • • • • • • • • • • • • • •

*Heather told Macca, Nunjikompita is 750 km from Adelaide.*

MACCA: 'You're pretty isolated out there.'

HEATHER: 'Not really—you're only isolated if you want to go to Adelaide or if there's something happening, but otherwise you think it's the centre of the Universe.'

### G'day, this is Macca

JEAN: G'day Macca. It's Jean from Maryborough. What I was going to say, being as it's Father's Day today, was I've got seven children and their dad went missing eighteen years ago. We've never ever heard from him or seen him and it's always a bit sad on this day when the kids want to buy him a present. They usually buy one for my brother because he's sort of been, I guess, a bit like their dad.

MACCA: Is this in response to what the bloke said 'You can't go missing in Australia'?

JEAN: Yeah, I think you can. Because we tried with Missing Persons and Social Security, Salvation Army, Australia Post and even Most Wanted. He never came forward, and he was always a really good Dad. We were always a really happy family. Just one day he walked out on seven children. The youngest was six and the eldest was nineteen.

MACCA: So that puts the lie to 'You can't disappear in Australia'.

JEAN: In those days eighteen years ago I suppose it was so easy to change your name and take on a new personality, or whatever, somewhere else if you sort of got a bit fed up with life.

MACCA: So you get a bit miserable on Father's Day, Jean?

JEAN: Yeah, and most other days during the year.

MACCA: What was his name?

JEAN: Gerry Whitefoot. An unusual name. There was only one in Melbourne. I've tried all the phone books. No, there's no others. Maybe he's listening. If somebody knows him or something…

# *H aving a yak*

from
BILL SCOTT
WARWICK
QUEENSLAND

IN THE DAYS BEFORE television and radio young people got their language and vocabulary from listening to their parents and elders; with the occasional addition of an apt phrase or word coined at the time. For instance, from the army in the Second World War we got 'pull your head in' and the expression to 'go through' or to 'shoot through like a Bondi tram', which lived on even when there were no more Bondi trams! These became part of our vernacular speech. But the never-ending bombardment of all our ears by especially Americanisms from both radio and television has led to much of the native pungency of speech being lost and replaced by imported slang, often of less vivid imagery than what was lost.

I've never heard any Americanism as apt or picturesque as the Australian 'as miserable as a bandicoot on a burnt ridge', for example. Young people seem to draw their slang vocabulary mainly from parroting catch-phrases from television series. These fads die quickly, of course; one rarely hears these times the catch-words from the Teenage Ninja Turtles like 'dude' and 'Cowabunga' that formed such a large part of children's vocabulary only ten years ago. Slang is such an ephemeral thing anyway, with few exceptions. The Sydney philologist Sidney Baker filled a lot of his definitive book *The Australian Language* with obsolete slang. But some local coinage still survives—'out past the black stump', 'in the mulga', the word 'swag' for your possessions you carry, 'muster' and 'billabong'. These remain with us though blokes have largely become 'guys' or 'dudes' and sheilas have perhaps become 'birds' (British slang, this) or even 'dames' (American). Whatever happened to 'chicks'? *That* came and went, didn't it.

•••••••••••••••••••

from
KEN BRINE
SOUTH PLYMPTON
SOUTH AUSTRALIA

I WAS INTERESTED IN your remarks about the use of the short and the long 'a'. I am seventy-one, born in Adelaide and educated at South Australian state schools until 1940. You may be surprised to learn that South Australians were taught to use the long 'a' and therefore I say 'ahnswer', 'chahnce', 'commahnd', etc. As far as I know it is still taught that way in South Australia.

The American accent was said to derive from the Irish immigrants. The Australian east coast attracted more Irish than South Australia which was largely settled by English people. The Aussie accent on the east coast has definitely changed during the past fifty years. During my army days I had trouble understanding the broad, nasal Sydney accent.

The flow of European and Asian migrants seems to be softening and modifying our accent. I wonder what it will sound like in fifty years.

•••••••••••••••••••

from
ROGER OXLEY
DENILIQUIN
NEW SOUTH WALES

I'D LIKE TO ADD MY two bob's worth on the subject of trivia associated with place names. You mentioned that Orroroo in South Australia was the only town spelt with seven letters that only has two letters in it.

Well Faulconbridge, on the Blue Mountains in New South Wales, is the only town that contains exactly half of the letters of the alphabet—with none of them repeated. What's more, it also contains all the five vowels.

•••••••••••••••••••

ON YOUR PROGRAM, you quoted a letter from a lady who claimed that the expression 'to have a kip' had something to do with kippers (the kippered herring variety, that is). I think she said it described the short naps the fishermen had between net hauling.

This view seems to be at odds with the *Shorter Oxford English Dictionary*, however, which claims that the word is from the Danish *kippe*, a mean hut; *horekippe*, a brothel. In English: 1. A brothel. 2. A common lodging house; a lodging in such a house; hence a bed 1879. Thus the verb 'to kip' means: to go to bed, sleep.

*Nuttall's Standard Dictionary* defines 'kip' as 'a cheap lodging-house, or a bed in one', with the phrase 'to kip down' meaning, to go to bed.

from
IAN D. ST G. LINDSAY
KEWARRA BEACH
QUEENSLAND

*Macca asked a Tasmanian truckie about the size of Tasmania:*
'We can never get into top gear or we'd go over the edge.'

ON TODAY'S PROGRAM MENTION was made that the word 'ripper' could have referred to a Japanese word. This reminded me of a story I recently heard on a coach trip south of Darwin. We were in an old gold mining area and the coach driver stated that in the last century the Chinese worked the fields and that the words 'fair dinkum' had their origins in this area. There was a Chinese gentleman on board who stated that a Chinese word pronounced similarly to 'dinkum' meant 'the best of gold'.

from
EARL SMITH
ASHMORE
QUEENSLAND

YOUR PIECE ON THIS morning's program re the word 'ripper' and the probable connection with Japanese pearl divers reminded me of something similar. Our Rotary district recently had a group study exchange team here from Pakistan and one member said our word 'tucker' is the Pakistan word for food. It seems to me that when Australia brought in camels and their drivers from the Afghanistan–Pakistan area to help with exploration the word 'tucker' or 'tucca' was possibly introduced into our language.

from
MAURICE DENSON
COBRAM
VICTORIA

COMEDIAN BILLY CONNOLLY's over-use of the f-word has been mentioned on your program. I thought you may be interested in the following. In Tamworth, New South Wales each year the beautiful blue Paterson's curse flower blankets the hills overlooking the town. One night someone took a lawnmower up there and cut a large f-word into the landscape which was visible for many miles around. Less than an hour after dawn the local authorities had slashed the word out. Consequently only a very few early risers actually saw it. So much effort to create something so spectacular for an hour's glory when the other four letter word 'love' could have remained splendiferous for all to see for the entire Paterson's curse season. There's a moral here that Billy Connolly could well learn, and his talent gives him neither licence nor excuse to overlook it. His persistent use of

from
LYN TOWER
MINDARIE
WESTERN AUSTRALIA

the word compels him to settle for a fraction of viewers when he could so easily enjoy a hundred per cent.

.....................

from
BETTY McLEOD
GORDON
VICTORIA

THIS MORNING I HEARD you read a letter from a lady who objects to the increasing use of gutter language, but who doesn't want to be called a 'wowser'. Well, I can assure her she is no wowser. We (five of us)—and I'm in my thirties—came from a home where gutter language was never used. No rule about it—we just never heard it in our home. Personally, I don't find any words 'shocking', but I do find that the same words used over and over and over with no real meaning make me think that the person is either too lazy or ignorant to know the meanings of many words.

.....................

from
CHRISTINA RATCLIFFE
BRUNSWICK
VICTORIA

I WONDER IF WE WILL ever pronounce Mount Kozchusko as it should be, and as you so rightly did on 22 September. If so, there may be hope for another correction—Mt Shtreletski. My stepfather was from Lithuania—one of the most highly decorated (RAF and Polish Air Force) bomber pilots in World War Two—he flew seventy-one missions. Franciczek Obush (Franscheeshek, O as in hot, and buch like Scottish loch). It's the spellings that confuse us, so let's go by the sound as spoken by the owners of the names. We could then extend the courtesy to our Aboriginal ancestors.

.....................

from
MARK DE GRAAF
CASUARINA
NORTHERN TERRITORY

EVERY NOW AND THEN mention is made on your program of an Aboriginal word and what it means. There were about 250 Aboriginal languages before 1788, so saying a word is 'Aboriginal' is about as meaningful as saying a word is 'Asian', 'African' or 'European'. Many Aboriginal words are claimed in popular writing to mean 'meeting place', or 'place of water'. Aboriginal people provide these sorts of 'broad' translations when they realise it is inappropriate or too difficult to explain the real meaning to a listener who is uneducated in the local culture and language. We should be very careful with the meaning and pronunciation of so-called 'Aboriginal' words, especially those listed in small dictionaries, popular accounts and tourist brochures. The dictionaries I am thinking of usually lump words from several or many languages together under the heading of 'Aboriginal'. The translations, which are often quite inaccurate, are generally taken from early records.

*Hilda Webb from Kilkivan, Queensland told of the local dances in the 1930s:*
'They'd put the babies down on blankets behind the band, and one night one wag swapped them all around. In those days there were few cars and fewer telephones and the babies weren't sorted out for a week.'

THERE SEEM TO BE an enormous number of people in my country who live in Austraya and are Austrayans, while I had always believed that I live in Australia, and am Australian. It's so entrenched. Many of the athletes returning from Atlanta were proud to have done their best for 'Austraya' and far too many of the radio and TV commentators were also Austrayans reporting to Austraya.

For what I regard as the obscene amount of money paid to the Institute of Sport, surely the coaches, psychiatrists, psychologists *et al.* could spend a little time pointing out that our country has an 'ell' in it.

from
JOY MCMORRINE
NORTH LAMBTON
NEW SOUTH WALES

• • • • • • • • • • • • • • • • • •

MY WIFE AND I spent about four years living in England and I would like to comment on the pronunciation question that you posed. The use of the short soft vowels in dance, transport and graph is very much a reflection of the cockney origin of much of Australian English.

The use of the long hard vowels such as in *darnce, trarnsport* and *grarph* reflects geographical and class variations of the English pronunciation. It stands to reason that Adelaide, with its lack of cockneys in the original years of its settlement, and relatively less population flux in subsequent years, would have a greater prevalence of the long hard vowel as in *darnce* and *trarnsport*.

Unfortunately it seems the use of the long hard vowel has developed as a badge of pseudo-sophistication in Australia, much the same way as one's fashion sense may send signals of sophistication, real or imagined! I think it is a tragedy as this type of class consciousness (especially as reflected in speech patterns) is something that I would hope we had left behind in Europe, as in 'Pygmalion' or 'My Fair Lady'. At least we have not yet taken on the Etonian *plarstic* for *plastic*!

My second point concerns newsreaders. I do not like them to be pretentious, but I do resent the way they say *mi'ion* (meeon) instead of *million* and *Austraya* instead of *Australia*. Pronunciation is one thing, but leaving half the word out is another.

from
IAIN FEATHER
BROADBEACH WATERS
QUEENSLAND

• • • • • • • • • • • • • • • • • •

DEAR MACCA
Believe it or not Mhaire is pronounced Moya, and Tiaro is pronounced Tie-ro, not Tee-ar-o.

from
MHAIRE ARMSTRONG
TIARO
QUEENSLAND

• • • • • • • • • • • • • • • • • •

REGARDING THE LISTENER FROM Tiaro who took you to task for your 'mispronunciation'. I have always thought you go to great lengths to ensure correct pronunciation of names. As a junior primary teacher, I teach my students that 'When two vowels go walking, the first one does the talking' (e.g. boat, snail, peach). However, I also teach them that there are exceptions to that rule. If the listener from Tiaro is correct, then for years I have been mispronouncing bias, diameter, diary, fiasco, giant, liar, piano, pliant, tiara and viaduct. I hope none of your listeners from places such as Diama, Miami or Kiandra now have an identity crisis!

from
D. W. MAGANN
REYNELLA
SOUTH AUSTRALIA

• • • • • • • • • • • • • • • • • •

from
FRANK BURKETT
CHILDERS
QUEENSLAND

Up north the good folk at Tiaro
pronounce their name like Cairo,
but after Macca's debate
they saw the mistake
and changed the name Cairo to Ciaro.

·····················

from
DAVID DONALDSON
LEEMING
WESTERN AUSTRALIA

THIS IS TO APPEAL to your love of Australian language and encourage your efforts to resist imported 'Americanisms' and other 'isms'.

A **kilo**metre (kill-o-metr) is a measure of distance (1,000 metres) as in **centi**metre, millimetre, etc.

A meter (note the spelling!) is a measuring device as in therm**ometer** (omm-it-r), baro**meter**, speedo**meter**, etc.

You will have noticed the tendency to pronounce 'kilometre' as a measure device by emphasising '**omm-it-r**'.

One wouldn't ask the shopkeeper for a 'kill-**ogg-ram**' of potatoes, would one?

Let's measure the 'wide brown land' in our own language.

····················

from
RAY THEES
VICTOR HARBOR
SOUTH AUSTRALIA

## ECCENTRIC METRICS

In 1966 with metrics we took the plunge
Old coins, measures and weights to expunge
Pennies for cents are okay I find
But some of the Metres are blowing my mind.

A Kilo's a 'keelo' whatever the rest
Add Grams or Watts for a simple test
Then why in telling the distance you're from
Does it suddenly change to sound like 'killom'.

And as for the yard and a bit that's a Metre
Whenever in use surely rhymes best with 'peter'
So I'm all mixed up and slightly bitter
To hear so many come up with 'mitter'.

So please can we halt this most strange delusion
That only in distance should we change the conclusion
Whenever 'Kilo' is used the unit's the same
A thousand metres—'keelometer' is the name.

Still unconvinced and not too clear?
Try the alternative sounds on your ear
'millimitters' and 'centimitters' could follow this trend
Even 'killogrims'—where would it end?

One for luck—'killossiccles'!

CAN YOU BELIEVE IT! The language polluters have been at it again. The Canberra bureaucrats have imported 'rangelands' from the good old US of A to describe the outback, inland, far west, back o' Bourke, interior, beyond the black stump and all those beaut Australian words we have used for two hundred years. When 'rangelands' crept into the jargon on ABC rural programs I wondered what the dickens they were referring to. I thought I had traced the perpetrator of this assault on our heritage when I heard a Dr Someone on one of these programs. He had an American accent and used the term repeatedly. But now I find that it has official sanction from Canberra.

from
LES SULLIVAN
PAMBULA BEACH
NEW SOUTH WALES

•••••••••••••••••••••

THERE IS NO DOUBT that the Broncos could have been better named. Would the 'Brumbies' have been an acceptable name to football followers? Probably not. *The Macquarie Dictionary* defines a brumby as a 'wild horse, especially one descended from runaway stock'. Not enough of the purebred about that name. It would have been an interesting experiment, however. Courageous, I think Sir Humphrey would have called it.

from
ROGER SCOTT
PETRIE
QUEENSLAND

In a current TV advertisement for a farm ute we are told that it 'don't look no different' (sic). This sentence contains two pieces of bad grammar, both of which are common in vernacular American English. The one which particularly concerns me both as an Australian and as a teacher is the double negative, whereby the literal meaning communicated is exactly the opposite to the one intended. Double negatives may have been around for years, but they are now very common in popular songs, especially American songs. Mick Jagger apparently got 'no satisfaction', but instead sang that he could not get no satisfaction. There is not a lot we can do about imported music, but do we need them in home-grown national television advertisements?

P.S. I have just heard some demonstrators chanting (on TV): 'One two three four, we don't want no nuclear war!' Somehow, I don't think they really mean what they are actually saying.

•••••••••••••••••••••

THIS MORNING I HEARD you speaking about 'blokes' and 'mates' and that awful word 'guys'.

The word 'guy', to me, conjures up a sort of androgynous person, especially as I've heard it used in a mixed group ('Hey, you guys') and in both male and female groups. So you see a 'guy' would be no substitute for a 'bloke' since a 'bloke' can only refer to a man. No 'bloke', no real blokes, would stand for it— or for quiche either for that matter—we all know what 'real' men don't eat, don't we?

from
HEATHER HASTINGS
ALBION PARK
NEW SOUTH WALES

Like many others I'm relieved that the word 'vulnerable' seems to have been 'vunnerbled' to death. I now look forward to the demise of the rash of apostrophes which besprinkle all our plurals. All around me are examples orange's and apple's (the orange's sometimes referred to as navel's) and this beauty: 'sallard bowl's for sale'.

•••••••••••••••••••••

<table>
<tr><td>

from

DENNIS PHILLIPS

BINALONG BAY

TASMANIA

</td><td>

**M**Y PRINCIPAL REASON FOR writing is to comment on the word 'gotten'. I am reading a book *Cromwell—Our Chief of Men* by Antonia Fraser. In it she quotes from a letter written in 1651: 'I bles the Lord I am safe gotten into Scot Land.' (Original spelling preserved.) It would appear that the word gotten was therefore in use in the UK in the seventeenth century and may not be the Americanism it is thought to be.

As a 'neutralised' Australian (ex-Pom) I am as keen as you to keep our Australian (English) language free of the insidious influx of American jargon words.

</td></tr>
</table>

• • • • • • • • • • • • • • • • • • • •

<table>
<tr><td>

from

MARY WILSON

SOMERVILLE

VICTORIA

</td><td>

**B**EING OF THE OLDER GENERATION I still use a number of terms which I have to explain to the youngsters of today. The word 'mikalonial' that my family used fairly frequently seems to have gone right out of use. It is pronounced like 'my colonial' with both words running together. It was used to register pleasant agreement. An example could be, 'Like to come fishing?' and the answer would be 'mikalonial'. It is definitely a 'strine' word and is actually shortened from 'my colonial oath'. That form was a variation of 'my bloody oath' which was shortened to 'bloody oath' or 'me blood'. We always referred to 'my colonial oath' as the 'stuck up' form.

</td></tr>
</table>

• • • • • • • • • • • • • • • • • • •

<table>
<tr><td>

from

DAVE OLIN

SAN PEDRO

USA

</td><td>

**I**T IS TRUE THE American media is an all-pervasive influence throughout the world, and more often than not I cringe at what it puts out. Indeed, it paints my home town of Los Angeles as some sort of 'crack shooting, everyone's gun toting' latter-day 'Dodge City', which it isn't.

I hear Australians whingeing over the use of the word 'guys' over 'blokes', suggesting it is the death knell of your local idiom. But I can assure you that many of your language patterns are intact judging from the number of times I have had to ask what a word or phrase means. An example is the word 'rort' which is not found in the American Websters or the English Oxford dictionaries I've looked in.

The only constant about language is that it is always changing. Thankfully we have scholars and writers who study and use contemporary idiomatic language to help preserve the cream of colloquialisms, the spice of the idiom. The yarns, poems and songs on your program go a long way in keeping your 'lingo' going.

</td></tr>
</table>

• • • • • • • • • • • • • • • • • • • • • • • • • • • • • • • • • • • • • • • • • • • • • • • • • •

*When Adrian Scott, the Dalby, Queensland, ABC rural reporter, retired after twenty-three years, a chap phoned in from Peekadoo:*
'We'll be sorry to see him go. He keeps people regular in the morning.'

• • • • • • • • • • • • • • • • • • • • • • • • • • • • • • • • • • • • • • • • • • • • • • • • • •

# Consult your maps!

from
JACK EVANS
RAPID CREEK
NORTHERN TERRITORY

# COUNTRY TOWNS

The country towns are dying, many lives have had to change
Folks left no choice but start again, to them so very strange

They centralised our banking, they centralised our health
People now don't matter as they centralise the wealth

When they closed our railways, we didn't ever get a say
Railways were once our lifelines and stations, centres of their day

They consolidate our councils, they consolidate our schools
They think that lives don't matter, they treat us much like fools

They closed Letona Cannery, they closed the one at Ky
The growers plus the workers just kissed their dreams goodbye

The pollies keep complaining of cities too large to cope
They seek the wrong solutions, they give us little hope

'Decentralisation' once an in-word, but nothing really done
The country towns still failing, they're failing one by one

Their hospitals are closing, the doctors they won't come
Everyone so selfish, looking after number one

The rural schools are closing, a real concern for us
To the nearest large school centre, the kids all go by bus

The grocers once delivered, the bakers did this too
They personalised their service, they looked after me and you

Our bakers now have vanished, the bread's transported in
Our bread is sliced, we still have a choice, between the thick and thin

The businesses gave credit, especially in a drought
Our ability to pay up, they never seemed to doubt

Our roads today are really great but take customers away
To the city supermarket, seeking specials of the day

Country towns that once we knew, again we'll never see
At times I love to ponder about those towns that used to be.

*A caller's suggestion for Bob and Blanche's much publicised union:*
'It's customary to throw sugared almonds at weddings, but at this one you'd better throw blanched hazelnuts.'

## THE JOY OF JUNEE

from
COL WHITE
INNISFAIL
QUEENSLAND

I got up early and made my cuppa tea
Tuned in to Macca—he was in Junee.
Early on we heard Neil Murray, Smacka Fitzgibbon and Ted Egan
A good start and chances of a great morning were much better than even.

In Junee it was round zero and that is pretty cool
A wallaby had fallen into Jenny's swimming pool.
The room was overflowing, they were cooking on the lawn.
John reckons he knew every pothole in town since before he was born.

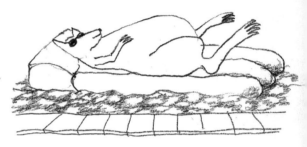

Rita remembered Junee station, her dad was the cook
We heard of other refresh rooms where the food was pretty crook.
Malcolm used to have lambs fry and bacon in the rest room
I think I can smell some more cooking—it should be ready soon.
I think I can smell something else too, think it might be Jaffles
I know that Graham, the Pear Man, is giving away his apples.

Alan, from Stawell, phoned up from the mine
Dr Frank rang from Germany, he's canoeing on the Rhine.
Ken called from Jakarta and talked about his cars.
One of these days, I reckon, we might get a call from Mars.

Janice talked about a bike ride when she was dressed up as a boy
Macca had Clifton the Wombat—wonder if that's his newest toy?
Vince bought a home in Junee on the cheap
The price he paid—it made us all weep.

Betty said she was nervous, but her voice was unwavering and clear
She told a remarkable story of her misfortune in a war year.
She was shot, lost a leg, but with support from Dad and Mum
She recovered, came back home, and kicked Billy Baxter in the bum.

Helen had some eggs that were cracked, decided it was time to bake
And she presented Macca with a double-tiered sponge cake.
I wonder if Macca forced it all down his gob
Or—maybe—he shared it with the rest of the mob.

There was plenty of live music, and wasn't it just grand
Didn't you just love the Wagga accordion band.
Larry and his group were there to give the show some zing
Boy, don't they know how to make a good tune swing.

Macca sang along—he was in good tone
He didn't enrich us by playing his trombone.
The Australian Army Band Vocal Ensemble sang perfectly in tune.
At Junee now the sun was slowly rising, replacing the sinking moon.

Gary Shearston came all the way from Hay
He drove through the night to be there for the day.
He has a resonant voice, lovely and firm and clear
Sings songs that to my heart at least, are just so near and dear.
He sang 'Shopping on a Saturday in 1945'
A great nostalgic song—and we all heard it live.

Did you know who was back on the job?
She was in the studio—yes—it was our Rob.
And didn't we all rejoice
To hear again her lovely Australian voice.
Her Mum and her Aunty were in the hall
Like the rest—they were having a ball.
Macca introduced his crew—gave them a good rap.
The crowd gave Perce a wonderful clap.
The entire program sounded like so much fun
If Junee wanted more fans—they've got them—put me down as one.

* * * * * * * * * * * * * * * * * * * * * * * * * * * * * * * * * * * * * * * * * * * * * * * * * * *

*Alec Pike, gold prospector of Western Australia, told how when he played his harmonica at night,
Aborigines would come and sit at the edge of the light from his campfire:
'I'd give them some tucker and they'd share it—it's communism without the nasties.'*

* * * * * * * * * * * * * * * * * * * * * * * * * * * * * * * * * * * * * * * * * * * * * * * * * * *

| from |
| T. A. BYRNE |
| NORTH PARRAMATTA |
| NEW SOUTH WALES |

## SMALL TOWNS

'Oh! the foetid air and gritty
of the dusty, dirty cities—'
Banjo's words keep ringing in my head
And I'd love to leave these places
See again the open spaces
And the small towns
Of the Western watershed.

I'd give heaps to hear the rattle
Of the stock yards and the cattle
And the ringers
crackin' whips and shoutin' curses
'Stead of listenin' to the cackle
And the everlasting prattle
Of the doctors and the inmates
And the nurses.

Me legs won't take me further now
Than the toilet down the hall
Where I sit and cry in solitude
Read the writin' on the wall
As I roam amongst the memories
Of the ones I loved the best
Those gemstones on the far out plains
The little towns out West.

Where morning breathes a gentle sigh
To call you from your sleep
Without the roar of angry traffic
Moaning in the street
And bush birds fill the opal sky
With the music I love best
How I wish that I was going
To a little town out West.

Perhaps a town with old time pubs
Like the Tambaroora Star
Where Banjo's ghost might join me
At a corner of the bar
We'd watch the old men drink slow beers
And roll slow cigarettes
And kiss the fragile Tally-Ho's
With lips that once caressed
A country girl with smiling face
In a little town out West.

I'd lounge around the broad main street
Just soakin' up the sun
And revel in the 'G'day' smiles
You get from everyone
They don't know me from a bar of soap
But that's what I like best
They won't let you be a stranger
In the golden towns out West.

It's a most unlikely dreamin' place
The 'lavvy' down the hall
Where I'm moved to contemplation
As I answer nature's call
And I sit and wonder what comes next
Is it God—or pension day
And if it's God, and should he say,
We'll try and do our best,
I'll ask him—
could he send my soul
To a little town out West.

*(With apologies to Banjo Paterson)*

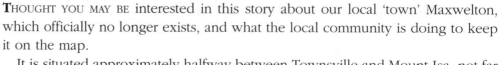

from
CATHY KENNEDY
MERRIULA STATION
MAXWELTON
(the town with
no postcode)
QUEENSLAND

THOUGHT YOU MAY BE interested in this story about our local 'town' Maxwelton, which officially no longer exists, and what the local community is doing to keep it on the map.

It is situated approximately halfway between Townsville and Mount Isa, not far from where the beginning of 'Crocodile Dundee' was filmed, and has slowly over the years, thanks to the drought, recession and micro-economics, died.

First the school went as there weren't enough pupils to keep the one-teacher school open. At one stage they put a pupil's pet roo, that he brought to school with him every day, on the roll in a bid to keep the numbers up! If an inspector came around that particular pupil was at home sick that day. (I think the roo's name was Matilda!)

Then the railway went, a victim of micro-economics and 'streamlining' to make the rail system more 'efficient'. The fact that the train passed through anyway didn't seem to matter. With its closure departed the families that lived there to work it.

Next the pub which obviously couldn't operate at a profit without clientele—no railway workers, and because of the drought graziers were no longer employing the married couples, ringers and cooks who were good customers.

Finally the post office was closed with little regard to the fact that the mail truck still called in to pick up mail from a post box kindly provided by Australia Post. Now we have to travel a further 100 kilometres round trip to get our mail!

We've decided to keep Maxi on the map and let people know we are still alive and kicking (up our heels in this case) by reviving the 'Maxwelton Ball of the North'. The ball was very big in the 1980s and was an annual event with a different theme each year. We've stuck our neck out to show the world we are still here and doing what we do best—besides produce beef and wool—and do it with style despite Maxwelton being a town with no postcode.

## EMPTY COUNTRY HOUSES

from
LESLIE A. GRIFFITHS
WEST WYALONG
NEW SOUTH WALES

The years have quickly passed since I first came this way
and things that I once knew and loved have irreversibly decayed.
The big cool wide verandahs, where wisteria once thrived
are now forlorn and rotting where rabbits dig their hide.
The once well kept orchards for making Mum's preserves
are now just dry old branches for resting little birds.
The stink of mice that scurry free and the dirty sparrows
that use the eves for trees.
The fallen gutters on the ground and crumpled tanks,
that are rusted out all around
The abandonment of empty homesteads, where mums, dads and kids
would listen to the wireless and wouldn't move for quids.
And sometimes on a special night Mum would play her piano just right.
And down the rough and rutted road the peppercorns the only sign
of schools that in another time, we once graced
have now become someone else's happy home, their place.
But now the dirt roads and tracks, which have all turned to black,
have trapped all life and family things,
from countryside where life begins.
We leave our big town life each morn our supermarkets, clubs and lawns,
to drive past the places we once knew
and think about the here and now and wonder . . . how?

---

*Jim phoned in from Elliston, South Australia. As they talked, Jim's voice had a strange echo.*

MACCA: 'Where are you ringing from?'

JIM: 'Elliston.'

MACCA: 'Are you in a phone box or something?'

JIM: 'I'm in the bath. On Sunday mornings I hop in the bath for an hour and a half and listen to you—I'm away from the wife and kids and I can relax.'

---

AS A KEEN FOLLOWER OF your program for many years now, I feel I have to take you to task over the myth that country people and towns are friendlier and safer than city people and towns. I am a city girl who has been living and working in five country towns of varying sizes for the past sixteen years and I have never found country people to be any friendlier than their city counterparts. In fact in most cases it is the opposite, they can be extremely cliquey. They do not accept people who are not born in the town. In two small towns I was told that I would not be accepted until I had lived there for forty years, that I was just a blow-in even though I lived in one town for eight years.

I have seen incredible cruelty and isolation forced upon itinerant workers and

from
LEONE DERRIMAN
WODONGA
VICTORIA

their children by locals. In the smaller towns, unless you drink at the local pub or are involved in the local football club you are not accepted no matter how good you are at any other sport—even if you get to representative level.

When we moved into my house in Sydney the people in the street threw a barbecue to welcome us, and they did the same when we left. That never happened in the country. When I return to the city, I am welcomed, but on returning to the country towns, I am looked upon as a traitor for leaving and usually ignored. I have been robbed four times, something that never happened to me in thirty-three years in the city. I have had plants pulled out of my garden. I have seen people pushing drugs in the main street, I have seen a man hold a gun to his wife's head and I have seen a gang-bashing.

Having said all that, I do love to live in the country, and have a wonderful lifestyle. I have made heaps of friends, all blow-ins like myself, who have given up trying to make friends with locals. I love the wide open spaces, the fresh air and the fact that it only takes me five minutes to get to work. Land and housing are much cheaper and therefore you are able to afford a better quality house and lifestyle than in the city. I have been able to complete a university degree, part-time, something I doubt I would have done in the city. I do miss the ocean, but this is compensated by snow skiing in winter.

What I am trying to say is that country people are just the same as city people. Some are nice and friendly—and I have met some great ones—and others are horrible. Country towns are no safer than city suburbs, it just depends who lives in them.

• • • • • • • • • • • • • • • • • • • •

from
DESLEY McDONAGH
STANTHORPE
QUEENSLAND

I'M ONE OF THOSE PEOPLE who lives in a country town and enjoys it. I listened to the letter you read from a listener who took you to task over what you said about country versus city living. I've lived in cities and the country, including Melbourne and the Gold Coast. It's the people around you that matter and I have been fortunate to have good neighbours wherever I've lived. For me the Gold Coast was the loneliest place, probably because of its holiday image, but Stanthorpe which is home is my favourite place! It's the people that matter and your attitude. If you go to live in a new place and don't make an effort to join in some of the activities and clubs there, then you can be left out.

*Chris from Gollan (between Dubbo and Mudgee), New South Wales, rang in:*
MACCA: 'What's Gollan like to live in?'
CHRIS: 'It's good. We've got a pub fifteen miles *that* way, and a pub fifteen miles *that* way, and no cops. It's bloody good.'

LISTENING TO LEONE'S LETTER about country people not being friendly to 'blow-ins', I agree! As a teacher who spent many years teaching in country schools I felt the same. On a recent farm holiday, as I wandered among the gum trees, I found myself singing:

from
PEG WEBBER
NEW LAMBTON
NEW SOUTH WALES

Give me a home among the Big Shops
With lots of Bus Stops,
A Club or Two, Lots of Things to Do,
K-Mart out the back
Big W out the front
and the Old Bank Card!

Graham rang in on a mobile phone:
MACCA: 'Where are you?'
GRAHAM: 'I'm on top of the Great Dividing Range—bit of a misnomer as it's only a slight rise—I'm near Gurulmundi, not far from Giligulgul and Guluguba's just down the road.'
MACCA: 'And what are you doing there?'
GRAHAM: 'I'm delivering papers—I've also got a mail run.'
MACCA: 'And why do you do that?'
GRAHAM: 'It's a slower way of going broke than farming.'

LEONE, YOUR WRITER FROM Wodonga, is quite right in one particular respect—country town residents generally don't accept people who haven't lived there for their entire lives. In some towns the inhabitants seem to be overly suspicious of newcomers and the perceived threat of change to 'their' town.

from
LYN DRIVER
ADELAIDE
SOUTH AUSTRALIA

Like Leone, I was told that I would not be accepted in a certain town until I had lived there for thirty years. Needless to say, I didn't stay! I am originally from Sydney and moved to Adelaide via lengthy stays of several years in New South Wales country towns. My children were well-accepted in the schools they attended but the local adults were usually a lot less friendly.

In spite of this I love country towns; by that I mean their physical situations: Leura, nestled among the trees in the Blue Mountains (although I would now class Leura and Katoomba as suburbs of Sydney); lovely Forbes on the Lachlan; Jindabyne and its lake—water rats and trout; little Jingellic, near the Murray, where you can stop for a pie and milkshake with not a single soul out on the main street.

Speaking of the Murray, I have fallen in love with the Riverland towns, especially Loxton and Waikerie. If you've never been to the Waikerie Bakery, you're missing the ultimate country bread, although it does have its equal in the bakery at Crystal Brook near Port Pirie. My favourite spot is the Waikeri camping ground, down by the Murray River. It's not 'politically correct', with its platoon of feral pine trees, but there's nothing more delightful than pitching your tent on the velvety green carpet beneath the evergreens, with a crackling fire roaring near-by and the scent of pine in your nostrils.

I dread the thought of the Murray drying up, as some people have suggested it may do. Is it possible? No more Queen's Birthday weekend canoe marathons; no more paddle-steamers; and what would happen to the hordes of pelicans, the curious water rats, the majestic Murray cod and of course the elusive bunyip?

## G'day, this is Macca

SHAUN: Good morning Macca, it's Shaun. Myself and Bruce are locomotive drivers on a freight train, and we've just gone through Stawell.

MACCA: Tell me more. What are you carrying, where are you from, where have you been?

SHAUN: We started in Dimboola about 5.15 this morning. My mate Bruce lives in Gerang Gerung and I'm from Jeparit.

MACCA: Gerang Gerung and Jeparit, there's a couple of great Aussie names!

SHAUN: They certainly are. We've a load of containers going to Melbourne from Adelaide. The train's running about three-and-a-half hours late. It had a bit of trouble in the Adelaide Hills. They get a lot of millipedes on the line—the guys with lots of legs—which make the trains lose traction going up hills. When they get squashed up it's like putting oil on the rails and the trains stall going up hills!

MACCA: I hear things on this program that I never hear anywhere else!

SHAUN: It's true! The suburban trains in Adelaide have little brushes in front of their wheels to brush the millipedes off the line, but we don't have anything like that.

MACCA: Isn't that a mighty little story. The millipedes must be committing harikari or something. How long have you been driving, Shaun?

SHAUN: Eleven years and I love it. It was my grandmother's fault. When I was a child she took me to the station and I rode my scooter up and down the platform, and that was the start of the sickness!

*Tommy Mac:*

'I come from the country — a place called Wedlock — I was born just out of it.'

## OUTSIDE BROADCASTS

### 1994
Darwin 7.8.94
Guyra 18.9.94
Allora 30.10.94
Melbourne (Southbank) 6.11.94
Geraldton 20.11.94
Narromine (Christmas Day) 25.12.94

### 1995
Winton 9.4.95
Kyogle 16.4.95
Mackay 30.7.95
Junee 13.8.95
Port Lincoln 17.9.95
Perth (RFDS) 8.10.95
Parramatta Park 5.11.95
Dalby 12.11.95

### 1996
Mildura 10.3.96
Brisbane 14.7.96
Leonora 29.9.96
Wodonga 6.10.96
Sydney Cricket Ground 20.10.96

### 1997
Broken Hill 2.3.97
Woomera 30.3.97

## OVERSEAS CALLS

Paul McCann, Bath, England 17.7.94
John Gaugary, Kansas, USA 24.7.94
Phoebe Frazer, Goma, Zaire 31.7.94
Lou Cooper, Dublin, Ireland 7.8.94
Scott Dolling, Devon, England 7.8.94
Peter Macleod, Isle of Skye, Scotland 7.8.94
John Hanlon, Edinburgh, Scotland 14.8.94
Tony Hirsland, Barrow, Alaska, USA 21.8.94
Trevor Newton, Lafayette, Louisiana, USA 21.8.94
John Moote, Portland, Oregon, USA 21.8.94
Johav, Israel 18.9.94
Lang Kidby, Singapore 9.10.94
Jane Borlin, Japan 9.10.94
Philippa Webb, Turkey, Umbria, Italy 16.10.94
Lang Kidby, Jakarta, Indonesia 16.10.94

Chris Higgins, Pittsburgh, Pennsylvania, USA 13.11.94
Lt Col Stuart Ellis, Mogadishu, Somalia 20.11.94
Phil, Idaho, USA 4.12.94
Ross Dominy, Auckland, New Zealand 18.12.94
Joe McMennamin, Killarney, Ireland 25.12.94
Bronwyn Toohey, Anchorage, Alaska, USA 25.12.94
Scotty, Scott Base, Antarctica 25.12.94
Bronwyn, United Arab Emirates 19.2.95
David, Kokoda Trail, PNG 26.3.95
Debbie Cox, Burundi, Central Africa 9.4.95
Gary, Sacramento, California, USA 16.4.95
Cyril, London, England 30.4.95
Tony Scranton, San Francisco, California, USA 30.4.95
Jack McLoughlan, New Orleans, Louisiana, USA 7.5.95
Bill Forrest, Ulaanbaatar, Mongolia 21.5.95
Fiona Campbell, Victoria, British Columbia, Canada 18.6.95
Brian, St Fleurs, France 25.6.95
Scotty, Antarctica 25.6.95
Kay Scott, Rovaniemi, Arctic Circle 2.7.95
Max Chambers, Lincolnshire, England 9.7.95
Wynette Horne, Thanllangothlin, North Wales 9.7.95
Ron Strahan, Berlin, Germany 16.7.95
Gil Webb, Juneau, Alaska, USA 23.7.95
Bill Mead, Washington, DC, USA 23.7.95
Kieran McNamara, Oshkosh, Wisconsin, USA 30.7.95
Margaret Gibson, Altona, Canada 30.7.95
John Shovelin, Hiroshima, Japan 6.8.95
Dr Frank Whitebrook, Dusseldorf, Germany 13.8.95
David Burt, Cape Town, South Africa 27.8.95
Ron, Beijing, China 27.8.95
Malcolm Crosse, Galway, Ireland 3.9.95
Janelle, Ooba Tooba, near Sao Paulo, Rio de Janiero, Brazil 10.9.95
John Davis, Beijing, China 10.9.95
Phillipa Webb, Oudtshurn, South Africa 17.9.95
Graham World, Port Moresby, PNG 17.9.95
Brian Rogers, Tongue, Scotland 24.9.95
Alastair, Banff, Canada 24.9.95
Graham Howie, Killarney, Ireland 1.10.95
Max Hitchens, Iceland 10.95
Sally, Cologne, France 1.10.95
Robin (from AAO), Chicago, Illinois, USA 15.10.95
Robert Tanelli, Blue Ridge Parkway, Virginia, USA 19.11.95
Bob Fulman, Dunedin, New Zealand 26.11.95
Tim Fischer, Thailand 10.12.95

Caroline Paul, Argentina   10.12.95

Rex, Auckland, New Zealand   10.12.95

Byron, Ottawa, Ontario, Canada   24.12.95

Amy, Sweden   24.12.95

Erin, Southern Alberta, Canada   24.12.95

Nick, Nishiwaki, Japan        4.1.96

Peter Donovan, Hamilton, New Zealand   4.2.96

Kerry, Port Moresby, PNG   18.2.96

Sgt Steve Wittel, Nicosia, Cyprus   7.4.96

Heather Hart (Woden Valley Choir), Zion Canyon,
   Utah, USA   4.4.96

John Flower, Port Churchill, Nevada, USA   21.4.96

Robert Latimer, Rome, Italy   21.4.96

Simon, Bogota, Columbia, South America   21.4.96

David, Parmukkale, Turkey   28.4.96

Joy, Ketchican, Alaska, USA   28.4.96

Rachel, Tiberias, Sea of Galilee, Israel   5.5.96

Anthony Taggart, Iquitos, Peru   5.5.96

Roslyn Blair, Wohan, Yangtze River, China   19.5.96

Roger, Jakarta   19.5.96

Noel Bentley, Cyprus   9.6.96

Katherine, Switzerland   9.6.96

Ronald Biggs, Rio De Janiero, Brazil   9.6.96

George and Robin, Chicago, Illinois, USA   16.6.96

Lt Cmdr Clive, Cambodia   16.6.96

Nicky Lee, Blagoveshenck, Russia   16.6.96

Kerry Bragg, Alberta, Canada   30.6.96

Clayton, Isle of Man, UK   30.6.96

Mike Zennerman, Port Moresby, PNG   14.7.96

Luciano, Solo Solo Village, Western Samoa   11.8.96

Helen, in a phone box, Niagara Falls, Ontario, Canada
   18.8.96

Danny Barnett, Brooking, South Dakota, USA   8.9.96

Barry Skipsy, Lucerne, Switzerland   8.9.96

Brad McCulloch, Hay River, Canada   1.9.96

Trevor Flugge, Beijing, China   1.9.96

Martin Benge, London, England   22.9.96

Graham, in a phone box, Narita, Japan   29.9.96

Vin, Taichan, Quon Dong Province, China   29.9.96

Kevin Leery, Papua New Guinea   29.9.96

Gwen Taylor, in a phone box outside St Paul's
   Cathedral, London, England   6.10.96

Stephen, Bali   6.10.96

Rhonda Carlow, Kilkenny, Ireland   6.10.96

Alby Harrison, Ankara, Turkey   13.10.96

Bruce and Robin Schultz, Eastern Highlands Province,
   PNG   20.10.96

Graham Mitchell, Tanzania, East Africa   20.10.96

Roberto, Calcutta, India   20.10.96

John Prince, Port Moresby, PNG   27.10.96

Trevor Bowen, New York, NY, USA   3.11.96

Robin Gilbert, Fujian Province, China   3.11.96

Steve Angel, Perth, Scotland   10.11.96

Janelle Marsden, Kansas, USA   17.1.96

Helen Hasst, New Zealand   12.96

Tania, Levee, Finland   8.12.96

Mike Mackay, Oxford, England   8.12.96

John, Broughton on Water, the Cottswolds, England
   8.12.96

Emma, Sharjah, United Arab Emirates   15.12.96

Steve Angel, Heaven Lodge, Zimbabwe   22.12.96

Peter Mack, Stockholm, Sweden   22.12.96

Sarah, Iceland   22.12.96

Lila, Wewak, PNG (Australia Day)   26.1.97

Brian McQuillan, Futuvut Tuvulu, 750 km north of Fiji
   9.2.97

Annie, Vanuatu   9.2.97

Scott Parry, Doncaster, England   16.2.97

Trevor Flugge, Cairo   9.3.97

David Stuart, Port Moresby, PNG   16.3.97

Tim Fischer, Khyber Pass, Pakistan   6.4.97

Frank Deans, Tullyvin, Ireland   13.4.97

Andrew O'Brien, Villiers Brettoneaux, France   27.4.97

Henry Gray, Kupang, Indonesia   27.4.97

Rewe Matthews, Anchorage, Alaska, USA   4.5.97

Trevor Davey, Bay of Plenty, Tauranga, New Zealand
   4.5.97

Greg Keegan, Qingdao, Shandong Province, China
   11.5.97

George Battese, Göteborg, Sweden   25.5.97

Matthew and Joy, Kalimnos, Greek Islands   8.6.97

Commander Andrew Cawley, Guangzhow City, China,
   180 km north west of Hong Kong   15.6.97

Bev McGrath, in a phone box, Coventry, England,
   opposite statue of Lady Godiva   15.6.97

Bev McGrath, Kensington, England   22.6.97

Laurel Bell, Bergen, Norway   29.6.97

Charles, Kent, England   29.6.97

Bev McGrath, Killarney, Ireland   29.6.97

## CALLS FROM PLANES

John Nixon, near Goondiwindi, Qld   24.7.94

Peter, Bass Strait, heading to Flinders Island   21.8.94

Richard Kingston, between Rockhampton and Bedourie, Qld 9.10.94

Owen Nelson, over Bass Strait 19.2.95

Dan Doyle, RFDS Polaris plane over Woomera, SA 9.4.95

Ted Rudge, over King Island Tas 20.8.95

Michael, near Launceston, Tas, 15,000 ft 18.2.96

Denis Gibbons, Qantas 747, heading to Antarctica 1.12.96

John, flying over South Australia in a helicopter 8.12.96

## CALLS FROM BOATS AND SHIPS

Captain Chris Blake—*Endeavour* replica, Port Lincoln, SA 23.10.94

Noel Geck, crabbing near Fraser Island 6.11.94

Flt Lt Marcus McGregor, HMAS *Melbourne*, Japan, 6.11.94

Captain Slim Hughes, *Iron Whyalla*, Great Australian Bight 4.12.94

Captain Chris Blake, *Endeavour*, North Head, Sydney 18.12.94

Nigel Scullion, *Reliance*, Gulf of Carpentaria 9.4.95

"WAS", on a ferry, Queenscliffe, Sydney 16.4.95

Commander Richard McMullen, HMAS *Sydney*, Vladivostok, Russia 21.5.95

Laurie Lawrence, HMV *Challenger*, near Magnetic Island 18.6.95

Don Hooke and John de Teligra, on the Australia Remembers ship, Mikael Shokohov, East Coast PNG. 9.7.95

Rod Oliver, rowing on Tamar River, Tas 9.7.95

Lt Michael Marley HMAS Submarine *Ovens*, near Byron Bay, NSW 6.8.95

Geoff Herriot, off Fraser Island 20.8.95

Mick, on a trawler, Torres Strait, off Cape York 27.8.95

Ben De La Costa, trimaran, off Brampton Island, Qld 10.9.95

Doris, on the Bollon River, Bicca, Qld 1.10.95

Nigel Scullion, *Reliance*, Port Essington 1.10.95

Noel Jones, *Tasman Venture*, off Maroochydore, Qld 15.10.95

Roz, *Cat Ballou*, off coast of Eden, NSW 29.10.95

Nigel Scullion, *Reliance*, north east of Bromby Islands, NT 12.11.95

Fred Christy, Skipper *Lady Nelson*, near Coffs Harbour, NSW 3.12.95

Ian Brown, on a cruise boat on the Amazon 10.12.95

Peter, on *Ballyando*, Hay Point, Qld 17.12.95

Kevin Williams, yacht *Prelude*, Macquarie Harbour, Tas 4.12.96

Captain Rob Ray, the *Curlew*, between Dunk and Fitzroy Islands 12.5.96

Alex, oil rig, Java Sea, 100 miles out of Bali 9.6.96

Kelly, *Shore Fire*, 300 miles north of Broome, WA 16.6.96

Ron Johnston, yacht *Temple Maid*, Gove, NT 30.6.96

Sandy Williams, the *Mulga*, Woods Inlet, Darwin, NT 14.7.96

Ted, *Lake Gardiner*, 100 miles west of Port Augusta, SA 11.8.96

Bill Walsh, prawning, Snapper Island, Qld 25.8.96

Kim, Suva, Fiji 8.9.96

Trish Hawkins, on a yacht, Long Island, WA 3.11.96

Harry, cray boat *Robert Nicholas*, Warrnambool, Vic 17.11.96

Nigel, *Reliance*, north east of Arnhem Land 24.11.96

Graham Cornish, 707 Steamer, Newport, Vic 24.11.96

Colin, off Phillip Island, Bass Strait 2.2.97

David ('Biggles') and Melissa, *Rig Seismic*, Australian Research ship between Heard Island and Antarctica 9.2.97

Shane, oil rig, *Karratha*, 750 km north-west of Onslow, WA 16.2.97

Irene, *Lady Nelson*, Strahan, Tas 23.3.97

Nobby, sailing boat, Koongul Creek, Fraser Island, Qld 30.3.97

John, yacht *Marchioness* between Durban and Fremantle, 2,500 miles from Fremantle 8.6.97

John, on 37-foot schooner anchored at Thomas Island, Whitsundays 8.6.97

Judy Benson in catamaran travelling from George Town to Devonport, Tasmania 8.6.97

Pat Comden, *Rum Runner*, on Coral Sea heading to Herald Cays 350 km from Cairns 15.6.97

Commodore Tim Cox with Australian Navy in Sea of Japan near Korea. Four ships, *Westralia*, *Hobart*, *Canberra* and *Darwin* 22.6.97

John, yacht *Marchioness* 70 miles off Fremantle 22.6.97

## CALLS FROM TRAINS

Colin Taylor, *Spirit of the Outback*, Longreach, Qld
19.11.95

Sean, on a freight train, heading to Adelaide, SA
9.6.96

Graham, diesel train, Junee, NSW   9.6.96

Rocky Wayne, freight train, Cootamundra, NSW
8.9.96

Graham Hind, steam loco, Zig-Zag Railway, Lithgow,
NSW   20.10.96

Gary Bellhouse, 3801, just out of Bathurst, NSW
6.4.97

Keith, heading through south west Victoria, Dimboola
to Cressy   15.6.97

## CALLS FROM ISLANDS

Jan, Elcho Island, off Arnhem Land, NT   11.12.94

Ray Jones, Lord Howe Island   18.12.94

Carol, Thursday Island, Qld   25.6.95

Jonathon Mitchell, Elcho Island, Arnhem Land, NT
10.8.95

Noelene Wall, Fraser Island, Qld   20.8.95

Steven Trelfo, Karkar Island, off PNG   15.10.95

Alison Johnson, Flinders Island, Tas   29.10.95

Les, Norfolk Island   24.12.95

Barry Baker, Centre Island, Gulf of Carpentaria
3.3.96

Bill Keats, Kangaroo Island, SA   7.4.96

Malcolm French, Flinders Island, Tas   28.4.96

Gail, Montague Island, off Narooma, NSW   5.5.96

Doris, King Island, Tas   23.6.96

Cecily, Boyne Island, Qld   1.9.96

Roger, Neptune Island, SA   8.9.96

Lindon Rae, Willis Island, 450 km due east of Cairns,
Qld   24.11.96

Greg, Thursday Island, Qld   24.11.96

Lisle Smith, Bruny Island, Tas   15.12.96

Leedham Walker, Flinders Island, Tas   2.2.97

Alan Long, Lord Howe Island   2.3.97

Don, Shetland Islands, Scotland   20.4.97

Kelly and Tom Maher, Christmas Island   4.5.97

Tom, Norfolk Island   1.6.97

## MISCELLANEOUS

David, ambulance driver, and patient Dan in the back
of an ambulance, Stanthorpe, Qld   16.7.95

Kim Gillette, in the bath, Elliston, SA   24.9.95

Ian, up a ladder picking oranges, Leeton, NSW
19.11.95

Suzanne, playing carillon bells in a tower forty metres
above Lake Burley Griffin, ACT   17.12.95

Barry, from public phone in caravan park toilet block,
Boorooloola, NT   13.4.97

David Hillen, Gulf of Carpentaria, sitting on a sandhill at
Camp 120, Burke and Wills   1.6.97

Kevin, in Rudall River National Park, WA, in between
Gibson and the Great Sandy Desert—a very remote
spot   22.6.97

## G'day, this is Macca

GREG: This is Greg Keegan speaking from Qingdao in China. It's in Shandong Province on the coast in northern China and I can hear you on short-wave radio surprisingly clearly. There are quite a few Australians working up here. The city has about six million people and it is one of the nicest spots in China. It's got beautiful mountains in the background, a lovely coastline and the people are really good. You'd be surprised how many listen to Radio Australia— we don't need to lose it!

I'm originally from Adelaide and have been here for nine months. My wife joins me shortly; as there's no schooling for older children here they have to remain in Australia.

You were talking about apples. The apples here are of superb quality. The farmers bring their goods in every morning from miles around on their three-wheeler motorbikes, and it's chock-a-block! Every day the place is changing, improving.

MACCA: Improving how, Greg?

GREG: The standard of living. When you compare what they had ten years ago to what they have today there's a big gap. A lot of Australian students are up here learning the language and they'll be a big asset in years to come.

*What Macca says:* 'If you've got one of those houses where the doorbell's connected to the electric kettle, I'm coming over!'

*What Macca says about government jargon:* 'We don't have droughts any more, we have "rain deficiencies".'

*A Macca question on air:* 'Where are you from originally...or recently...or roughly?'

*And from Stan Mellick, Brisbane:* I was overseas in San Francisco and it was time for your program so I had to beetle out and get some copper wire. I don't know if many people know this, but in my army days when we wanted to pull in a program or a distant station we'd take the wavelength, and in your case I think it was on the twenty-nine-meter band. So I took a quarter of that, went out and bought thirty feet of copper wire, strung it up in a tree and attached it to the little radio I had—and in you came, booming!

So there you go...

· · · · · · · · · · · · · · · · · · · · · · · · · · · · · · · · · · · · · · · · · · · · · · · · ·

*Kevin phoned in and Macca spoke to him about Barry from the same district.*
KEVIN: 'Aw, *him!* He's been around for a fair while. He was born when the Dead Sea was only a little bit crook.'

· · · · · · · · · · · · · · · · · · · · · · · · · · · · · · · · · · · · · · · · · · · · · · · · ·

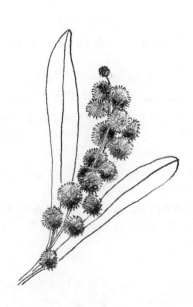